SHAME AND SOCIAL WORK

Theory, Reflexivity and Practice

Edited by
Liz Frost, Veronika Magyar-Haas,
Holger Schoneville and Alessandro Sicora

P

First published in Great Britain in 2021 by

Policy Press, an imprint of
Bristol University Press
University of Bristol
1-9 Old Park Hill
Bristol
BS2 8BB
UK
t: +44 (0)117 954 5940
e: bup-info@bristol.ac.uk

Details of international sales and distribution partners are available at
policy.bristoluniversitypress.co.uk

British Library Cataloguing in Publication Data
A catalogue record for this book is available from the British Library

ISBN 978-1-4473-4406-3 hardcover
ISBN 978-1-4473-4408-7 paperback
ISBN 978-1-4473-4409-4 ePub
ISBN 978-1-4473-4407-0 ePdf

Cover design: Robin Hawes
Front cover image: istock-490549852

Contents

Notes on contributors

Marie Demant is a research assistant and doctoral student in the Department of Educational Sciences at Goethe University Frankfurt, Germany. She has been working in the fields of child abuse prevention and sexual rights as a practitioner and as a researcher. Her areas of specialisation are violence and power in pedagogy and education, collective memory and media studies. Her current research examines the characteristics of child sexual abuse in the family, reappraisal and recognition for survivors.

Liz Frost is Associate Professor of Social Work at the University of the West of England, Bristol, UK. She has two main areas of scholarly activity. The first is developing European perspectives in social work, through research, publication, creating networks and undertaking pan-European projects. She is on the board of the European Social Work Research Association, and the *European Journal of Social Work*. Secondly, she has developed the profile of psychosocial theory, particularly in relation to social work. She has pioneered a psychosocial curriculum for social work students, edits the *Journal of Psychosocial Studies* and is a board member of the Association for Psychosocial Studies. Her chapter 'Why psychosocial theory is critical' was published in *The Routledge Handbook of Critical Theory* (ed. S. Webb, Routledge, 2019).

Matthew Gibson is Senior Lecturer and Researcher in the School of Social Policy at the University of Birmingham, UK. His research interests relate to emotions and professional practice, and particularly the emotions of pride and shame. He is the author of *Pride and Shame in Child and Family Social Work: Emotions and the Search for Humane Practice* (Policy Press, 2019) and *Reassessing Attachment Theory in Child Welfare* (with Sue White, Policy Press, 2019). Matthew is a qualified social worker with professional practice experience in statutory child protection social work in the UK and around the world.

Mark Hardy is Senior Lecturer in Social Work at the University of York, UK, where he teaches social work theory, research philosophy and method and criminology. His practice experience was in mental health and work with young and adult offenders, both areas he retains an active interest in. His major publications include *Evidence and Knowledge for Practice* (with Tony Evans, Polity Press, 2010) and

Governing Risk: Care and Control in Contemporary Social Work (Palgrave Macmillan, 2014). Mark has current interests in the impact of risk thinking in practice, the role of personality disorder in offending behaviour and the potential of American pragmatism as a philosophy for practice. He is also associate editor of the journal *Evidence and Policy*.

Friederike Lorenz is a researcher in the Department of Educational Sciences, Social Work Division, at Freie University Berlin, Germany. She wrote her PhD on the practice of silence in the context of staff violence in residential care. Her recent research projects are a study on the processing of sexual violence in the Protestant Church in Germany, an ethnographic study on teachers participating in further education about the Shoah and a study on antisemitism in schools.

Veronika Magyar-Haas is Professor of Educational Sciences at the Faculty of Philosophy of the Université de Fribourg, Switzerland. She was interim professor with focus on social pedagogy and family research at the Goethe University Frankfurt and researcher and senior lecturer at the University of Zurich. Her research has been situated in the areas of philosophy of education, social work and childhood studies. This includes anthropological concepts in educational science, social-scientific research on body, emotions and vulnerability, as well as qualitative-empirical research on education and social inequality. She is co-editor of the book series *Kindheit – Bildung – Erziehung: Philosophische Perspektiven* (Metzler, since 2019) as well as the books *Zum Schweigen. Macht/Ohnmacht in Erziehung und Bildung* (Velbrück, 2015) and *Education and the State. International Perspectives on a Changing Relationship* (Routledge, 2015).

Sighard Neckel is Professor of Sociology at the Department of Social Sciences at the University of Hamburg, Germany. Before taking his chair at Hamburg University he held professorships for sociological theory at the German universities of Gießen and Frankfurt and the University of Vienna, Austria, and was research director at the Frankfurt Institute for Social Research. He took up visiting professorships in the USA, South Korea, Japan, Australia, Poland and Greece. His research covers a wide range of sociological topics in the fields of social inequality, economic sociology, cultural studies, social theory and sociology of emotions. Among his most important publications are *Status und Scham* (Campus, 1991), *Flucht nach vorn* (Campus, 2008), *Strukturierte Verantwortungslosigkeit. Berichte aus der Bankenwelt* (Suhrkamp, 2010), *Sternstunden der Soziologie* (Campus, 2010), *Burnout,*

Fatigue, Exhaustion (Palgrave, 2017), *Die Gesellschaft der Nachhaltigkeit* (transcript, 2018), *Die globale Finanzklasse* (Campus, 2018).

Holger Schoneville is Senior Lecturer of Social Work at Faculty of Educational Sciences at Dortmund University, Germany. His expertise includes research on poverty and social exclusion, subjectivity and vulnerability in relation to social work theory and the transformation of welfare (state) arrangements. The design of his research is rooted within a qualitative-reconstructive methodology. He is a qualified social worker and worked in research and teaching at various universities and research institutes in Germany, Europe and the USA.

Carsten Schröder is a research associate at the Faculty of Education at the University of Dortmund. His research focuses on the field of child and youth welfare, theories of social work, the phenomenology of emotions, child protection and children's rights. Carsten has developed a particular expertise in his ethnographic study on the analysis of the relationship between emotions and professional action in social work.

Alessandro Sicora is Associate Professor in the Department of Sociology and Social Research at the University of Trento, Italy. He is a qualified social worker with professional practice experience in geriatric social work and youth social work. He is Secretary of the European Social Work Research Association and President of the Italian Society of Social Work. His research interests relate to international social work, reflective practice, professional mistakes, emotions and professional practice. Alessandro is the author of *Reflective Practice and Learning from Mistakes in Social Work* (2017).

Shame and social work: an introduction

Liz Frost, Veronika Magyar-Haas,
Holger Schoneville and Alessandro Sicora

Shame is a powerful emotion in the context of social work. It affects individuals and attacks their subjectivity from within, and yet is also experienced in the here and now as a thoroughly social emotion that enmeshes the individual within society. It is therefore highly potent within the field of social work, both with regard to service users and in social work practice itself. People who become service users often live in social situations in which they are confronted with shame: the emotion can occur by virtue of them being in the social work system, and shame can also be experienced by those recruited to alleviate social problems – the social workers. This book will try to make sense of the complex relationship between the social conditions, norms and expectations that co-produce shame in the context of social work, and will highlight the impact that shame has on those who are affected by it. We hope that our readers, whether academics, researchers, students, practitioners or policymakers, will find this useful.

Despite its importance, the topic of shame has until recently received little attention within the multiple discourses that constitute social work. This book seeks to address this gap by drawing on scholarship from across Europe to examine theory, reflection and practice. Shame is, often literally, an 'unspeakable' emotion: this book encourages a broad and open discussion of shame, and how it can be sensitively addressed through social workers' own reflexivity and in relationship-based practice with service users. Importantly and uniquely, the book discusses the socio-political roots of shame, challenging the notion that individuals are responsible for their own shame suffering. This volume sets out to highlight the systematic relevance of the emotion 'shame' in theoretical terms and at the same time will offer the reader detailed examples of the impact of shame on service users and workers in specific contexts.

Although focusing on experiences in four European countries, there are overarching themes which emerge in the book, emphasising the commonalities of much shame thinking across the continent. As we will discuss in more depth, the book is divided into three parts,

1

each with a specific focus: on shame theory, shame in relation to service users, and shame and social workers. However, core themes also emerge across these sections, as they do across national borders, interlinking the chapters offered here. The meaning of the concept of shame, the issue of subjectivity, and the theme of power and control are three such themes.

The combined chapters that constitute the overall text offer considerable focus on the slippery nature of the meaning of shame. While acknowledging the paradoxical nature of shame as both the most social and most unspeakable of emotions (Chapters 1–3) a theme emerges of creating some form of order – some form of intelligibility – in relation to this dynamic, shape-shifting concept. It is not just in Part I, which focuses on theory, that Frost, Neckel and Magyar-Haas (in Chapters 1, 2 and 3, respectively), formulate shame within a three-part schema (the three dimensions of political, social and individual shame; the subject, normativity and the other, respectively). Schoneville, in Chapter 4, in seeking to analyse poverty and subjectivity, also highlights that through shame, the structure of society, the individual's position in it and subjectivity are all interlinked. Hardly a chapter fails to offer a rich contribution to clarifying our understanding of shame (for example, the thorough analysis to be found in Part III in both Chapters 7 and 8). Interestingly, the proffered perspectives do not obviously represent national or disciplinary differences, but rather the commitment of scholars to formulate a richer understanding of the unsettled meanings of shame. However, a multiplicity of ideas and perspectives: from philosophy, sociology, pedagogy, psychology, historical-sciences, political-sciences, anthropology, research on social policy and organisational studies, are variously combined and deployed to illuminate this opaque concept.

The individual as the object, product, victim and/or target of shame in its various applications also arises as a recurrent theme across the chapters of the book. Shame is named as an attack on subjectivity in the very title of Chapter 4, in which Schoneville demonstrates from primary research findings the damaging impact of social structural oppressions on the formation of a shamed subjectivity. Demant and Lorenz in Chapter 5 equally powerfully analyse the destructive application of shaming practices, including violence, on children in residential care. One could almost think of this as the weaponisation of shame. Through social and philosophical perspectives, both Magyar-Haas and Hardy (in, respectively Chapters 3 and 8) bring us closer to the self-relationships of social workers in practice today, while Sicora's work in Chapter 9 humanely considers how shame damages the identities and esteem of social workers in relation to the all-pervasive shame of not being good enough as they struggle with the ramifications of making ordinary errors in the context of contemporary organisations.

Shaming as a power strategy also emerges as a uniting theme, though it is seen from at least two different perspectives. On the one hand, power in relation to the enforcement of social norms (in other words to insure conformity within groups, cultures or societies) is theoretically explored by Neckel in Chapter 2 and empirically analysed by Demant and Lorenz (Chapter 5) in all its pervasive influence on the life of children and young people in residential care. Emotional labour, serving just this purpose, is discussed by Schröder in Chapter 6, who suggests it is a potent force harnessed by social workers and their institutions to instil conformity and apply normative expectations to service users. Gibson in Chapter 7 similarly uses the notion of 'emotional regulation' in constructing feelings of shame in others. On the other hand, in doing so, leaders and managers of social work services create a risk-averse climate whose outcomes may annihilate most of the positive effect of social work on the life of service users. 'Risks' – as Hardy declares quoting Anderson (2019, p 496) – 'are not simply dangers we face, but things individuals must take'. At the same time, shame and fear of transgression drastically reduces any space for innovation and creativity, as Gibson points out.

Other themes worth mentioning also emerge from the text. For example, the importance of paying greater attention to issues of shame in the whole field; keeping the individual who is experiencing shame at the centre of one's considerations; developing a practical understanding of the relational dimension of shame in the social work arena; and keeping to the fore an understanding of shame as a socially generated phenomena.

But before the structure of the book is introduced, it may be useful to explore in more depth the overarching theme of the meanings of shame: what it is, what it is like, and the areas of conceptual disagreement about this. In other words, we will offer a brief guide to the complex terminology deployed in relation to shame and some of its related emotions.

Shame as a social emotion

In his work, Thomas J. Scheff proposes a broad definition of the term shame. Such a definition is promising because it illustrates how the emotional constitution, the emotional reactions of people are linked to society, to social bonds. Referring to Lewis' analysis of shame as an inherent social emotion and Goffman's interpretations of embarrassment, Scheff proposes a conceptual definition: 'I define Shame as the large family of emotions that includes many cognates and variants, most notably embarrassment, guilt, humiliation, and related feelings such as shyness that originate in *threats to the social bond*' (Scheff, 2003, p 255). In this sense, these emotions are different forms of shame, they indicate shame on different levels: 'embarrassment' is considered as weak and transient, 'shame' is stronger and more durable, while 'humiliation' is powerful and has a long duration (Scheff, 2003, p 254). Here Scheff uses shame in a narrower and wider sense. He pleads for a broad definition of the term in order to be able to perceive the manifold social sources of shame in a broad and differentiated way.

The 'social nature' of shame is ubiquitous in most major studies of the subject. From the early 20th century, Cooley (1902) was able to advance the notion of 'the looking glass self': the idea that it is what we understand is being reflected back at us that sets in motion our feelings of either shame or pride. The reflection of ourselves is therefore an indirect one, that is mediated through the other and entails judgements of others (see also Scheff, 2003, p 242). Similarly, albeit three generations later and on a different continent, Landweer argues 'When feeling ashamed, we feel ashamed for something in front of somebody' (1999, p 2).[1] The ideas this simple statement contain are useful: she emphasises the social nature of shame while at the same time pointing to three aspects which – although weighted differently – are crucial references when it comes to analysing shame across different scientific disciplines: the significance of the self (*I* feel ashamed), the significance of the (potential) view of the others (*in front of somebody*) and the significance of normativity (for *something* which has been violated and which I insist be respected) (see Magyar-Haas 2012, 2015). From an education-philosophical perspective, as Schäfer and Thompson (2009, p 7) point out, these three relations are intrinsic to experiencing feelings of shame: thus – firstly – the relation of the bodily subject to itself and thus to its concept of self-ideal. Secondly, the relation of the subject to the present others: the 'witnesses of shame'. As well as, thirdly, the relations of those involved (the subject as well as the others) to shared social or moral norms and values. That the development of shame requires the violation of norms one accepts oneself, and that others must be physically, expectedly or supposedly present, are fundamental *structural features* of shame (Demmerling and Landweer, 2007, p 119; Demmerling, 2009; Neckel, 1993; Magyar-Haas, 2012, 2015).

Shame as a feeling, a subjective lived experience, has become a clear area of focus in contemporary analysis in the fields of philosophy, sociology and psychology. Notions of exclusion and expulsion are highlighted, as is the bodily response to shame. For example, shame can be understood as 'the visceral experience of being shunned and expelled from human connectedness' (Walker, 2011, p 452). The isolating effect of shame, which may further 'punish' those experiencing it with additional social expulsion or isolation, is frequently quoted as intrinsic to its destructive power. As Neckel (1993, p 94) points out, shame is 'rooted in the "social fear" of being left alone or expelled'. Shame impacts on social being by separating individuals from each other and silencing them through fear of denigration and degradation (Nussbaum, 2004). Shame is a repressive and disconnecting state, a point also made by Scheff (2014) in relation to alienation and separation.

Neckel further emphasises that the feeling of shame develops if a person perceives themselves as having been devalued or have experienced a 'value reduction'. Through the feeling of shame, he argues, a person becomes aware of being 'in a state which he/she perceives as unsatisfactory or undignified' (Neckel, 2009, p 104). Tangney and Dearing make a similar point in relation to poverty and shame: '[people have] profoundly experienced personal feelings of social marginality and worthlessness at being excluded from these resources' (2004, p 20). As Sicora (2018, p 29) emphasises in his work on shame: 'In shamed states we are never enough.'

Shame, then, has an existence, on the one hand, as a set of behaviours which are supposed to be avoided and, on the other hand, as concrete feelings. In this context, shame as a 'regulation mode' (Meyer–Drawe, 2009, p 38) is based on social norms and values which have been internalised by the concerned subject. These norms and values are powerful, because they are *socially accepted* and enforced through power: both when it comes to their internalisation and to their sanctioning. Hegemonic discourse emanating from and reproducing systems of social power casually ascribe 'unacceptability' to those groups who vary from the defining hierarchy: part of the process of 'othering'. Shame accrues easily to 'outsiders' and the 'othered' in all societies: the aged, the disabled, the vulnerable in a range of different ways are stigmatised and also imbibe these judgements of 'inferior' (Goffman, 1968).

Shame, then, is powerful also and most of all because the concerned human him/herself *accepts* the judgement. For example, Houston's recent work on recognition and shame acknowledges 'the repressive impact of shame on service users lives' (2016, p 13) because of their existence in a climate which is constantly defining the service user as inferior, a scrounger, dysfunctional, so that feeling inadequate – being shamed – becomes internalised as 'ashamed', a point we will return to.

This consideration of shame moves the discussion specifically into the realm of social work. We will now focus on shame and humiliation in this arena. As Frost (2016) comments in the context of England, having contact with a social worker is likely to be a source of shame – quite apart from the relational, identity or social structural struggles that may have driven (the need for) that engagement.

That this relates to the enforced status of the service user as dependent, 'needy' and vulnerable in an unequal relationship is certainly implicit in such shame (along with a sense of them having broken social values and norms), so the connection between dependency and shame is worth further consideration.

Shaming situations in the context of social work

Social work may, then, involve the kinds of social relations which challenge the subjects' self-perception to such an extent that they experience themselves as being somewhat deficient, as being 'lesser than' or inadequate (internalising the labels applied by services, for example, 'an inadequate parent'; 'a problem family') to the norm, and thus feel ashamed. However, the feelings of dependency and vulnerability themselves are accompanied by deeply uncomfortable 'feeling states' which are useful to consider.

The vulnerable and dependent subject

While it may seem that being in need and being 'dependent' is almost invariably accompanied by humiliation, from an anthropological perspective dependency is part of being human (see also Chapter 3). Not only are we as babies completely dependent on support, care and love, but as humans we are, throughout the course of our life, often in need of help in some form or another from others. At the same time independence can be understood as a social marker of the life stage of 'adulthood' in many cultures. This is, for example, illustrated in ideas of hegemonic masculinity, a concept which eschews all forms of dependency and vulnerability. This contradiction between the fundamental anthropological condition of the human being as a dependent being and the socially constructed expectation of independence and autonomy is part of the social background in which the emotion of shame becomes relevant.

But it is not only anthropological considerations about humans as bodily beings with needs that question the expectation of (full) independence and autonomy. In different terms social theory also contributes to the understanding of dependency: here it is not understood as an essential feature of bodily beings but is located in concrete intersubjective relations within which the process of becoming a subject is realised. Honneth, for example, suggests that 'the reproduction of social life is governed by the imperative of mutual recognition, because one can develop a practical relation-to-self only when one has learned to view oneself, from the normative perspective of one's partners in interaction, as their social addressee' (1995, p 92). The self-relationship (their subjectivity) is developed in relations of recognition with others – or the lack thereof. Because of this fundamental dependency to develop a sense of self, 'the other' is in a powerful position. The subject is a vulnerable subject, by virtue of its dependency on others, and is at the same time made subject through the other's power.

Against this background, when it comes to shaming the subject, acts of shaming by others are attacks on the individual's subjectivity. This can be based on the fact that, if subjectivity is created only by way of intersubjective relations, and thus the subject is genuinely dependent on the other, people are, at the same time, subject to the power of the others who may exploit this dependency for their own purposes (see also Chapter 2).

Relationships to others are, of course, socially contextualised, and social structural theorists also contribute a great deal to understanding how almost all forms of actual dependency have become demonised and reviled. Hoggett (2001), for example, argues that within the context of the highly individualised, narcissistic and ego-driven societies of late consumer capitalism, there is no place for the frail, the disabled, the old: those who are not able to achieve full empowerment are socially invalidated.

Shame in helping contexts

Social work is active in a field of society where experiences of humiliation are never far from the surface. Bohn (2007), for example, localises feelings of shame within the service users' lifeworlds. Contrary to Houston, cited in the section 'Shame as a social emotion', she tends to conceptualise them as something the service user brings with them into the social work encounter.

Also in contrast to Bohn, Bolay goes beyond the assumption of an already shamed service user and takes a more critical view, which examines the ambivalences of *providing* professional help in the field of social work. For him, feelings of shame are not just something service users bring with them into the field of social work, but that instead 'help' and 'shame' are themselves constitutively connected. The relation between dependency and shame, already mentioned, is at the heart of this formulation. Bolay (1996, p 80) assumes that being dependent on professional help means 'basically admitting or accepting that, through one's own (lack of) capacity, one's own (lack of) power, or one's own (inadequate) performance, one is not sufficiently capable of acting'. Professional help has the potential to create feelings of shame on the side of the 'addressees' – the (potential) service users – of social work. Even *'before any actual help ... the possibility of shame and humiliation is already structurally connected to professionalised help'*. Thus, Bolay (1996, p 81) identifies potential feelings of shame and their concomitant 'attacks' on the subjectivity of the service user within the actual structure of the helping relationship.

If a helping relationship requires somebody in need of help to reveal his/her own incapability and dependency, we may well assume that help itself may structurally come along with feelings of shame. At the same time this perspective seems to be too narrow. As explained, internalised feelings of shame (also) develop from not meeting social norms. The admission of being not or only moderately able to do this or that must thus, in each case, be considered in the context of the respective expectations each subject holds, which, in different historical and social contexts, may be quite different from each other. Contemporary, neoliberal expectations and demands of the 'empowered' subject are based on the myth that the subject alone, by his/her own performance and will – independent of others – is capable of doing almost everything. The subject's awareness of not being capable of meeting socially demanded – internalised and thus considered relevant by the subject – norms (such as: being indeed *in*dependent of others) may trigger feelings of shame.

Feelings of shame are neither simply what service users bring with them to the social work encounter as 'something to be solved' nor can they be understood just as an automatic product of helping relations: it is oversimplified to suggest help relations are – per se – humiliating. 'Help' does not 'automatically' come along with feelings of shame, the social norm which insists we 'should' be capable of doing a certain thing makes not meeting the norm an intrinsic component of shame. If being dependent on a certain kind of help violates a certain socially constructed norm (such as, eg 'self-sufficiency' in contemporary Western countries) then shame may ensue. For example, the meaning-laden, emotionally saturated and culturally reinforced norm of 'self-sacrificing motherhood' can mean, for women who are subject to family interventions by social services, that shame is likely to be a very powerful and intensely affective state. In a similar way, Schoneville (2019) was able to show that the lack of financial resources for parents who are faced with poverty meant they also see themselves as confronted with the question of whether they are able to fulfil their own ideas of good parenting – a question that comes with feelings of shame.

The internalisation of social norms

Shame, like all emotions, is experienced individually, but what makes this emotion a *social* emotion is that its foundation lies in the core of society. Shame is based on shared social norms and it occurs when a norm that is shared by and became part of the individual is violated. Social norms have to be understood not as just issues of knowledge but as internalised components of individuals' emotional worlds: their internal landscapes. Theorists such as Elias (2000 [1939], pp 365–78) argue that as a result of the 'process of civilisation' norms do not only function as an external force of order, but that the internalisation of norms can be understood as the 'social constraint towards self-constraint'. While norms are usually stabilised by powerful forces within society and the deviation is met with various kinds of sanctions, internalised norms have a self-disciplining function. The subject him/herself is permeated by society, is the bearer of social norms and values, and understands these to be part of him/herself. The feeling of shame is an internal force to sanction the violation of social norms and values – and in doing so the norms are confirmed and stabilised. As Goffman puts it:

> the stigmatised individual tends to share the same beliefs as we do ... The standards he has incorporated from the wider society equip him to be intimately alive to what others see as his failing, inevitably causing him, if only for moments, to agree he does fall short of what he really ought to be ... shame becomes a central possibility. (1963, pp 17–18)

Shame, then, refers to each person's respective social reality and is an emotional expression of internalised social sanctions. Accordingly, Neckel (2009, p 112) argues that 'an individual's feelings of shame always concern the person's position amidst a larger social context' and are thus 'the emotional nexus between the individual and the social structure, between the social hierarchy and the person's own status position'. Hence, considering feelings of shame provides the potential for looking back at the social embedding of these individuals. It draws attention to the connection between the reproduction of social inequality and emotions. And, furthermore, it opens possibilities to question the significance of social situations for each respective subject. Following this thought, Schoneville (2013, 2016) has shown that poverty, unemployment and social exclusion forces people into living situations that differ immensely from the way they want to live and how they think they should live. This contradiction is reflected in the emotion of shame. These thoughts and research results lead to the wider question of whether members of other socially denigrated groups (people from ethnic minorities, LGBT groups, asylum seekers etc) are more likely to be affected by shame.

When it comes to social work, this allows for understanding the forms of social humiliation (such as degradation or social exclusion) individuals or indeed groups are subjected to, while reflecting on both the contributory social context and what existing shame accompanies the group or individual into the helping context.

Shame theory in practice

Shame theory in social work, or indeed various other helping contexts, attempts to conceptualise the phenomena of shame and the feelings of shame across the interlinked dimensions of the individual subject, intersubjectivity (relatedness, in other words) and social-theoretical perspectives. The *feeling of shame* indicates that the subject's self-concept as well as his or her relevant, internalised norms have been attacked. This analysis allows for a greater understanding of the humiliated subject, as the latter becomes more recognisable in their vulnerability and genuine dependence on others and other things. It is also possible, by adopting these multilayered theoretical approaches, to critically consider the subject's social inclusion and exclusion, their social situation generally and the way they relate to these.

For social work in particular, it seems to be crucial to clarify the connection between help relationships and service users' feelings of shame. This raises the question of whether experiences of humiliation are in fact a constitutive element of the help relation: to what extent is humiliation structured into the helping relationship? And to what extent is this connection due to social expectations and to the institutional embedding of the intersubjective, professional relationship?

These questions prevent reductionist binary approaches, which know only two possibilities: either one thing or the other.

Against the background of our arguments so far, the question of how far do supporting measures (does social work intervention, in other words) have a stigmatising and devaluating effect emerges as fundamental. Equally important is to ask in what ways social work service users experience their living situations, as well as help, as humiliating and burdening? And perhaps most importantly for the practitioner, is it possible to help in ways that offer recognition which might support the respective subjects' self-esteem instead of attacking it?

Simply focusing on the question of whether subjects are humiliated or not in itself does not say much about whether the organisations and structures through which help is conceptualised and operationalised may still be potentially humiliating. What emerges from theoretical accounts propounded across several disparate countries and more than one continent is that these three levels – that of the subject, that of his/her (intersubjective) relations to others, as well as that of institutionally grounded and socially demanded norms and values – are best understood not as separate but as systematically related to each other. From this perspective, different ways of helping and supporting people provided by social work are not limited to single-focus interventions to eradicate a (socially defined) individual's problem, but, through a more interrelational application, can encompass issues of integration, and may thus support a broader consideration of ways of participating in society.

The structure of the book

The contributions presented in the book illustrate the theoretical perspectives outlined. Within the three main parts of the book we are going to examine these dimensions in an exemplary way. The chapters presented within Part I try to clarify the basic theoretical dimensions of the feeling of shame and its relation and relevance within the theory and practice of social work. Those within Part II analyse, in a more focused way, specific dimensions of shame and their relevance for those who are addressed by social work: the (potential) service users. The final part, Part III, looks at the profession of social work itself and asks which ways the feeling of shame is relevant for professionals and their ability to act as such.

Part I of the book interprets the feeling of shame from different disciplinary perspectives, in terms of sociological, psychosocial, historical and anthropological analyses. Against the background of multifaceted and various interpretations and definitions of the concept of shame in sociological, psychological and philosophical literature, Liz Frost (Chapter 1) proposes a systematic classification of the levels at which shame could be considered. This three-part taxonomy was developed in reference to Honneth's theory of recognition, with the expectation of generating an analytical tool for social work theory, reflection and practice. Three levels are taken into account: political/national, group/social and individual/personal. Each category considers how and by whom this type of shame might be generated, some key ideas or arguments within its purview, and some effects and/or practices to which it leads. The importance of the proposed taxonomy is illustrated and clarified on the basis of the phenomenon of ageism.

In his contribution (Chapter 2) Sighard Neckel points out the social characteristics of shame. This emotion arises from the interweaving of social relationships and presupposes the difference between the self and its ideal image, just as much as a violation of the norm in the eyes of others. In this respect shame is tied to sociality, normativity and morality. The author illustrates the structural anchoring of the loss of self-esteem in social conditions. Analogous to the dimensions of status acquisition used in sociology in modern societies, such as material prosperity, knowledge, and one's position in organisations and in informal groups, different social shaming techniques are explained. Neckel shows that social devaluations arise when people's work is not valued or when their needs are ignored. The associated devaluations in material and social terms produce feelings of inferiority – feelings with which the addressees of social work are systematically confronted. The chapter concludes by arguing that by individualising social situations and interpreting social disadvantages as personal failure, shame and the experience of one's own unworthiness are generated. It is shame that indicates how heterogeneous respect and recognition can be distributed in society.

Veronika Magyar-Haas (Chapter 3) shows that from an anthropological point of view the possibility of the experience of the self in two modes – as a subject and an object, also to be considered as the difference between the 'I' and 'Me' – serves as a structural condition of feeling ashamed. Even if shame in this sense can be defined as a universal human feeling, the historical and cultural relativity of this phenomenon should be taken into account. Magyar-Haas argues that in shameful situations subjects become objects for others and for themselves, too. She points out that by analysing shame the existential difference of the self can be presumed – but the sources of shame, as well as its intensity and forms of appearance, are historically, culturally and socially varying. The contribution discusses the historicity of anthropological perspectives and the historical, cultural and social involvement of understandings of shame. It argues that in the emotion of shame the self reveals itself as a vulnerable self in various relationships to others and to their normative expectations. With reference to neoliberal expectations and 'workfare programmes', the chapter illustrates to what extent these generate shame among service users and how shame can be seen as a reproduction of power.

Part II of the book focuses on service users and their experiences. The arguments of the chapters in this part draw heavily on empirical research in different fields of social work. They highlight ways in which the emotion of shame is something that service users have to deal with in their everyday lives, and how institutional and organisational settings, as well as interactions within social work interventions, are (potentially) associated with shame.

In the first chapter of this part, Chapter 4, Holger Schoneville argues that a social work perspective on poverty has to be informed by a theory of subjectivity. He sets out to show what such a perspective entails and what role emotions, such as shame, play within it. He illustrates his argument through a research project that he conducted. One of the central questions of the project was how people who use food banks in Germany experience their life and what these experiences mean for them in terms of their self-relationship and self-conception. Interviews with food-bank users reveal that the emotion of shame is especially virulent when it comes to poverty. The analysis points out that poverty not only means that people are faced with a lack of resources, but that they are also forced into living circumstances in which they face contradictions regarding their (self-)expectations and their everyday reality. The chapter therefore highlights how the structure of social inequality, institutional forms of welfare and shame are interlinked.

Within Chapter 5, Marie Demant and Friederike Lorenz discuss the role of shame in the context of violence against children in residential care. Their work is based on two empirical projects and includes reports of survivors of sexual violence, from hearings conducted by the German 'Independent Inquiry into Child Sexual Abuse', which started its work in 2016. It furthermore includes empirical material from a research project on systematic violence by a team of professionals in a residential care home for children with disabilities. Both perspectives indicate how young people experienced shame and humiliation as part of the institutional setting. Furthermore, the chapter shows the negative impact these practices have on children and adolescents in situations of dependency, seeking help and disclosure. It points out practices of humiliation as a part of the violence and shows to the extent to which shame can affect the likelihood that young people in these situations are able to be heard and get help.

Within Chapter 6, Carsten Schröder analyses the production of emotional atmospheres as part of professional social work. He argues that emotional work, as work on professionals' own emotions and the emotions of others, is an integral part of social work. He provides examples from a project in which he ethnographically observed social workers within a residential care home. His work focuses on how professional social workers create emotional atmospheres through and as part of their interventions. In his example he focuses on the production of an emotional atmosphere that aims to reinforce a rule within the setting of the care home in order to discipline the young residents. Schröder points out how harmful the experience of shame can be and therefore raises the question of whether these interventions can still be viewed as professional interventions.

Part III of the book is focused on shame when felt by social workers. Matthew Gibson (Chapter 7) considers how those invested in an organisation seek to regulate feelings of shame in employees in order to generate compliance and conformity to organisational rules, standards and expectations. This chapter outlines a framework for understanding how leaders and managers seek to contain or divert employees' feelings of shame as a result of undertaking required tasks while ensuring shame is evoked as a result of any transgressions. This perspective extends and deepens themes developed within shame in professional practice, both within social work and in other professions.

In Chapter 8 Mark Hardy argues that the highly charged context in which practice occurs means that because of unrealistic expectations of infallibility social work decision-making has taken on an existential character. He elaborates on why this is so, accounting for how risk, blame and shame intersect both practically and emotionally, as well as the value of existential thinking in enabling practitioners to preserve the authenticity of their practice.

In the final chapter of Part III, Alessandro Sicora argues that even for social workers the shift from 'I/you made a mistake' to 'I am/you are a mistake', that is, 'I am/you are a failure as a practitioner or even as a person' is easy and common, and shame may be the resulting feeling. This chapter also presents some examples of short reflective writing by social workers and social work students who undertook an in-depth structured reflection on some of their most relevant experiences in relation to this issue.

Note

1 Within the chapter we refer to quite a few contributions by German academics, whose works are available only in German. The quotes from papers and books have been translated from German into English to the best of our ability.

References

Anderson, A. (2019) 'Parrhesia: accounting for different contemporary relations between risk and politics', *Journal of Sociology*, 55: 495–510.

Bohn, C. (2007) 'Zur Bedeutung der Scham im professionellen Kontext sozialer Arbeit', *Theorie und Praxis der Sozialen Arbeit*, 4: 51–3.

Bolay, E. (1996) 'Scham und Beschämung. Subjekttheoretische Überlegungen zur Prozeßqualität in helfenden Beziehungen', *Widersprüche. Zeitschrift für sozialistische Politik im Bildungs-, Gesundheits- und Sozialbereich*, 61: 75–91.

Cooley, C. H. (1902) *Human Nature and the Social Order*, New York: Scribner's.

Demmerling, C. (2009) 'Philosophie der Scham', in A. Schäfer and C. Thompson (eds) *Scham*, Paderborn: Ferdinand Schöningh, pp 75–101.

Demmerling, C. and Landweer, H. (2007) *Philosophie der Gefühle. Von Achtung bis Zorn*, Stuttgart: J. B. Metzler.

Elias, N. (2000 [1939]) *The Civilising Process: Sociogenetic and Psychogenetic Investigations*, Oxford: Blackwell.

Frost, L. (2016) 'Exploring the concepts of recognition and shame for social work', *Journal of Social Work Practice: Psychotherapeutic Approaches in Health, Welfare and the Community*, 30(4): 431–46.

Goffman, E. (1968) *Stigma: Notes on the Management of Spoiled Identity*, Harmondsworth: Pelican.

Hoggett, P. (2001) 'Agency, rationality and social policy', *Journal of Social Policy*, 30(1): 37–56.

Honneth, A. (1995) *The Struggle for Recognition: The Moral Grammar of Social Conflicts*, Cambridge, MA: Polity Press.

Houston, S. (2016) 'Empowering the "shamed" self: recognition and critical social work', *Journal of Social Work*, 16(1): 3–21.

Landweer, H. (1999) *Scham und Macht. Phänomenologische Untersuchungen zur Sozialität eines Gefühls*, Tübingen: Mohr Siebeck.

Magyar-Haas, V. (2012) 'Beschämende Vorgänge. Verhältnisse von Scham, Macht und Normierung in Kontexten der Sozialpädagogik und Sozialen Arbeit', in S. Andresen and W. Heitmeyer (eds) *Zerstörerische Vorgänge. Missachtung und sexuelle Gewalt gegen Kinder und Jugendliche in Institutionen*, Weinheim: BeltzJuventa, pp 195–214.

Magyar-Haas, V. (2015) *Grenzverhältnisse. Spiel-Räume der Bildung und Verhandlung von Grenzen in pädagogischen Kontexten*, Dissertation, University of Bielefeld.

Meyer-Drawe, K. (2009) 'Am Ursprung des Selbstbewusstseins: Scham', in A. Schäfer and C. Thompson (eds) *Scham*, Paderborn: Ferdinand Schöningh, pp 37–49.

Neckel, S. (1993) 'Achtungsverlust und Scham. Die soziale Gestalt eines existentiellen Gefühls', in S. Neckel (ed) *Die Macht der Unterscheidung. Essays zur Kultursoziologie der modernen Gesellschaft*, Frankfurt and New York: Campus, pp 92–109.

Neckel, S. (2009) 'Soziologie der Scham', in A. Schäfer and C. Thompson (eds) *Scham*, Paderborn: Ferdinand Schöningh, pp 103–18.

Nussbaum, M. (2004) *Hiding from Humanity: Disgust, Shame and the Law*, Princeton, NJ: Princeton University Press.

Schäfer, A. and Thompson, C. (2009) 'Scham: eine Einführung', in A. Schäfer and C. Thompson (eds) *Scham*, Paderborn: Ferdinand Schöningh, pp 7–36.

Scheff, T. (2003) 'Shame in Self and Society', *Symbolic interaction*, 26(2): 239–62.

Scheff, T. (2014) 'The ubiquity of hidden shame in modernity', *Cultural Sociology*, 8(2): 129–41.

Schoneville, H. (2013) 'Armut und Ausgrenzung als Beschämung und Missachtung. Hilfe im Kontext der Lebensmittelausgaben "Die Tafeln" und ihre Konsequenzen', *Soziale Passagen*, 5(1): 17–35.

Schoneville, H. (2016) *Armut, soziale Ausgrenzung und die Neugestaltung des Sozialen. Die Lebensmittelausgaben 'Die Tafeln' in Deutschland*, Dissertation, University of Kassel.

Schoneville, H. (2019) 'Familien in Armut. Erziehung im Widerspruch von Armut', *Grundschulzeitschrift*, 314: 28–31.

Sicora, A. (2018). 'Vergogna e servizio sociale. Esplorazioni intorno a un'emozione poco considerate', *Prospettive sociali e sanitarie*, 4: 29–32.

Tangney, J. P. and Dearing, R. L. (2004) *Shame and Guilt*, New York: Guilford Press.

Walker, J. (2011) 'The relevance of shame in child protection work', *Journal of Social Work Practice*, 25(4): 451–63.

PART I

Theoretical dimensions of shame

Making sense of shame theory: a psychosocial structure

Liz Frost

Introduction

Shame is an overwhelming emotion, and its use in theory and practice, for example in the sociology of emotions, psychosocial theory and applied social sciences such as social work, is also burgeoning and complex. Within sociology, how shame is generated through class inequality in education, health and poverty is the focus of much careful analysis (Reay, 2005; Wilkinson and Pickett, 2009; Chase and Walker, 2012; Peacock, Bissell and Owen, 2013). Social work literature on shame in relation to service users and social workers is beginning to emerge (eg Walker, 2011; Gibson, 2016; Frost, 2016).

Noticeably, the sheer volume of versions and approaches to the concept of shame circulating contemporarily, and the ubiquity of its use, renders the concept both confusing and opaque. It is a term used to describe very personal, even confessional, experiences of feeling unworthy within oneself, but it can also mean feeling negatively evaluated by social groups (as with internet shaming). It is further used in broader contexts, for example being ashamed that unassisted refugees drown on one's national shores in attempts to flee war zones. Social workers report that, for their service users (and sometimes themselves), of all the complex psychosocial human states they encounter, the most prevalent, entrenched and obscure is shame. This chapter proposes a framework for making sense of the many contemporary uses of shame.

Ways of 'ordering' shame (eg definitional, comparative) are specifically formulated in a great deal of seminal work on the subject. For example, the notion of shame as either 'external or internal'; shame in contrast to other significant negative emotional states such as guilt or stigma; as either individual or social/group; and as comparable across cultures and epochs, do much to guide readers through this complex topic (Stearns, 2016). This chapter advances a structure, not by establishing contrast or comparison with other experiences or across time, but by focusing on meaningful differences within the existing ideas of shame in circulation. Axel Honneth's (1995, 2012) work on recognition is the prototype of this model.

One of the reasons that recognition theory, and Honneth's version in particular, has become visible in a broad range of disciplines, including social work (eg Houston, 2010, 2016) might be that it formulates a pragmatic (three-part) taxonomy. It develops both an analytical framework and, potentially, a normative critique. It can be deployed as a hypothetical enquiry and in formulating a specific understanding of what humans need, and in what areas resources, practices and even ethical codes fail to achieve this (Taylor, 2002; McNay, 2008; Garrett, 2010).

The concept of shame, and that of recognition, can contrast, 'mirror' or illuminate each other. They can be productively comparatively examined, through an equivalent theoretical focus (Connolly, 2014; Houston, 2016; Frost, 2016; see also Chapter 2). In terms of subjective experience, for example, the absence of the one might suggest the presence of the other: if I am recognised, my shame may be ameliorated. Honneth (1992) was also concerned to consider shame. Nancy Fraser's (2013) notion of misrecognition can function as a reading of collective shaming, though less concerned with subjective experience than social structures.

This chapter formulates a tripartite approach to understanding shame, following in the footsteps of Honneth's (1995) three-part organisation of a complex, psychosocial phenomena (recognition). It advances categories of 'political, social and personal'. But firstly, prior to this central undertaking, the chapter sets out some of the parameters of the discussion. It then explains the taxonomy itself, before discussing each category of shame in more depth: particularly the key ideas and arguments in its purview and through what mechanisms it is generated. Finally, the chapter illustrates, through the example of ageism/ageing, how a comprehensive analysis of shame in each of its three domains may be accessed to inform social policy and social work in this complex area.

Before introducing the framework, it seems helpful to draw attention to the ethos and some of the intellectual challenges which affect this enterprise. Of primary importance here is that the underlying perspective is psychosocial. Although familiar to many readers, this can still be a confusing approach, not least because of its rather different meanings in psychology, psychiatry and medicine to contemporary psychosocial studies (see eg Woodward, 2015). The body of work developed by mainly UK psychosocial theorists since the 1990s or so holds a fundamental tenet that the social contexts of people's lives permeate their identities at a conscious and unconscious level (see eg Elias, 2000 [1939]; Lucey and Raey, 2002; Jimenez and Walkerdine, 2011; Frost, 2015). For example, structural inequalities such as class or gender profoundly impact how people are able to manage in the world: something like Pierre Bourdieu's (1973) notion of habitus is often referenced in psychosocial scholarship. Equally, the body of work argues, early childhood relational experiences lay down a dynamic unconscious that will form the 'lens' through which people can perceive the world. Honneth chose to use psychoanalyst Donald Winnicott's object relations theory to explain how this first and fundamental form of recognition – loving and caring – become incorporated into the person (Winnicott, 1958). Winnicott's theory can also productively be applied to shame (see the section on how shame is generated individually). Psychosocial scholars utilise Kleinian and Lacanian theory as well as Freud's foundational oeuvre. They argue that social structures and the affective unconscious constantly interact with each other to construct and reconstruct subjective experience and dynamic identity. They also position subjective experience as central to forms of psychosocial research and academic enquiry. This can be of value to social work (Frost and McClean, 2014; Froggett, Ramvi and Davies, 2015). This chapter reflects this disciplinary perspective.

Secondly, dividing complex and ubiquitous human 'states' like shame into three categories (or five, or eight) is an introductory strategy, offering initial access to identification, discussion and analysis. But it requires ignoring invariable overlaps and similarities: an artificial simplification. Like Honneth's recognition theory, the linguistic trope of categorisation – 'there are three types of ...' – plays off comprehensibility against nuance, establishing a base line, or platform, of ideas to elaborate, discuss, critique and apply, in the classroom as well as during the case discussion and in the research team meeting. This chapter reflects just such entanglements.

Thirdly, although the three categories being suggested are not intended to mirror Honneth's, the act of structuring this material thus, for attempting a model which is analytical, critical and normative in its purpose and, further, for positioning the experiencing individual at the heart of the discussion, means the chapter is indebted to Honneth's work.

A fourth proviso that needs to be acknowledged is both conceptual and linguistic. Somewhat paradoxically, some of the most enduringly trenchant and powerful theory in the area of shame sidesteps the word itself. Erving Goffman's work, though recognising the importance of shame, develops 'stigma' as his central analytical framework (1968b); Richard Sennett and Jonathan Cobb (1973) recognise the ordinary working-class experience of being treated as unworthy of respect and seeing oneself as culpable as a devastating exemplar of 'the hidden injuries of class', though without specifically naming this as shame. Fraser's (2013) concept of 'misrecognition', in which institutionally some people are constituted as of less importance and worthy of less respect, likewise powerfully invokes the concept without the word.

This, of course, begs the question: 'if these careful theorists mostly do not use the word shame, then why would anyone?' Scheff (2000) suggests that the taboo in relation to shame means that it is rarely mentioned by those subject to the state, and this seems to also extend to those who study it. This may also be a disciplinary issue. These sociological/political science authors (except Goffman, a social psychologist) may prefer not to use such a 'psychologised' term and such a personalised affect as shame. Fraser states that 'misrecognition is an institutionalized social relation, not a psychological state. In essence [it is] a status injury ...' (2013, p 177). Psychosocial theorists would question that these are alternatives, and also question the need to keep a disciplinarily distance from the latter.

Finally, it is important to acknowledge that there is a vein in shame theory which considers its positive role in national and personal conduct: in other words, the act of 'shaming' can be regarded, potentially or in reality, as a mechanism to punish culturally unacceptable behaviours, whether corporate or personal (eg carbon footprints, bullying) (Jacquet, 2015). There is not the scope here to include this perspective, but this chapter does focus on negative shame. Ethically, it is aligned with those theorists whose position on shame is that it is overwhelmingly a negative and destructive human force (eg Nussbaum, 2004).

Having made these provisos, the chapter will now briefly define each of three categories of shame, before going on to discuss them in more depth.

Three categories of shame

The position of this chapter can be outlined thus. In contemporary 'developed' countries, people are vulnerable to feelings of shame in three distinct realms:

> People are vulnerable to shame in relation to their *political* selves. This is likely to mean through their memberships of states/nations. These are contexts in which power relations are fundamental. The

actions of governments, for example, may generate collective shame. Agency may be experienced as limited or non-existent. A category, then, of *political/national shame*.

People are vulnerable to shame as *group* members: of classes, communities, cultures, identity categories, families and so on. Within and between these, meaning is fundamental: for example, norms which cohere and/or exclude; beliefs and discourses, all of which position some groups as shameful. Agency may seem possible in some contexts. A category, then, of *group/social shame*.

People are vulnerable to *individual* shame. Elements of their past and present experiences, imposed and chosen, can generate powerful visceral and affective responses. These may be experienced as personal, individual and, frequently, silencing and/or isolating. Agency is often assumed totally, and sometimes denied defensively. A category, then, of *individual/personal shame*.

These three categories comprise a structure for thinking about shame. It may be profitable to develop each in more depth through critical analysis and examples.

Political/national shame

'Political' is an amorphous category, into the meaning of which important inroads have been made in the preceding decades, for example, in highlighting 'the political' in many forms of relations, such as gender relations/intimate life (Benhabib, 1999; Clarke, Hoggett and Thompson, 2006). 'Political shame' as a concept also has a venerable literature, mainly in philosophy, from Socrates to Nussbaum (2004), concerned with, for instance, the identification of the state as not achieving its democratic ideals and the shame of this. This political shame is an invocation to reform: a moral category whereby the identification of which should lead to action. Thus, Honneth (1992) uses this: shame may be indicative of state injustices and *should* lead to political activism.

'Political' also includes notions of the tectonic shifts experienced in the 20th and 21st centuries as all 'Western' wealthy social democracies engage in individualisation, globalisation and the digital revolution. This is too vast a canvas to work on here. However, what does seem of importance are the ways in which it suits the state — certainly the neoliberal state — to promote individualism and individual responsibility (see also Chapter 3). Contemporarily, 'political' becomes easily subsumed in the idea of 'national' as an appeal to an identifying voice. The recasting of budgetary choices made by central governments as issues of 'national shame' is not without its uses for the state. The appeal to 'nation' may also strengthen such a voice. Political/national shame, then, works through complex mechanisms. The following examples serve to illustrate the concept:

In October 2013 Jeremy Hunt, then UK Secretary of State for Health, claimed a million old people in the UK suffered from loneliness and this was a 'national shame' (Hunt, 2013). Ryan (2017), in the *Guardian*, claimed that people trapped at home because they were wheelchair users was a 'national shame'. On a similar tack, Australia's National Children's Commissioner, Megan Mitchell, spoke in May 2016 of 50,000 children in care as 'A national shame' (Mitchell, 2016). The *Pakistan Express Tribune* and *The Times of India* regularly present editorials on 'honour killing' as a national shame. And so on.

These are certainly political issues – their specific national locations lead hence to an invocation of an 'us', the enfranchised members of this state, who are addressed as sharing in some way the responsibility for 'our problem' and by implication the moral imperative to rectify this.

Group/social shame

Much of the classic literature of shame in the social sciences takes for granted that it is in relation to one's immediate social group that shame is most relevant. Thus, Cooley's (1902) notion of the 'looking glass self' has each person reflected back by those in their particular social world. Scheff and the symbolic interactionists developed this (Scheff, 2000, 2014). Goffman (1959) is helpful here, and so, too, is Giddens' (1991) work.

Socially and/or group-generated shame includes prejudice and the unthinking circulation of prejudicial ideas; the exclusion of some groups by 'othering'. It is the kind of thinking we might associate with 'red-top' journalism: 'they [insert any category of 'outsiders'] take all our jobs and bankrupt the NHS …'. The attribution to some groups of what are actually social problems and experiences also frequently generates shame, for example the 19th-century policy category of the 'undeserving poor'; education's notion of being a 'school refuser'; and, in social work, categories such as 'dysfunctional families' and 'the hard to engage'.

Particular sections of society might be shamed by the circulation of ideas of their worthlessness, as in the term 'benefit scroungers'. Owen Jones' (2012) popular analysis of the category 'Chavs' offers an extended example of what Fraser calls 'misrecognition' and he calls 'demonisation'. Shame is category damage from the disrespect, hostility or even patronisation shown to certain groups, through such an imposed definition of its identity: 'tasteless, loud and vulgar'; a 'welfare cheat'; the infamous, and racist, Donald Trump accusation that Mexicans are rapists and drug dealers.

Individual/personal shame

As noted in the introduction to this chapter individual experience is at the heart of psychosocial enquiry. Here it is also important to understand that any or all of the concepts mentioned are likely to be experienced as individual shame. The relationship among how individuals believe themselves to be perceived by the group, as set out in the previous section 'Group/social shame', by another person and/or by some internalised voice that is identified as their own, is enmeshed.

Damming judgements may relate to membership of a social group or a generalised category, for example being poor, but may also be specifically targeted at a particular individual. Jon Ronson's (2015) book on internet shaming mainly concerns named individuals, though that does not preclude the additional impact of wider social structural oppressions on these judgements, for example, misogyny.

Individual shame, in the same way as individual being, resonates with issues of identity generally. People's perceptions of their 'social selves' form part of their being as surely as their infant experiences do (to a psychosocial scholar). An individual's particular and general internal worlds, developed from birth onwards and affecting how they will perceive life, contain the potential for and, some would argue, the reality of, shame.

Thus shame is an individual issue. However, it is, in tandem, profoundly socially generated, though individually 'lived'. For example, the self-loathing a women might experience if she feels 'fat', or the diminishment of an ageing man the first time someone offers him their seat on a bus, are still experienced individually as shaming however much the individual is aware these feelings exist because of social attitudes. Sennett and Cobb (1973) recognised that the class injuries working men experienced were the product of both being disrespected *and seeing themselves as responsible*.

Shame, then, is experienced by individuals as failure to live up to socially generated expectations that have been incorporated into their selves and may well be experienced as of the self. Indeed, writers such as

Connolly (2014) would argue that the powerful nature of the emotion of shame is located precisely in that experience. 'Failure to control the body' examples are particularly evocative: the social imperative of self-control and bodily containment is strong and impossible to separate from a person's subjectivity. 'Incontinence' of feeling is also thus experienced as shaming, for example: to be seen to be frightened in conflict or combat; to be in tears in the office; to be too dependent or 'needy' in relationships. The visibility of these humiliations to loved ones, friends and communities of value exacerbates this. To be labelled 'a slag' on Facebook may be experienced as devastating humiliation. To have a social worker call round, likewise.

Through what processes is shame generated?

Having outlined the three categories of shame and offered some illustrative examples, the chapter now looks more specifically at the processes through which these types of shame are generated.

How is shame generated? Political/national shame

This considers shifts in zeitgeist and in social policy – the broad contexts of contemporary existence and contemporary social work – and examines ways in which these national and international changes may impact on the issue of shame.

As mentioned, meta-social changes, affecting states and nations and enacted in that realm, may make the experience of shame more likely in the present era than at any other time. For example, the rapid acceleration over a century from (relatively) collective societies to greater social individualisation sets in place the potential for this. Individualisation, which privileges choice, autonomy, self-determination and indeed determination, includes not just the imperative of individual responsibility/choices but also individual blame/shame if 'success', by whatever standard, is not achieved. Within an era of individualism, shame silences and isolates further. Nussbaum (2004), for example, comments on how shame impacts on social being by separating people and silencing them, as contact with others may expose the individual to degradation or denigration. Loneliness may proceed from this. Chase and Walker's (2012) analysis understands shame as not just a threat to the social bonds within which people live, but as potential social damage of 'an atomization of modern society' (p 739). Loss of collective and community contributes to a cycle of disconnection, alienation and exclusion. Scheff, for example, argues that, as the traditional rural society gave way to the 'dehumanisation' of the city and its new complex worlds, the social bonds between people decreased. As people became decontextualised from each other, condemnatory judgements could then be made easily and quickly on superficial understanding and slight evidence.

Changes in socio-economic practices at state level, then, can produce alienation and the loss of collectivism, while separation, disconnection and the potential for shame intensifies. This continues to be relevant as individualism becomes more intense under neoliberal regimes. Contemporary political economic theorists like Fraser advance an analysis of how political contexts degrade some sections of those who live within them.

Fraser's notion of political change and how it exposes people more intensely to misrecognition forms part of her thesis of much of the Western world shifting from 'a politics of redistribution' (in which the focus is on economic equality; for example, the reduction of child poverty, improvements in benefits systems) to that of 'recognition' in which the focus is on the socio/political recognition of difference: in other words the full inclusion of diverse identities). She considers, for example, governmental (including UK) turns to Third Way politics in the 1980s, and their promotion of recognition issues at the expense of, and/or as a distraction from, issues of economic distribution. The whole focus on issues of 'choice' rather than redistributive equality would also fit this analysis. Individuals are thus flatteringly addressed – 'your choice; you know what's best' – while many experience no access to 'the best' choices, as actual resources are unfairly distributed or severely limited.

Structural explanations, which understand the shamed individual as a product of a hierarchical and profoundly unequal state, are, then, of explanatory value. Using a Bourdieusian analysis, the issues of class oppression, social marginality, social suffering and symbolic violence are profoundly political/national, and similarly to Fraser's analysis, seen as products of the injustices of distribution and also sites of misrecognition – of institutional demeaning and disrespect. Bourdieu, similarly, in both early work on the symbolic violence perpetrated in the education system to working-class children rendered outsiders and eventually outcasts in a bourgeois system (1973), through to his later analysis of social suffering (1999) as socially (and symbolically) generated, analyses the mass damage of powerful social shaming.

This chapter has limitations in terms of scale, and the political changes of the 20th–21st century that link to the notion of shame are numerous and complex. Globalisation, for example, and particularly global capitalism, has an insidious impact on many areas of people's lives – and not only through its subtle reinforcement of Western individualism. One example feminist research generated was that the homogenised, normative version of the 'desirable' female body (blond, white, thin) circulating round the world induced feelings of inadequacy and shame in those women who did not fit it, and instigated consumption of all the possible 'fixes' (eg skin lighteners, diets, cosmetic surgery) on the market (Bartky, 1990; Frost, 2005). Drawing on Gilligan's (2001) work with violent offenders, Wilkinson and Pickett (2009) link inequality levels to a range of social ills, not least of which, violence, they connect to shame: the shame of being derogated through lack of status and lack of those goods – those very expensive goods – which demonstrate to the world of consumer capitalism that a person is 'respect-worthy'. Violence may be a claim for respect when poverty is shameful (for a different connection between violence and shame see Chapter 5 on violence against children in residential care).

The reach of the global digital revolution into all aspects of contemporary life is another meta-issue here – as a medium but also as message. The individualised nature of much of its consumption, the disinhibiting of ordinary human consideration afforded by its anonymity and, paradoxically, the exposed nature of any interchange allows for such levels of intense verbal derogation of the individual by its mass audience/voyeurs/participants that humiliation and shame constantly lurk (Ronson, 2015).

How is shame generated? Group/social shame

Issues of class, as discussed, usefully hand us across the boundary between the first and second categories here. The re-enforcement of class differences can be seen as the state's power at work through a range of mechanisms, but with equal validity elided to the membership of a particular group or category. In the individualised societies of late modernity, though, it is easy to bypass notions of the group altogether and focus solely on the relationship between state and the individual. Certainly, the modernist theorists who embedded shame thinking put 'the social' at the heart of their analysis, for example, what messages from their social sphere impacted on people, and this analysis has continued to be useful for understanding how and by whom groups may become demeaned.

Social groups and social relations form the basic unit of analysis for Honneth's (1995) work: recognition from their 'community of value' is a crucial ingredient of people's psychological well-being. Houston

(2010), directly concerned with issues of the emotions in the social work sphere, utilises the premise of 'the generalized other' (Mead, 1967) to consider how the experience of being in social groups and contexts form people's self-judgements – including the harsh ones, such as shame.

Scheff's work on alienation and integration offers one analysis of group membership and shame, and it is a concern of further symbolic interactionist work, with both Goffman and Giddens' differing versions useful here. Goffman, through the notion of stigma, formulates a version of shame in which self-definition is undermined by the negative definition of the group, and looks at how this becomes incorporated into identity (1959, 1968b). For example, if someone has a background of mental illness, their attempts to define themselves as recovered may be undermined by their community's or potential employer's continuing to treat them as 'unstable'. Forms of subaltern identity are thus ascribed, shaming the individual and becoming incorporated into self-image.

Giddens (1991), though locating his analysis within late modernity, considers similar themes to Goffman and Scheff. He identifies shame as a powerful affect within individual and group relations, through the ontological insecurity generated by the lack of capacity to sustain a coherent identity ('narrative of self') in the face of struggles with social definition.

Thinking more structurally: oppressed social groups are devalued, disrespected and shamed. These are the excluded, marginalised sectors of a society about which there may be little understanding or concern, and with whom social workers are often involved. The working class, as mentioned, women, people from black and ethnic minority groups, the disabled, gay, binary neutral, old, and those who may additionally be further inscribed in categories of need: poor, the homeless, the mentally ill. This is not exhaustive, but gives some indication of where shame is likely to be induced and respect mostly lacking.

In addition to a social structural analysis, Kleinian psychoanalysis has been much used to understand intergroup hatreds and denigration. Based on the residual unconscious affect from early childhood material, it considers the 'splitting' of groups and the projection of all unwanted feelings and ideas from one group to another. Thus the 'bad' is located in a group or groups that are not 'ours' or 'mine' but 'those others'. Useful for thinking about racism (Clarke, 2003; Gadd and Dixon, 2010) and 'othering' as a more general strategy of group exclusion (Kapur and Campbell, 2004), the excluded or 'subaltern' are likely to be exposed to derogation and insult – to a battery of shaming ideas and beliefs. Constructing certain categories – 'the work-shy' or 'social security scroungers' – can be understood as just such a group process.

Psychosocial scholarship drawing on both structural and psychoanalytical accounts has contributed much to understanding group affect (Frosh, Phoenix and Pattman, 2003; Woodward, 2015). Central to, for example, Jimenez and Walkerdine's (2011) account of shame and masculinity are individual identities dynamically and intersectionally constructed, including class, gender and community, as well as intergenerational family relationships. Their work is a social structural analysis, which considers class relations, social inequality and gender. However, as psychosocial scholarship, it also understands the (shamed) individual, as constituted by dynamic unconscious, defence mechanisms and affect, to be the subject of the study. In this research, the closure of a steelworks – the traditional working-class male employer – in a Welsh town means that not just jobs but the working-class male identities constituted in relation to these jobs – strong, 'hard' and hard-working, proud, collective – are no longer available to the younger generation of men. What jobs are available are seen by the previous generation – their fathers and uncles and the older men in the community – as 'girls' jobs'. The alternative of unemployment (such as the service sector) some are forced into is equally humiliating in a milieu where 'real work' is respected. Jimenez and Walkerdine's research discovered significant levels of shame and anxiety, as the young men saw themselves as doing demeaning jobs.

How is shame generated? Individual/personal shame

The psychoanalytical and psychosocial, as discussed, and indeed much symbolic interactionist work, concern themselves with the individual subject positioned by the negative reflections and demeaning opinions through which they understand themselves. Shame is then simultaneously both individual and social.

In this section, two theoretical mechanisms are deployed, through which the individual's position within interpersonal relations is the primary site within which the potential or actual experience of shame can be understood: object relations theory and Giddens' work on reflexive narrative identity.

Shame, like recognition, is experienced differentially by individuals to some extent. Like recognition, there is an agentic recipient. From a psychosocial perspective, this is an experiencing subject with a dynamic unconscious which forms the basis of their identity (as does their social structural location). Early childhood relational experiences lay down affective possibilities, and the unconscious may contain propensities to experience the world as persecutory through to benign (as a spectrum, not alternatives). This will impact on how (much) shame is felt: how sensitive an individual is to shame. For example where early parent–child relations did not nurture a child's sense of 'mattering' – of being worthy of love – they may be unable to develop a strong internal sense of themselves as essentially respect-worthy or important. The cause of this can be theorised as an 'attachment' issue. Walker (2011), for example, understands shame in the context of attachment theory, as the result of early childhood experiences of the prolonged/severe rupture of parental attunement (meaning understanding and/or empathy), or more broadly as lack of parental empathy or capacity to prioritise a baby's needs. The developing internal self lacks feelings of worth: a sense of shame becomes more likely.

However, the object relations author frequently turned to by shame and recognition theorists – Winnicott – argues that all individuals have a potential for feeling ashamed. Certainly, he too argued that the relationship between the mother (figure) and her baby at the early stages of infancy was formative.

The establishment of trust, from which the infant can move from 'other' trust to self-trust, and from dependence (when it is met by the mother figure) to self-confidence is part of these early processes. Where needs are met, a baby can internalise the meeting of needs and develop the capacity to meet them from their own psychic resources. This, Winnicott (1958) argues, has profound implications for whether, as an adult, he or she can trust, nurture, love and also receive love (or indeed friendship, closeness etc).

However, Winnicott (1958) also reasons that this intense, symbiotic parent and baby phase necessarily establishes the potential for shame universally. The baby's initial sense of omnipotence and centrality in relation to his or her expanding universe is necessarily revised in the light of small (but not to a little child) failures, everyday limitations and gaps in competence, and so on. 'The toddler learns itself to be vulnerable, dependent and frail, not omnipotent: a basis for shame' (Frost, 2016, p 436).

These painful feelings, this suggests, are part of the ordinary make-up of adults. Present in their dynamic unconscious are dependence, failures and vulnerability: the kinds of feelings that are the essence of a sense of shame.

The individual's identity development, then, is the mechanism which makes the experience of shame a reality. This is not just at the heart of psychoanalytical approaches but also symbolic interactionist theory.

Giddens' work, for example, offers a further approach to understanding the individually internalised nature of shame.

Giddens (1991) less specifically focuses on issues of the unconscious, but still connects the individual and their 'identity formation' through their capacity to sustain a coherent and credible self-narrative. He talks of shame as the positive side of the person's 'motivational system', with something like pride or self-esteem as its opposite. The potentially shaming state in Giddens' analysis is not Scheff's 'alienation' but 'ontological insecurity'. The individual's reflexive narrative constructs a viable identity which is then 'themselves in the world', as experienced by others and in close intimate relations with a specific other. Shame is experienced when this falls apart – when the coherence of the narrative is shattered by actions which do not fit this sustained story of the person one is (Giddens, 1991).

Shame, Giddens suggests

> is a negative side of the motivational system of the agent. The other side is pride or self-esteem: confidence in the integrity and value of the narrative of self-identity. (1991, p 66)

Giddens understands this as becoming integral to one's understanding of self, and self-reinforcing through reflexive narratives of self: shame is dependent on feelings of insufficiency and inadequacy, and shame generates shame.

Winnicott and Giddens both seem to offer productive ways of considering the subjective and individual experience of shame, particularly if one situates these individuals in the context of the neoliberal zeitgeist. Other mechanisms may also play a part. For example, one might consider the notion of 'identification', and how people come to identify with the versions of self they are being offered. However, this is outside the scope of this particular chapter. The final section, 'A tripartite analysis of shame and ageing/ageism', will now offer an example of the three-part shame structure being formulated here, and ask the question: 'how might one analyse the phenomena of ageism through this tripartite lens?'

A tripartite analysis of shame and ageing/ageism

At a political/state level

Politically and nationally (and internationally), various forms of rhetoric have become so commonplace in relation to older people that they have ceased to be metaphors or tropes, and are circulated as truths, for example, in the context of social policy. Each is derogatory, victim-blaming and shaming.

In the UK old people are spoken of as a burden on the economy, responsible for draining care budgets and for bankrupting the NHS, and for taking up valuable hospital beds (that could, one is left to assume, be given to more valuable people). Ideas of a 'plague' of dementia coming down the tracks (Zeilig, 2014 and the young and middle-aged having to pick up the cost are much repeated. That the 65-year-olds and above contribute £61 billion to the economy through work (£37 billion) and informal care, child care and volunteering are statistics far less circulated. At a national level, older people are regularly now represented as the group source of a range of economic problems, deflecting attention from the need for government action to produce, for example, a fairer universal tax system.

At a social/group level

The battle between the millennials and baby boomers, currently being talked into existence in the UK, seems mainly to be an ill-informed and politically convenient notion that older people wrecked the lives of younger people by, for example, forcing up housing prices, voting to leave Europe and so on. This avoids thinking about the rich, or about class, and feeds into already existing ageism. Readily circulated prejudices include the idea that older people 'refuse to vacate' jobs. They are also casually judged as being 'stuck in their ways', slow at learning, incapable of adaptation to new skills and so on. Stigma (Goffman, 1968a) and 'misrecognition' in Fraser's (2013) sense, are ordinarily generated: ridiculing, derogating and shaming older people.

At an individual level

There are many examples one might use here, but shame and the ageing body – ageing people's experience of their bodies becoming less under their control – may be illustrative. Ageing bodies are shamed by their perceived (and subjectively experienced) lack of masculine strength and feminine beauty (see eg de Beauvoir, 1972; Featherstone, Hepworth and Turner, 1991).

The ageing body in its social context has implications for social policy, social welfare and social workers' practices. Incontinence, disability, failing hearing or any range of aspects of the ageing body are hidden where possible, causing the acute discomfort, silencing and social avoidance that shame brings. Connected to this, but also to a wide range of factors, loneliness is another unmentioned, internalised, painful source of shame. This is also frequently the product of political decisions (transport; housing; benefits), but is experienced personally. Dependency and vulnerability are socially constructed as highly undesirable states: the need for help in itself is regarded as shameful.

The responses of the social work profession to this example of older people (and other oppressed groups) are of profound importance. These too can be focused at political, social and individual levels. For example, the tool of social work research impacts on understanding the political context and can attempt to influence policy; anti-discriminatory practice in all its forms can fight to combat ageism and stigma; and profoundly careful social work encounters, such as relationship-based practice, can support individuals to re-evaluate their part in their shame and find a voice to name the 'real culprits'.

Conclusion

This chapter has introduced a three-part structure to consider shame, and specifically the conditions under which different types of shame are likely to be generated. It has argued, overall, that making sense of shame can be challenging, and that conceptualising the multiplicity of ideas about this concept as a three-part structure can render it comprehensible. The demarcation of shame firstly as a set of political/national ideas reinstates a meta-perspective that in itself challenges casual contemporary assumptions that individuals themselves must be mostly the focus of understanding shame, and indeed can be seen as mainly responsible for shaming and being shamed. The second category, group and social shame, is then reviewed, drawing on symbolic interactionism and structural approaches and also introducing psychoanalytical and psychosocial perspectives on 'othering' and intersection shame experiences. The third dimension of this tripartite structure considers shame as an individual phenomenon, using object relations theory and Giddens' contemporary work on narrative identity. Finally, the three-part analysis is very briefly applied in relation to ageing and ageism, and how social work might respond to this is referenced.

Initially the point was made that although taxonomies must invariably be less than perfect, where overlaps and repetitions in reality make boundaries between categories contingent, nonetheless such a strategy allows an accessible initial examination, and indeed a re-examination of this important but nebulous set of ideas. Overall, the chapter has attempted to offer a multi-stranded analysis, with perhaps some additional normative implications for exercising judgement in relation to issues of understanding and praxis. For example, insisting on the inclusion of the national/political as a category that reaches into all aspects of shame implies a refutation of the neoliberal tendency to consider individual experience as individual responsibility. Paradoxically, the chapter has attempted to make stronger connections among political, social and individual shame via highlighting the divisions.

References

Bartky, S. (1990) *Femininity and Domination: Studies in the Phenomenology of Oppression*, London: Routledge.

Benhabib, S. (1999) 'The personal is not the political', *Boston Review*, 1 October.

Bourdieu, P. (1973) 'Cultural reproduction and social reproduction', in R. Brown (ed) *Knowledge, Education, and Cultural Change*, London: Tavistock, pp 257–71.

Bourdieu, P. (1999) *The Weight of the World: Social Suffering in Contemporary Society*, Cambridge: Polity Press.

Chase, E. and Walker, R. (2012) 'The co-construction of shame in the context of poverty: beyond a threat to the social bond', *Sociology*, 47(4): 739–54.

Clarke, S. (2003) *Social Theory, Psychoanalysis and Racism*, Basingstoke: Palgrave Macmillan.

Clarke, S., Hoggett, P. and Thompson, S. (2006) *Emotions, Politics and Society*, Basingstoke: Palgrave Macmillan.

Connolly, J. (2014) 'Shame and recognition: the politics of disclosure and acknowledgement', *Global Discourse: An Interdisciplinary Journal of Current Affairs and Applied Contemporary Thought*, 4(4): 409–25.

Cooley, C. (1902) *Human Nature and the Social Order*, New York: Charles Scribner's Sons.

de Beauvoir, S. (1972) *The Coming of Age*, London: André Deutsch and George Weidenfeld & Nicolson.

Elias, N. (2000 [1939]) *The Civilizing Process: The History of Manners and State Formation and Civilization*, Oxford: Blackwell.

Featherstone, M., Hepworth, M. and Turner, B. (eds) (1991) *The Body: Social Process and Cultural Theory*, London: Sage.

Fraser, N. (2013) *The Fortunes of Feminism: From State-Managed Capitalism to Neoliberal Crisis*, London: Verso.

Froggett, L., Ramvi, E. and Davies, L. (2015) 'Thinking from experience in psychosocial practice: reclaiming and teaching "use of self"', *Journal of Social Work Practice: Psychotherapeutic Approaches to Health, Welfare and the Community*, 29(2): 133–50.

Frosh, S., Phoenix, A. and Pattman, R. (2003) 'Taking a stand: using psychoanalysis to explore positioning of subjects in discourse', *British Journal of Social Psychology*, 42(1): 39–53.

Frost, E. (2015) 'Why social work and sociology need psychosocial theory', *Nordic Social Work Research*, 5(1): 85–97.

Frost, L. (2005) 'Theorising the young woman in the body', *Body and Society*, 11(1): 63–85.

Frost, L. (2016) 'Exploring the concepts of recognition and shame for social work', *Journal of Social Work Practice: Psychotherapeutic Approaches in Health, Welfare and the Community*, 30(4): 431–46.

Frost, L. and McClean, S. (2014) *Thinking about the Life Course: A Psychosocial Introduction*, Basingstoke: Palgrave Macmillan.

Gadd, D. and Dixon, B. (2010) *Losing the Race: Thinking Psychosocially about Racially Motivated Crime*, London: Karnac.

Garrett, P. (2010) 'Recognising the limitations of the political theory of recognition: Axel Honneth, Nancy Fraser and social work', *British Journal of Social Work*, 40(5): 1517–33.

Gibson, M. (2016) 'Social worker shame: a scoping review', *British Journal of Social Work*, 46(2): 549–65.

Giddens, A. (1991) *Modernity and Self Identity*, Cambridge: Polity Press.

Goffman, E. (1959) *The Presentation of Self in Everyday Life*, New York, Random House.

Goffman, E. (1968a) *Asylums: Essays on the Social Situation of Mental Patients and Other Inmates*, Harmondsworth: Pelican.

Goffman, E. (1968b) *Stigma: Notes on the Management of Spoiled Identity*, Harmondsworth: Pelican.

Honneth, A. (1992) 'Integrity and disrespect: principles of a conception of morality based on the theory of recognition', *Political Theory*, 20(2): 187–201.

Honneth, A. (1995) *The Struggle for Recognition: The Moral Grammar of Social Conflicts*, Cambridge: Polity Press.

Honneth, A. (2012) *The I in We: Studies in the Theory of Recognition*, Cambridge: Polity Press.

Houston, S. (2010) 'Beyond Homo Economicus: recognition, self-realization and social work', *British Journal of Social Work*, 40(3): 841–57.

Houston, S. (2016) 'Empowering the "shamed" self: recognition and critical social work', *Journal of Social Work*, 16(1): 3–21.

Hunt, J. (2013) 'Our national shame', *The Independent*, 17 October.

Jacquet, J. (2015) *Is Shame Necessary? New Uses for an Old Tool*, London: Penguin.

Jimenez, L. and Walkerdine, V. (2011) 'A psychosocial approach to shame, embarrassment and melancholia amongst unemployed young men and their fathers', *Gender and Education*, 23(2): 185–99.

Jones, O. (2012) *Chavs: The Demonisation of the Working Class*, London: Verso.

Kapur, R. and Campbell, J. (2004) *The Troubled Mind of Northern Ireland: An Analysis of the Emotional Effects of the Troubles*, London: Karnac.

Lucey, H. and Raey, D. (2002) 'A market in waste, psychic and structural dimensions of school choice policy in the UK and children's narratives of demonized schools', *Discourses: Studies in the Cultural Policy of Education*, 23(3): 23–40.

McNay, L. (2008) 'The trouble with recognition: subjectivity, suffering and agency', *Sociological Theory*, 26(3): 271–96.

Mead, G. H. (1967) *Mind, Self and Society*, Chicago: University of Chicago Press.

Mitchell, M. (2016) '50,000 children in care: "a national shame"', *The Australian*, 16 May, http://www.theaustralian.com.au/news/nation/national-shame-nearly-50000-kids-in-care-and-numbers-growing/news-story/eb386f0b91e7c7afc429756b5c2adaa5.

Nussbaum, M. (2004) *Hiding from Humanity: Disgust, Shame and the Law*, Princeton, NJ: Princeton University Press.

Peacock, M., Bissell, P. and Owen, J. (2013) 'Shaming encounters: reflections on contemporary understandings of social inequality and health', *Sociology*, 48(2): 387–402.

Reay, D. (2005) 'Beyond consciousness? The psychic landscape of class', *Sociology*, 39(5): 911–28.

Ronson, J. (2015) *So You've Been Publicly Shamed*, London: Picador.

Ryan, F. (2017) 'The UK's hidden shame: disabled people trapped at home in wheelchairs', *The Guardian*, 3 August.

Scheff, T. (2000) 'Shame and the social bond: a sociological theory', *Sociological Theory*, 18(1): 84–99.

Scheff, T. (2014) 'The ubiquity of hidden shame in modernity', *Cultural Sociology*, 8(2): 129–41.

Sennett, R. and Cobb, J. (1973) *The Hidden Injuries of Class*, New York: Vintage Books.

Stearns, P. (2016) 'Shame, and a challenge for emotions history', *Emotion Review*, 8(3): 197–206.

Taylor, C. (2002) 'The politics of recognition: interview with Simon Thompson', *Newsletter of the Centre for Critical Theory*, University of the West of England, August.

Walker, J. (2011) 'The relevance of shame in child protection work', *Journal of Social Work Practice*, 25(4): 451–63.

Wilkinson, R. and Pickett, K. (2009) *The Spirit Level: Why Equality is Better for Everyone*, Harmondsworth: Penguin.

Winnicott, D. (1958) *The Maturational Process and the Facilitating Environment: Studies in the Theory of Emotional Development*, London: Hogarth Press.

Woodward, K. (2015) *Psychosocial Studies: An Introduction*, London: Routledge.

Zeilig, H. (2014) 'Dementia as a cultural metaphor', *The Gerontologist*, 54(2): 258–67.

2

Sociology of shame: basic theoretical considerations

Sighard Neckel

Sociologists who concern themselves with emotions immediately face the difficulty of expressing themselves properly. Scientific language provides us with neither the vividness nor the sophistication needed if we are to appreciate the full meaning of the reality that a person experiences in all its depth and scope. For some levels of the human stream of experiences, this is even true of language in general. The world of emotions is one of those spheres of our existence that are so close to us that separation by verbalisation hardly appears possible.

The most accomplished pages of literature can at times offer us images which represent emotions that are difficult for us to access by means of language. What Dostoevsky tells of the emotional torment of the 'poor clerk' in the writing rooms of tsarist Russia, what Virginia Woolf reports about the feeling of cruel ridicule after a failed self-presentation, what Stefan Zweig is able to convey about the fear of a hidden tendency of the self being discovered or what Franz Kafka reveals about his shame in relation to his father – these are condensed representations of a collective experience that leaves every single person speechless. In this context, science is but a paltry concentrate that translates the full content of the experiences into meagre concepts and, in doing so, succeeds in capturing neither the acuteness of the inner anguish of shame nor the metaphysical indecisiveness that characterises this sensation of a momentary loss of the world.

We habitually speak of shame as something quite personal that does not really incorporate historical or social aspects. Other than perhaps fear and love, shame is perhaps the emotion that is most closely attached to the character of a person, that is positively inscribed to the body. And yet shame is also a social emotion, which is consistently present in the everyday societies and which, in these societies, plays a crucial role in human self-image and behaviour.

What is common to all emotions is that while feeling them we immediately assign a certain meaning to reality as we experience it. Shame is the feeling of having lost one's self-esteem in this reality.

This is what makes shame a social phenomenon: it arises from the network of social relations and from the low degree of recognition that we receive from others. In the feeling of shame, a person understands that he/she is in a state which he/she perceives as unsatisfactory or undignified. This is what makes shame normative: it presupposes an ideal of one's own self, which a person's actual behaviour or appearance then fails to match. Shame ultimately cannot be separated from the feeling of having violated a norm. This is what makes shame a moral emotion: the loss of personal worth that is felt is always accompanied by a feeling of guilt, by the feeling that the individual is responsible for their own inadequacy.

Shame breeds insecurity and entails a burden; shame isolates: feeling ashamed makes us lonely. It attacks our self-esteem, and we fear others will see this. This is why people tend to keep their feeling of shame to themselves. This may be the reason why sociologists have at times opined that emotions such as shame no longer matter much to life in modern societies.

This hunch is nourished by the fact that – at least in adults – shame is hardly visible in our everyday lives, it appears to be constrained to rare situations that become embedded deep in our memories and that, however, precisely because of this bear witness to the singularity of feeling shame. Everyone can probably recall a situation from their childhood or adolescence when they felt terribly ashamed. Back then, we still had to learn the norms, so there was scope for 'misbehaving'. There is also something old-fashioned about shame. Modern people may be embarrassed, but are they ever ashamed? Being invisible does not mean that something cannot exist. This also applies to shame, perhaps the most private and clandestine emotion in modern society, which not only in itself already bears the desire to hide but which is furthermore hidden itself because it is so strongly at odds with the modern maxims of one's own self-esteem. Being hidden, denied and seemingly entirely personal, the social characteristics of shame only reveal themselves gradually, reluctantly and not without obstacles on the way.

To these difficulties, we may also add something else: 'And they were either of them naked, both Adam and his wife, and were not ashamed' (Genesis 2:25). We know that this state was not to last, which is why shame appears as an ontological topic, being fundamental to an individual as such and therefore rather unsuited for analysis from a societal perspective. So what do we make of shame in a social sense, what are the social properties of shame and, finally, how is it that we are able to discern in the varied manifestations of shame a consistent pattern of experience that leads us to perceive our own selves as worthless or contemptible, as petty or filthy, as ridiculous or ugly, as shabby or pathetic?

Sociology would be a presumptuous science if it were to attempt answers to these questions that seek to provide a coherent explanation for every single person's feeling of shame. They who do not know the limits of a theory know nothing about life, but equally nothing about science. The sociological perspective itself already constitutes a reduction. It does not strive to discuss the value content of shame, and it cannot say what shame or shamelessness tells us about the inner life of an individual person; however, it will at least be cautious when formulating its own hypotheses about the anthropological origins of shame. In the world of emotions, the sociologist is well advised to treat the object of his research as a 'social fact': socially omnipresent, embedded in norms and interactions, and therefore scarred by the applicable forms of sociation. From this perspective, shame refers to the specifics of each social process that can trigger this feeling and to the consequences for the personal interaction from which the feeling of shame arose.

Norm and identity

Conscious of the resulting limitations, a path to answering the question about the social nature of shame offers itself, and that path leads us to the type of everyday behaviour that has us signalling mutual assessments of one another. As readers will quickly be able to confirm on the basis of their own emotions, and as evidenced by all conceptual variants of shame, the feeling is associated with negative assessments of the nature of a person's own being – whether these assessments are entirely internal or occasioned by someone else. Shame is a feeling of (un) worthiness. It indicates that one's sense of self-worth is depressed or threatened. The loss of worth that we become aware of in a shameful situation presupposes that we have an image of ourselves as altogether sound and likeable – notwithstanding injuries and weaknesses that are incorporated in our image as tacit knowledge. If a person's self-esteem is affected, their whole person, their innermost essence, becomes open to debate. If we find our self-image confirmed or if we at least think it unlikely to be damaged, we feel the security of being able to safely live among others as the person whom others see.

In the throes of feeling shame, that subjective security loses its basis. Undeniably, the self-consciousness becomes aware that it has been depreciated, which calls into question our habitual or expected participation in life with those around us. According to Sigmund Freud (2014 [1914]), shame is based on the 'social anxiety' of being abandoned or rejected. What matters here is the assessment by others or by the group, irrespective of whether that assessment is real or anticipated in our own imagination. The inner self-perception of being personally devalued then mobilises all the somatic reactions of inner inhibitions including blushing, which by virtue of the feeling of shame are part of the basic anthropological configuration of humans.

According to an expression by the American sociologist Norman Denzin (1984), shame is simultaneously a 'self-feeling' and a 'sensation of the body' – a value-laden emotion centred on one's own self, and a social affect that grows from the fear of losing existential security. The fact that shame still harbours the remains of an instinct also limits our ability to 'control' feelings of shame, to make them accessible to our consciousness. Bodily and existentially, shame overcomes us rather than announcing itself. Shame manifests itself, it is not negotiable; 'controlling one's feelings' (Hochschild, 1983) will typically not work. Sometimes one feels shame about having been shamed earlier. Then our self-consciousness reflects on our own vulnerability and appreciates how fragile and porous the borders of our own self are after all.

The emergence of shame is always tied to a person's self-ideal. This personal ego ideal provides us with a model of our own person, which we would like to see preserved or confirmed in our interactions with others.[1] In the feeling of shame, this ego ideal suddenly collapses. While a minute ago I was quite sure of myself and of the situation I was in, the shameful incident denies the identity that I showed others in my behaviour. A conflict erupts between the claimed I and the actual I, an inconsistency arises that allows others a glimpse down into the abyss of the shamed soul.

Three anxieties govern those who feel ashamed: to have lost their coherence as an actor, their acceptance as a fellow human being and their integrity as a person. In the moment of shame, an individual loses all the protection that he or she was able to build around him/herself. They lose protective distance because strangers have penetrated into hidden spheres. They lose dignity if their body, their urges or their neediness are open for inspection, if the subject was forced to make that 'inner return' (Scheler, 1957, pp 78ff) to their mere bodily existence, which the intellectual-moral person considers to be an inferior mode of being. Finally, he or she loses his/her honour to the extent that his/her claimed status within a group is no longer covered by his/her actual behaviour, jeopardising the basis for mutual esteem.

The occasion for such exposure is usually found in the personal failure to comply with a norm whose observance is part of one's self-image. According to the German sociologist Georg Simmel, shame arises whenever a person experiences 'a rupture between the norm of the personality and its actual state' (Simmel, 1983 [1901], p 142)[2] or if the person violates a norm which with their self-image expects them to comply. This presupposes that the person knows the norm and intends to follow it. Someone who is ignorant or indifferent about a rule lacks the cognitive or moral capacity, respectively, to feel ashamed about breaking the rule. Therefore, a child's shame differs from an adult's: children are uninhibited where older people are embarrassed, they are cruel where an adult shows restraint, yet they are touchy about things which a mature person can easily overlook. A child's inner map has different areas flagged for risk of embarrassment.

The same also applies to those who stand out from others not because of age-related knowledge levels but because of cultural differences, be they due to ethnicity, social position or gender. Different interpretations of life will qualify episodes of the everyday world as harbouring the potential for shame in different ways. For example, according to traditional norms, a man need not be ashamed of his body odour. By contrast, many cultures regard women as fundamentally impure and therefore expect higher standards of physical hygiene of them, which implies that they should feel sustained shame at any bodily uncleanliness. The gender-related shame of a man, by contrast, traditionally revolves around the shame that he brings upon himself through his own cowardice – even though many women hold that a brave man is a rarity anyway. The descendant of the established bourgeoisie, who quite naturally was already familiarised with the world of culture by his musical mother, in turn need not have read every single piece of commentary on the latest opera performance in order to feel at home in legitimate cultural circles – whereas the social climber, the autodidact, who had to work hard for everything he has achieved, is immediately embarrassed by any indication of cultural ignorance. Examples such as these reflect the spirit of historic times, with the patterns of civilisation as they applied then, the self-constraints that they imposed, and the idols, moods and ideals.

The hypothesis of a simple 'advance of the threshold of shame and repugnance', which the sociologist Norbert Elias (2012 [1939], p 457) formulated in his theory of civilisation, ceased to be undisputed long ago. The signum of the history of the development of civilisation appears to be not a constant increase of self-constraints and shame but rather a shift in the objects of shame with respect to which personal self-constraints must prove themselves. In the development towards a bourgeois society, the self-constraint of persons increasingly found its role model in the ideal of sovereign individuality that everyone should project – a modern ideal that slowly but steadily replaced the priority in terms of public esteem that the group traditionally enjoyed.

Moral and social shame

Whatever flaw may be historically associated with shame, and in whatever form – nudity or uncleanliness, cowardice or greed, sacrilege or poverty (see also Chapter 4), stupidity or failure – the individual who becomes such a disappointment to him/herself that he/she wishes the ground would swallow him/her up implicitly bases this sentiment on a norm whose lack of fulfilment through failure or defeat can give rise their his feeling of shame. It is not the violation of a norm itself that has us blushing, it is the thought that others know of the violation. This is where guilt and shame – the two psychological sentries of a person, which often salute each other – part ways. 'Conscience anxiety', the basis of guilt, does not necessarily require a third party to effectively punish the self. By contrast, 'social anxiety', the basis of shame, only comes to life via the fear of being found out.

Guilt is the feeling of being responsible, through one's actions, for the infringement of a norm; shame is the feeling of having received damage to one's identity. Guilt arises from overstepping rules; shame arises from failing one's own ideals, from the discrepancy between the actual and the ideal self-image. The American psychoanalyst Helen B. Lewis (1987, p 18) has phrased this distinction in the following fitting formula: 'Shame is about the self; guilt is about things.'

Guilt and shame are not absolute opposites; in many situations they will be inseparably linked. However, conscience anxiety eo ipso has a moral quality that shame need not have. Infringements of moral norms, too, cause a feeling of shame only if the individual relates these infringements to the consequences they are expected to have on the way in which others assess him or her. Conversely, not every instance of feeling shame is preceded by an immoral action. We often feel ashamed about something that is not morally reproachable, such as about our looks or a lack of competence. Human shame is directed not just at the wickedness in us, but also at our weakness, ugliness and deficiency.

To facilitate our orientation in the maze of guilt and shame, we may differentiate a moral zone of shame from one that can only be referred to as social.[3] Moral shame corresponds to an internal imperative, social shame to external pressure. In individual cases, it may be difficult to distinguish between social and ethical, moral and conventional causes of shame. Conventions have a tendency to be moralised; the morals themselves are a product of society, their value content is permeated with social characteristics. Also, any feeling of shame can be an internal call for us to look for a moral transgression as the cause of the ashamedness, to consider the incident that made us ashamed in the light of a personal aspiration or action that is morally reproachable. And yet the distinction between moral and social shame makes sense: it reveals to our attention those processes of social contempt and disparagement whose occasions or causes cannot be ethically assessed for their moral character because they are not due to a damnable, evil action but rather to an infringement of social conventions. Moral shame is the companion of guilt and presupposes action, responsibility, harm to others.[4] By contrast, social shame depends on none of these. It leans on a person's 'appearance', their 'negligence' and their own harm as occasions for their disparagement and lack of self-esteem.

We find occasions for social shame hidden in a range of different contexts and constellations of life. Here they represent a latent undercurrent to our experiences, which is covered by awkward silence because these occasions cannot be shared without depreciating our self-esteem. To use a simple classification, occasions for social shame can arise from a person's body, their personality or their status – the person as reflected in their physical nativeness, in their self-claimed identity and in their social esteem.

Rejection that we experience in our bodiliness or as sexual partners, violence that we physically endure, loss of control in the presence of others – these are experiences that undermine the self-confidence with which we inhabit our bodies. The shameful effect of social degradation is generally at its strongest if it concerns the body, as it affects that sphere of a person that appears most closely associated with their nature. Here the social disparagement is linked organically, as it were, to the individual, which therefore appears fundamentally and altogether worthless. Especially in modern society, which celebrates the body as the last province of meaning of a person's existence, the body carries the symbolic meaning of, in a sense, being the person's decisive representative organ. To look healthy or sick, beautiful or ugly, groomed or sordid, lean or fat is considered a visible expression of a person's inner characteristics, as a merit or a flaw of their being.

A second area of social shame is the disparagement of the identity we claim for ourselves. Unkindness received from an otherwise close person, reproach or derision suffered from others, a tactless invasion of my privacy or insults will damage the integrity of one's personality and denigrate one. All rites of passage that, for example, a new arrival to a group must endure rely on the temporary destruction of a person's identity, which is exposed, with any flaws put on display for inspection.

Finally, failure or defeat in social competition, poor performance in relation to social norms of achievement or appearance, being discriminated against in lieu of the group that a person belongs to or the deprivation of his or her rights will threaten the status that a person was conceded or has assumed for him/herself. This is why many cultures refer to persons without any status as being 'shirtless' – they have no rights that might cover their human nakedness.

The special burden of shame, however, consist in the fact that it can be 'endless', that it can migrate from one sphere to another and then become generalised. The entire self appears worthless, fraught with errors, flawed. If the feeling of shame is in accordance with norms that a person expects him/herself to uphold, it triggers the mechanism of self-reproach. Even indignation at the disparagement cannot supplant the central experience that the perception of a person's identity in the eyes of others has become the image that this person has of him/herself. In feeling ashamed, we accept the external assessment as our self-appraisal, and we justify our humiliation as self-induced. Jean-Paul Sartre (1992 [1943], p 350) said in this context: 'my shame is a confession' (for an intensive discussion of Sartre's theory see Neckel, 1991; and also Chapter 3). This is why social shame, too, demands its own moralisation: to obtain an explanation for the meaning of the injury that one has received.

Self-confidence and humiliation

If we now enquire about the substantive content that such injuries consist in, we must look for the central experience that the ashamed subject has under the eyes of others. I propose to describe this experience as a loss of esteem, dignity or respect. To be shown respect is an expectation that people naturally have when entering into interactions with others; self-respect is an aim that a person has vis-à-vis their own self. Disrespect in turn signifies that others have thwarted these aspirations. As we feel shame, this lack of respect then manifests itself in our body and in our inner self-perception.

Sociologically, a gain or loss of respect may be reconstructed as the positive or negative prospect of being able to preserve the conditions of one's self-respect in the perception of others. Shame indicates the breakdown of self-respect under the pressure of a situation in which the actual or imagined perception by others has the subject worrying that they will lose the respect of the group. The need for self-respect may but need not be undermined by the subject himself. It may be subjected to conditions of esteem stated by others, and meeting these conditions then becomes the price of self-esteem. This is the case, for example, with shaming rituals, which typically play off the shamed person's interest in self-preservation against their need for self-respect, so that those who state the conditions can then revel in the subject's lost dignity.

A person may also be denied all respect, which means there is no longer any opportunity for them to experience appreciation through the perception of others. He or she would then recognise the maxims of their own esteem in others, where they serve precisely as the occasion for his or her humiliation. If an individual proudly reveals something about him/herself that others consider ridiculous, then he/she have not deprived him/herself of their self-esteem through their own actions; rather, the condition for the possibility of self-esteem has been taken from them. Again, Jean-Paul Sartre is the modern philosopher on this tragic constellation. He has described like no one else the idea that humiliation is based on making someone the object of their own freedom, so that they lose their freedom and autonomy to the same extent. Humiliating a person is the most subtle form of taking possession of them because it means that the criteria of the person's self-respect have been provided by others.

This is the most negative variant of the basic anthropological situation that the human self-confidence is dependent on the perception of others, and is therefore vulnerable to that perception. A person's self-confidence does not form according to the logic of that person's self. A person's self-confidence takes reassurance from the appraisal of others, and due to them it may perish.

Status and shame

Shame refers to a person's self-esteem, which is inseparable from the esteem that others have for that person. Thus, an individual's feelings of shame always concern the person's position amid a larger social context; they are the emotional nexus between the individual and the social structure, between the social hierarchy and the person's own status position.

Sociology knows four dimensions along which status can be acquired in modern society, and these dimensions at the same time represent the social sources from which esteem in society springs: material prosperity (as evidenced by 'money'), knowledge ('certificate'), and a person's position within organisations ('rank') and informal groups ('belonging') (see Kreckel, 1982). If we map the occasions of social humiliation ideally to these possibilities of acquiring status in modern society, the following techniques of humiliation can be distinguished:

Firstly, the technique of excluding a person prevents or terminates them belonging to informal groups. Exclusion penalises and at the same time creates strangeness – be it for social, physical or cultural reasons. To label a person as 'strange' is a particularly drastic form of contempt. It can amount to dismissing the last remaining common ground among individuals, or in the words of Georg Simmel (1950 [1908], p 408), to denying another's 'precisely general attributes, felt to be specifically and purely human'.

Loss of respect can grow into an existential feeling of shame, whose archetype is the unloved and unwanted child. The victim of this existential shame is the person who feels useless and worthless, and whose mental state the psychologist Helen Merrell Lynd (1961, pp 46f) has described as follows: 'We have become strangers in a world where we thought we were at home. ... With every recurrent violation of trust we become again children unsure of ourselves in an alien world.'

Secondly, the technique of degrading someone deprives them of the rank they held within a hierarchical organisation. It serves to create subalternity, which can permanently damage a person's sense of social value. Here, shame arises from the discrepancy between a person's self-evaluation and the public role they have been conceded. The public persona undermines the personal ego ideal and obliges the individual to present him/herself to others in a position that is at odds with his/her own maxims of self-respect. In this context, shame comes from the obligation to serve.

Thirdly, examination is the strategy for challenging someone's cognitive competence in order to demonstrate their ignorance to others. For the humiliation to be justifiable in public, the examination must be objective, so its contents must be codifiable, its procedure must be valid and its goal must be formally attainable. It is precisely its objectivity which makes the technique of assessment so effective at obliterating self-confidence – it being an unquestionable institution which in its indifference regarding the candidate's character only pushes that character all the more fiercely into the light of latent denigration. As the French sociologist Pierre Bourdieu (1989, p 387) analysed, the educational system

transforms social classifications into academic classifications, with every appearance of neutrality, and establishes

> hierarchies which are not experienced as purely technical ...
> but as total hierarchies, grounded in nature, so that social
> value comes to be identified with 'personal' value, scholastic
> dignities with human dignity ... so that privation is
> perceived as an intrinsic handicap, diminishing a person's
> identity and human dignity, condemning him to silence
> in all official situations, when he has to 'appear in public',
> present himself before others, with his body, his manners
> and his language.

Finally, social devaluation refers to all processes that deprive a person's work or their needs of social recognition in the form of material values, or that never grant this recognition in the first place (for a detailed discussion of the question of recognition see also Chapter 1). Devaluation ultimately produces poverty, which at the same time stigmatises the affected persons. As we know, Karl Marx stated that wages also have a moral component: someone's pay reflects, not least, the social esteem that is attributed to their work. The material disparagement of the human work effort constitutes a humiliation just as much as the denial of a decent material subsistence for those who cannot make their living from work – those who, before they can expect any help, must have their own weakness appraised by the modern state (see Walker, 2014). From poverty research and from analyses on unemployment and social policy we are familiar with the stigmatising effects of such appraisal systems. The result has been described as a feeling of inferiority in those whose social situation, way of living or competence is characterised as substandard in relation to the prevailing norms. The prototypical situation of such socially caused shame is the 'means test' conducted by authorities before the disbursement of any public welfare. In this situation, the client is in a sense forced to play off his material interests against his claim to personal self-respect. Standing in a line of competing petitioners, he must present himself as someone who is in particular need of assistance with his livelihood, thereby stigmatising himself at the same time.

Humiliations such as these serve as social techniques to preserve one's own benefits in the face of foreign claims, to classify deviant ways of life or characteristics as inferior, to increase one's power in the interaction with others. Situations of shame may be triggered by a person's own actions, by someone else's doing or by random events. For the act of humiliation to achieve its purpose, however, the responsibility for the shameful flaw must be transferred to the person to be humiliated. Throughout history, the criterion of personal responsibility has been construed quite differently. Only in the modern world have incidents that may be attributed to a person's actions come into focus as justifiable reasons for shaming. Traditional societies derive shame from chance events, which are considered a sign from the gods. In the world of status groups, an individual will blush for his collective. In modern society, by contrast, shaming for random events or 'social circumstances' is questionable, at least officially. This reflects a historical change in the social construction of shame, a change that is internally driven by the development towards the human sense of individuality.

Individualism and self-respect

In a traditional class society, for example, people's shameful faults are only comparable to an extent because each class has its own set of norms to observe. By contrast, in modern Western society, the reference framework for social esteem is standardised to those characteristics that determine the success an individual makes of their life in a market society. In this context, a central role falls to the achievement principle as the formally indifferent but in reality socially selective guiding norm of bourgeois society. If there are no longer any legal barriers based on one's ancestry to accumulating wealth, knowledge, title and competence by virtue of one's performance, then a person's failure to possess certain resources is regarded as their personal flaw. 'Inferiority' (Neckel, 1996) – which in a class society was still a collective status that was due to unequal rights – has now become assignable to a person.

Present-day modern society has dissolved its former social milieus and continues to individualise itself. Individualisation in this context means the liberation of people from the traditions and social references as provided by class cultures, family ties, professional traditions and regional milieus. The experience of inequality and disrespect now receives the social meaning that a deficit in status is in each case attributed to the very particular characteristics of a person's biography. The subjects have the events of their social fate attributed to them as the consequences of their individual decisions. Social forms of shame are based on making social disadvantage the occasion for the moral assignment of personal failure. The individual is forced to explain a personal deficit to him/herself because collective patterns of interpretation of social inequality are losing their persuasiveness. The individual's responsibility for his/her social circumstances is declining but – it appears – so is the responsibility of the social circumstances for the individual.

This process of the individualisation of social status and social consciousness (Beck, 1992) creates the structural conditions under which social shame survives in modern society. As a person's individual responsibility for his/her own biography grows, the fear of personal failure grows by the same measure. As society increasingly sheds its traditions, the social areas in which the validity of a norm is uncertain grow. Because of the 'intersection of social circles' (Simmel 2009 [1908], pp 367ff), the spheres of unquestionable security of behaviour shrink, which increases the risk of misguided self-portrayal and 'inappropriate identities'. A central institution of the distribution of status in modern society is the labour market. In an individualised competition for opportunities in the markets and in life, the characteristics that are relevant to someone's status are not limited to the person's formal qualifications. More than ever, these characteristics refer to the 'whole person', their appearance, their lifestyle and their personal properties such as their demeanour and their communication skills; and this development thoroughly institutionalises the reference frame of shame within the labour market. Social inequality has ultimately become a biographical experience that is subject to cyclical changes over a person's life course. Periods of being tolerably established in the employment and status system more frequently alternate with instances of dropping out of the system, at which point a person will experience at first hand how unequally respect and recognition can be distributed in society. Status anxiety can thus establish itself as a constant background experience in modern life.

Because the value of individuality increases, the subject perceives shame as the sensation of impaired self-worth no less acutely than in times when every person thought of themselves not as an individual but as the representative of a group. Furthermore, the less a moral conscience determines the image of personal identity, the more the ego ideal tends to open up to external influences of social evaluation. Using the example of the American society of the 1950s, this hypothesis of a growing importance of shame in modern society was already formulated by US social psychologist David Riesman (1961), who recognised 'the fear of being shamed' as an attribute of the other-directed personality. This observation was later taken up again by social theorists such as Agnes Heller (1985) and Anthony Giddens (1991).

According to Riesman, Heller and Giddens, everyday life becomes the domain of shame, which in the course of this development once again changes its own nature. Fuelled by the social fear of inferiority, this domain absorbs the values of the societal scale of prestige, which first and foremost rewards success. The feeling of shame loses its meaning as a virtue and value in large parts of everyday life, just to come to the fore all the more strongly as a social sanction. The modern individual thus faces a widespread expectation of shamelessness. After all, the feeling of shame documents that one is affected by the expectations of others. It means that we have allowed our emotional state to be dependent on the judgement of others, or in other words, that we have not achieved the aspired degree of sovereignty that has become the ideal today. Amid a culture that has created more space than any other for the expressivity of the individual, shame thus becomes the 'secret rest' of the personality, it becomes an unpresentable emotion for which rituals of relief are hardly available any longer. To the same extent that individuality is considered an achievement in its own right today, society expects of an individual creativity, initiative, self-esteem and confidence in their role. In this context, shame assumes the character of a secret emotion that punishes its own expression because it is so strongly at odds with the ideal of self-confident individuality. Shame is covered by awkward, oppressive silence.

Today, the fear of shame pervades modern society because the danger of losing esteem threatens the value of uniqueness. This is precisely where the old technique of social control now ties in, the technique of directing the individual towards conformity by means of signals of contempt. The fact that individualism is the conformity norm of the present age does not disperse the dichotomy of standard and deviance. To appear sufficiently individual becomes the condition for social esteem and personal self-respect. Not being capable of individualisation, be it for material, cultural, cognitive or aesthetic reasons, thus constitutes the most modern form in which shame is associated with a person in social terms. Using the example of a failed personal self-presentation on the occasion of an evening party, Virginia Woolf has left us the soul image of shame in the age of individualisation. In 'The New Dress', she writes about the feelings of her protagonist:

> What she had thought that evening when, sitting over the teacups, Mrs. Dalloway's invitation came, was that, of course, she could not be fashionable. It was absurd to pretend it even ... – but why not be original? Why not be herself, anyhow? ... But she dared not look in the glass. She could not face the whole horror. (Woolf, 1962 [1944], p 49)

Acknowledgements

This text is the translated and slightly modified version of my contribution 'Soziologie der Scham', published in the anthology *Scham* by Alfred Schäfer and Christiane Thompson in 2009 by Schöningh, Paderborn. The publishing house expressly agreed to the publication of this paper.

Notes

[1]   According to Freud, the 'ego ideal' is the mental instance by which an individual 'measures his current self'. It emerges in early childhood and changes from the narcissism of the ego into a normative self-commitment by means of which the ego seeks to preserve its 'self-respect'. The ego ideal is not identical to the superego, the conscience. The latter rather works as an internal censor to ensure that the current ego actually corresponds to the ideal ego (see Freud 2014 [1914]).

[2]   Translated from the German by the author.

[3]   The genesis and phenomena of 'social shame' are discussed extensively in Neckel (1991), where the focus of the analysis is on the meaning of social shame in the age of new forms of social competition.

[4]   See also Heller (1985, pp 4ff), who differentiates 'shame-guilt' as a 'social affect' felt by one's conscience, and thus ties in with ethnological studies that reported on the separation between 'deep shame' and 'shame on skin' in tribe societies. Lewis (1987, pp 15ff) also distinguishes between a 'moral' and a 'nonmoral stimulus of shame'. In the separation proposed in the present contribution between moral and social shame, we do not share the assumptions that already underlie the earlier distinction between cultures of shame and cultures of guilt in cultural anthropology. According to those assumptions, the feeling of shame lacks any internalisation of norms, whereas the sense of guilt is characterised precisely by such internalisation. The objections to this, which have been formulated in disciplines ranging from ethnology to modern psychoanalysis, are overwhelming. They may be summarised to the effect that moral drivers of shame constitute a variant in the triggering of this feeling that is not unknown even to 'primitive societies'.

References

Beck, U. (1992) *Risk Society: Towards a New Modernity*, London: Sage.

Bourdieu, P. (1989) *Distinction: A Social Critique of the Judgement of Taste*, London: Routledge.

Denzin, N. K. (1984) *On Understanding Emotion*, San Francisco: Jossey-Bass Publishers.

Elias, N. (2012 [1939]) *The Collected Works of Norbert Elias*, vol. 3: *On the Process of Civilisation: Sociogenetic and Psychogenetic Investigations*, Dublin: University College Dublin Press.

Freud, S. (2014 [1914]) *On Narcissism: An Introduction*, London: White Press.

Giddens, A. (1991) *Modernity and Self-Identity: Self and Society in the Late Modern Age*, Cambridge: Polity Press.

Heller, A. (1985) 'The power of shame', in A. Heller, *The Power of Shame: A Rational Perspective*, London: Routledge & Kegan Paul, pp 1–56.

Hochschild, A. R. (1983) *The Managed Heart: Commercialization of Human Feeling*, Berkeley: University of California Press.

Kreckel, R. (1982) 'Class, status and power? Begriffliche Grundlagen für eine politische Soziologie der sozialen Ungleichheit', *Kölner Zeitschrift für Soziologie und Sozialpsychologie*, 34: 617–48.

Lewis, H. B. (1987) 'Introduction: shame – the "sleeper" in psychopathology', in H. B. Lewis, *The Role of Shame in Symptom Formation*, Hillsdale, NJ: Lawrence Erlbaum, pp 1–28.

Lynd, H. M. (1961) *On Shame and the Search for Identity*, New York: Science Editions.

Neckel, S. (1991) *Status und Scham. Zur symbolischen Reproduktion sozialer Ungleichheit*, Frankfurt and New York: Campus.

Neckel, S. (1996) 'Inferiority: from collective status to deficient individuality', *The Sociological Review*, 44(1): 17–34.

Riesman, D. (1961) *The Lonely Crowd: A Study of the Changing American Character*, New Haven, CT: Yale University Press.

Sartre, J.-P. (1992 [1943]) *Being and Nothingness: A Phenomenological Essay on Ontology*, New York: Washington Square Press.

Scheler, M. (1957) 'Über Scham- und Schamgefühl', in M. Scheler, *Gesammelte Werke*, vol 10, Bern: Francke, pp 67–154.

Simmel, G. (1950 [1908]) 'The stranger', in K. Wolff (ed) *The Sociology of Georg Simmel*, New York: Free Press, pp 402–8.

Simmel, G. (1983 [1901]) 'Zur Psychologie der Scham', in G. Simmel, *Schriften zur Soziologie. Eine Auswahl*, Frankfurt am Main: Suhrkamp, pp 140–50.

Simmel, G. (2009 [1908]) *Sociology: Inquiries into the Construction of Social Forms*, Leiden: Brill.

Walker, R. (2014) *The Shame of Poverty*, Oxford: Oxford University Press.

Woolf, V. (1962 [1944]) 'The new dress', in V. Woolf, *A Haunted House and Other Short Stories*, London: Hogarth Press, pp 49–58.

3

Shame as an anthropological, historical and social emotion

Veronika Magyar-Haas

In his study *The Mask of Shame* (1981), Léon Wurmser posits that scholars of psychoanalysis have paid insufficient attention to the topic of shame. The work of Thomas J. Scheff (2003) also aligns with this viewpoint, albeit from the perspective of a different discipline: he traces the persistent taboos associated with the phenomenon of shame, and the lack of an explicit attempt to get to grips with the term 'shame' in the field of sociological analysis, from a historical and systematic perspective. With reference to Goffman, Elias and psychoanalytic literature, he describes that, for the US in particular, the understanding of shame as a taboo topic is demonstrated in scholarly works either through other terms (such as 'embarrassment') being used to refer to the phenomenon, or through the muted reception of studies exploring questions of shame. Scheff makes the reader aware that shame is cloaked in taboo in the modern age, both on a social level and within academic reflections. In light of these discourses, it would be possible to view shame as being openly concealed.

Wurmser's identification of researchers' disregard for shame is pushed to its limits in the present day: there are now a host of different studies on the topic in the context of psychoanalysis and psychology, while philosophy, sociology and cultural studies have also considered this phenomenon to be a relevant research area over the last twenty years. In the English-speaking world, Scheff's work has contributed just as much to this as the sociological and philosophical studies on emotions published in the German-speaking sphere in the 1990s (Neckel, 1991; Landweer, 1999). The sheer number of recent publications, not to mention conferences, on this subject imply that shame, as a topic, is experiencing a resurgence within academia. Across a broad range of research areas and debates within psychology, theology, history and literature studies, the phenomenon of shame is paired with a variety of concepts, such as guilt, honour, trauma, body, age and poverty, with the ultimate aim of bringing the issue of 'shame' into focus and creating a clearer definition of this term. This phenomenon is not merely psychological: it is primarily social. Indeed, the research mentioned has illustrated its multidimensionality and complexity, while also highlighting the problems associated with getting to grips with the specifics of shame (see Magyar-Haas, 2020).

Given the range of disciplines that have researched questions of shame, it is worth noting, with regard to the German-speaking world, that the topic is of marginal relevance, at best, in education studies. While the Max Planck Institute for Human Development has looked at the 'history of feelings' from a cultural and socio-historical perspective, thereby targeting various contexts within which the feeling of shame can arise (see Frevert, 2009), and while individual papers have been written on the topic of shame, primarily in the field of educational philosophy (see Schäfer, 2000; Meyer-Drawe, 2008; Ruhloff, 2009; Schäfer and Thompson, 2009), it is hardly possible to suggest that the field of education studies has engaged with this topic in a systematic manner.

Within the context of psychoanalysis and psychotherapy, Micha Hilgers (1996, p 21) theorises that scholars' delay in researching shame as an effect, or effects in general, is astonishing, since an individual's first visit to a therapist can trigger feelings of shame just as therapists are 'frequently associated with shameful topics'[1]. With regard to the lack of attention paid to shame in this context, Wurmser (1981, p 3) emphasises 'the danger of neglecting whatever does not fit neatly into the traditional system'. The history of the profession and discipline of pedagogy has not escaped the danger of largely ignoring shame and humiliation, both as issues in themselves and topics of research, either – as is the case for the phenomena of failure and lack of success: in the field of pedagogy, this sense of 'repression' of the topic of shame can be explained in that different practices of humiliation (whether in the shape of corporal punishment or in the form of more subtle techniques that see power and dominance exerted in the guise of equality) call professional acts themselves into question. Furthermore, the necessity of researching this can be illuminated just as convincingly from a historical perspective by virtue of the traditional, predominant, pedagogical concept of the modern, rational and autonomous subject that legitimises the discipline: the very act of reflecting on and analysing these phenomena of shame and feelings of shame reveals that this concept of the sovereign subject is an illusion (see Schäfer and Thompson, 2009, pp 25–32), if not even pushed to the limits of absurdity. This chapter does not go into further detail as to why topics of shame and humiliation have received little attention in pedagogical contexts (for further analysis, see Magyar-Haas, 2020). Rather, it focuses explicitly on these phenomena themselves.

In her phenomenological study about shame and power, the philosopher Hilge Landweer (1999, p 2) uses a phrase that highlights the sociality of shame, revealing the three key dimensions of this term: 'When we feel ashamed, we feel ashamed of something before someone.' Firstly, this reveals the dimension of the subject who feels shame, namely, the relevance of taking into consideration the embodied subject's relationship to itself when analysing shame. Secondly, the phrase 'of something' underscores the significance of normativity: the matter of which we are ashamed is based on the violation of norms and values that the subject itself views as important and worth respecting. The formulation 'before someone', thirdly, emphasises the Other's (potential) look, that is, that of the individual witnessing the instance of shame and the breaching of norms (see Magyar-Haas, 2012, 2020). In contemporary analyses of shame, these dimensions almost serve as central reference points across disciplines, although they are emphasised differently depending on the field in question.

This chapter uses these dimensions to draw on perspectives from the fields of philosophy, sociology and cultural studies, with the aim of demonstrating how far shame can be viewed as an anthropological, social and historical phenomenon. It opens with an investigation of the significance attributed to shame in selected analyses within the field of philosophical anthropology that deal with questions of being human, and by extension, the possibilities of experiencing the self in the modes of subject and object. What assumptions about being human are brought to the fore when shame becomes the focus of analysis and is capable of being described as a universal human phenomenon? How are subjects conceptualised in works of educational philosophy – and what is the significance of shame in these works? However, the inverse of this is also worth exploring: what do analyses of shame, such as Sartre's formulation that 'my shame is a confession' (1992 [1943], p 350; see also Neckel, 1991, p 29 and Chapter 2), say about the concept of subjects themselves? When Alfred Schäfer and Christiane Thompson (2009, p 9) describe the feeling of shame as 'a reaction to the breakdown of the individual's relationship to their ideal self-image', it is worth questioning how this 'ideal self-image' comes into being: if this self-image is viewed as the provisional outcome of rational, emotional dealings with, and perceptions of, relevant Others in certain ever-changing contexts, then it testifies to internalised expectations and normative concepts, as well as social control (Magyar-Haas, 2012, 2020). This demonstrates that viewing shame as a purely anthropological phenomenon is an insufficient approach, unless this draws on works from the domain of philosophical anthropology that take into account the historicity and sociality of humans' self-relations and, consequently, shame, as well as the historicity of humans' own statements and anthropological constructs themselves. This chapter makes explicit reference to works that refer to these insights, such as those by Helmuth Plessner, as they consider that both the grounds for shame and the intensity of it vary historically, culturally and socially.

Against the backdrop of the sociality, normativity and morality of shame, the section 'The shamed subjects of social expectations and pedagogical norms' of this chapter focuses on the areas which have significant resonances with social work. It attempts to answer the question of the extent to which a range of social and socio-political expectations (of performance) can serve as triggers for shame, with the threatening potentiality of inadequacy of the self that is inherent to them. In this regard, the chapter focuses on the normativity of pedagogy, as well as the normative 'activating' mandate of social work, as embedded within normative, socio-cultural and economic expectations in terms of performance and fulfilment. Subsequent to this, this chapter sounds out how far humiliation can be understood as a power strategy, as a form of the reproduction of power structures and conditions of adequacy. It takes into account the significance of attributions, allocations of responsibility and instruments of control in the context of social work, which can be problematised as the monitoring gaze[2] of a society (of performance) construed by 'homogenous norms'. These discussions are underpinned by a rather controversial thesis, namely, that moments of humiliation within social work are evoked on a structural level and, consequently, are latently inherent to this field. The chapter closes by considering what this interpretation of shame reveals with regard to the relationship between social workers and addressees of social work, as well as with regard to approaches in the field of social work that deal with situations giving rise to feelings of shame.

Anthropological analyses: on the dividedness of the self

Within the context of German-language work on philosophical anthropology, Max Scheler explicitly addresses the topic of shame and feelings of shame in his 1913 essay 'Scham und Schamgefühl'.[3] In this essay, Scheler confronts the ways in which a person can feel shame, focusing not on the various causes of shame but on 'human beings' themselves. Shame, as the 'clair-obscur of human nature', is seen by

Scheler (1957 [1913], p 67) to be a genuine human characteristic. It is not merely human beings alone who can, and must, feel shame: 'ultimately, they are ashamed of themselves "before" the God within them' (Scheler, 1957 [1913], p 69). In line with this, *inadequacy* in attaining a goal is, in Scheler's eyes, the common denominator of all shame-related experiences from an existential point of view. In Scheler's anthropology, shame can be summarised as 'the feeling of falling short of spirituality, specific to the embodied individual', as the 'appreciation of the fractures and wounds suffered by our existence, the feeling of the brokenness, woundedness, and fragility of the self' (Zwierlein, 2011, pp 163, 168). Scheler (1957 [1913], p 68) describes shame as being characterised by the 'contradictory experience which sees the ideal self that "ought" to exist turn into the "actual" one'. However, this formulation of the conflict between 'life' and 'spirit' is not unique to Scheler: rather, it appears to be paradigmatic of philosophical anthropology in the early 20th century.

Helmuth Plessner's end point of 'eccentric positionality' also makes reference to this ontological rupture – albeit without extolling spirituality, in opposition to Scheler. Using categories gained through phenomenological analyses, Plessner (2003 [1928], p 363) makes a metaphor out of humans' ability to distance themselves from their embodied connection to the here and now. In this regard, interpreting 'eccentric positionality' as the ability to engage in reflexivity would involve abbreviating his approach to an impermissible extent. Instead, this is intended to mark out a double relationship: acting at a distance (ie ec-centrically) from one's own (centric, embodied) positioning within the world means standing both within and without one's self. Within this, viewing oneself as a 'self' makes it possible, and indeed necessary, to view the Other as a 'self', too (see Ricken, 2006, p 133). In Plessner's anthropology (2003 [1928], pp 383, 385, 391), an 'eccentric way of life' at once refers to 'brokenness', 'constitutive lack of a home', 'dividedness', 'incompleteness' and 'constitutive imbalance'. On the one hand, these characteristics point out that 'humans', when removed from themselves, are ambivalent and located within an undetermined relationship to themselves, and, on the other hand, they refer to the existential relevance of sociality, culture and artificiality: 'With knowledge, human beings … have lost their directness; they see their nakedness, *are ashamed of their nakedness*, and must, therefore live indirectly via artificial things' (Plessner, 2003 [1928], p 384, emphasis added). This statement contains two significant elements.

The first is that it does *not* pave the way for a theory of shame. Instead, Plessner uses it to clarify that this 'knowledge', and thereby the potentiality of emerging from the embodied 'centre', the non-coincidence of the subject with itself, the existential human brokenness, are precisely those things that ground life in the mode of indirectness and partial shortfall of the self. The reason for intertwining the self with the Other lies in the self's broken relationship with itself. In line with this, 'eccentricity', as a kind of outside perspective looking at oneself, is viewed as a prerequisite for an intersubjective social being that is reliant on Others. Standing in this 'gap', within the brokenness of the self's relationship with the possible and the real, enables the reader to recognise the conflict between Plessner's theory and any attempt to pin down humanity – which can, in fact, be associated with humiliation. This topic will be returned to subsequently, in the section 'Existential-philosophical interpretations'.

Secondly, creating a direct association between shame and nakedness in Plessner would be failing to do this issue justice, in light of the statement cited. Unlike Scheler, Plessner does not explore questions of embodied/physical shame. Indeed, this would be impossible from a purely logical standpoint, as Plessner views the relationship between 'spirit' and 'body' neither as one marked by a duality nor by a hierarchy, but rather as an entanglement. Instead, nakedness can be understood symbolically here, in the sense of vulnerability, helplessness and dependence.

However, Anja Lietzmann has indeed drawn on Plessner's philosophical anthropology to develop a theory of shame. She turns to the structural feature of 'eccentricity' to illustrate the conditions that open the door to shame: 'Insofar as humans are eccentric beings, they must invariably find themselves in situations associated with shame' (Lietzmann, 2007, p 53). She continues with the slight contradiction that 'the eccentric existence [is] the same moment that causes shame' (Lietzmann, 2007, p 86). However, Lietzmann is also interested in challenging a perspective that turns shame into a dichotomy and views it either as a universal phenomenon or a cultural and historic one.

Consequently, this chapter argues that eccentricity, or existential brokenness, does indeed serve as a condition that enables shame to be experienced. In turn, this can be viewed as genuine *potentiality*: it is not the sudden realisation that the self is different that functions as a reason for shame: instead, humans' own brokenness, their own contradictions (and simultaneously, their existential referentiality to Others) are first recognised during the shame triggered in that particular *situation*, and this shame causes the self to experience itself as different. Becoming aware of this rupture, suddenly realising the difference between how I would like to appear and how I actually appear to myself and Others in the situation, might limit the available options for action. In this situation, a person's relationship to their self, to Others and to these relationships, usually balanced, lived and a matter of habit, fall apart or suddenly cannot be maintained.

These are situations in which the subject sees itself as an entity that is pinned down and objectified by Others, or, in other words, in which the subject itself becomes an object. Jean-Paul Sartre paid particular attention to these kinds of situations in his phenomenological ontology, *Being and Nothingness* (1992 [1943]), thereby laying bare the phenomenon of shame.

Existential-philosophical interpretations: the production of shame through the look of the Other

One area of great significance, and one which has taken on near-canonical status in philosophical and sociological explorations of intersubjectivity and shame, can be found in the 'keyhole scene' of Sartre's magnum opus (for a detailed analysis see Neckel, 1991, pp 25–40; Magyar-Haas, 2020). In this scene, a person who believes themselves to be alone is suddenly seen by the Other as they engage in behaviour that is viewed as socially unacknowledgeable or illegitimate because it deliberately oversteps the boundaries of the private sphere:

> Let us imagine that moved by jealousy, curiosity, or vice I have just glued my ear to the door and looked through a keyhole. I am alone and on the level of a non-thetic self-consciousness. This means first of all that there is no *self* to inhabit my consciousness, nothing therefore to which I can refer my acts in order to qualify them. (Sartre, 1992 [1943], p 347)

Sartre depicts how the person peering through the keyhole almost loses themselves, dissolving into the situation, and how their consciousness is 'glued' both to their acts and to the spectacle unfolding behind the door. The person is 'drunk in by things', transcends into jealousy, they are not distanced from themselves at all, as it were: they are at one with themselves and the situation (Sartre, 1992 [1943], p 348). It is only once they have heard footsteps and recognised that they are being watched that the person is 'suddenly affected', in terms of their own existence: 'First of all, I now exist as *myself* for my unreflective consciousness. It is this irruption of the self which has been most often described: I see *myself* because *somebody* sees me ...'

(Sartre, 1992 [1943], p 349). For Sartre, an individual 'is presented to consciousness in so far as the person is *an object for the Other*' (Sartre, 1992 [1943], p 349, original emphasis). The person only becomes aware of his/herself and sees him/herself within the situation 'from an external perspective' *because* they hear steps and thereby anticipate the Other's look. Or, as Sighard Neckel (1991, p 27) puts it in his analyses of Sartre's phenomenology of the look: 'Only within the Other's perception can the subject relate to itself to the extent that they can gain consciousness of itself.' Sartre almost goes so far as to deconstruct Descartes' '*cogito ergo sum*': the self is not, or does not exist, because it thinks. Rather, it can think about itself (or reflect on itself) because it is, for the Other, an object, no less. The self can turn itself into an object because it becomes an object through the Other's look. 'In this sense, intersubjectivity refers to the process of the mutual objectification of subjects, which sees them become the objects of their own perception' (Neckel, 1991, p 27). Consequently, it is the Other who uproots a person from their world – and who divides the self into an 'observing' part and an 'observed' part, as Georg Simmel (1983 [1901], pp 144–5) puts it. The Other also sees something that the voyeur fails to glimpse: it has a kind of an exterior perspective on the part of the world into which the voyeur has merged.

In his analyses of the look, Sartre (1992 [1943], p 350) considers shame to be the 'recognition that I am indeed that object which the Other is looking at and judging' (see also Neckel, 1991, pp 28–9; for another concept of recognition see Chapter 1). When shame is experienced, the self is ashamed of what it is – and this is what the other person has seen of it during the moment within which it was looked at: 'Imprisoned within the look of the Other, my projects of existence are arrested, my freedom is lost and the original orientation of my being as an in-itself becomes dis-oriented and dis-placed' (Elveton, 2007). In this object status, the Other's appraisal is accepted. As a result, the subject represents the object of the Other's appraisal, although the person at whom the Other looks has no influence on this. Ariane Schorn (1998, p 57) references that this admission during the experience of shame ('I am how the Other sees me') has little to do with truth; after all, the shortfall that has been made visible merely shows that we are this *too*, and not, however, that *we are all this already*.

Like Neckel (1991, p 30) argues, in Sartre, the feeling of shame testifies that humans' being is located 'outside'. This does not invoke reciprocity, that is, mutual recognition, as with Hegel; instead, it invokes *conflict* as the 'fundamental structure of all intersubjectivity' (Neckel, 1991, p 30). In Neckel's reading, Sartre's exposition does not revolve around the belief that the self somehow is revived or recognises itself through the Other; rather, it sees everyone become foreign to themselves as a result of the Other (Neckel, 1991, p 30). As, for Sartre, a person's own subjectivity cannot be recognised in the subjectivity of the Other, because the look does not turn the self into a subject, the relationship of recognition is shaped differently in his work: the subject itself becomes the object due to the Other's recognition of it. For Sartre, shame, or the moment in which a person is caught out and looked at, is when the Other is recognised, albeit 'not in terms of a subjectivity that reflects me to the same extent, but rather as an "inaccessible subject" that gives me the status of an object' (Neckel, 1991, p 30). In this sense, Sartre views shame structurally, as follows: 'shame is a unitary apprehension with three dimensions: "*I* am ashamed of *myself* before the *Other*."* If any one of these dimensions disappears, the shame disappears as well' (Sartre, 1992 [1943], p 385, original emphasis).

In summary, it is possible to discern that, for Sartre, being looked at involves the subject's self-understanding be scaled down in a stigmatising manner, with the subject being objectified and taking on an external interpretation. This interpretation is experienced as the documentation of a deficit rooted in their very person. For Sartre, the Other's look, or even the very possibility of being observed, consequently helps to constitute the self and one's own consciousness, on the one hand, and, on the other hand, objectifies it and enables it to be shamed.

Sociological additions: the social, embodied self of shame

From a social sciences perspective (see Neckel, 1991, pp 31–4), it is rather problematic that Sartre's phenomenology of the look and his analyses of the feeling of shame see the philosopher exclude consideration of the normative references found within social situations. For Sartre, shame merely requires the look of an Other who is present and situated in a more advantageous position: it is not viewed as an *admission* of having breached assimilated norms and value patterns. Rather, shame is testament to a different admission: that I am precisely how the Other sees me. As a result, shame could be deemed the 'subjective reaction to the fear of being able to be turned into an object for Others at any time, which is situationally rooted in the consciousness of the self', and this feeling (the state of always being exposed to the look) is brought up to date by shame (Neckel, 1991, p 32).

Perspectives of this kind from the field of existential philosophy manage to get by without reflecting on the normative expectations that come into play with the Other's look. Conversely, as Neckel (1991, p 31) points out, symbolic interactionism, and George Herbert Mead in particular (1972 [1934]), dwelt on this issue. Mead distinguishes between the 'significant' Other and the 'generalised' Other as a way to refer to the viewpoint that has been ascribed relevance and is represented by one particular interaction partner or all interaction partners within a society. Social norms are exerted in the latter perspective, in particular (Mead, 1972 [1934], pp 152–64). The self may not only empathise with the significant Other: it can also take on the position of the generalised Other, to the extent that this is associated with the 'internal representation' of normative expectations to which the assessment of one's own acts, and the acts of Others, refers (Neckel, 1991, p 32).

In his comparative analysis of Sartre's and Mead's approaches regarding the contexts of looks, shame and normativity, Neckel (1991, pp 32–3) states that, for Mead, in the situation of being looked at, the stranger's *expectation* comments on one's own behaviour, with this expectation only able to trigger the feeling of shame if the stranger's expectation corresponds to the self's expectations of itself. Conversely, for Sartre, interactions 'are determined by the ontological situation, namely that I am only able to be certain of myself as the object of an Other, even prior to any interpretation by the actors involved' (Neckel, 1991, p 33). However, from a sociological and pedagogical perspective, it is difficult to disregard the evaluative interpretations (whether mistrust, agreement, scepticism or confirmation) that are assigned to 'the look' in social interactions, and which in turn evoke normative ideas and expectations. In addition, Thomas J. Scheff (2003, p 242) draws on Charles H. Cooley's thesis from 1922 to argue that 'shame and pride both arose from seeing oneself from the point of view of the other'. This 'point of view' already includes the self's imaginings of the judgements of the Other about the self; judgements which have been made against a backdrop of the applicable norms and expectations that are of relevance to the self.

However, Sartre does not focus his attention on norms. Instead, he looks at power structures in conjunction with the phenomenon of subordination, that is, what being exposed to the look means for subjects and subjectification. In the situation of being looked at, this reduction and pinning-down of the self to a *certain* existence, namely to the snippet of being that is perceived by the Other, occur to a near-total degree in that the freedom of the Other during the look sublates the freedom of the self (see Elveton, 2007). For Sartre and for Plessner, too, this type of objectification, *the pinning-down of the self to a particular state of 'being like that'*, is what produces shame. However, Sartre's main work (1992 [1943]) unfolds its understanding of shame as an ontological condition of human subjectivity, and thereby ignores that 'the prospects of abasement are just as unevenly distributed across society as the power to abase someone' (Neckel, 1991, p 33). Conversely, for Plessner, the shame-inducing character of pinning people down is grounded in a particular state of 'being like that'.

Plessner's concept of 'eccentric positionality' goes hand in hand with viewing a person as 'masked'. By emphasising the brokenness of human beings and their inability to be at one with themselves, he challenges the concept of a sovereign, autonomous self that scholars of pedagogy have gladly passed down. For Plessner, the existential foundation of intersubjectivity, reliance on others, art and culture, first reveals itself when the self is thought of as broken. With this, and with his 'anthropological law' of 'natural artifice', that is, the idea that human beings can be social and artificial due to their 'nature', Plessner seems to have anticipated the central approaches followed the psychoanalyst Helen Lewis. As Scheff (2003, p 247) puts it, Lewis 'asserted that human beings are social by biological inheritance'. This underlying assertion also leads Lewis to consider shame to be a biopsychosocial feeling.

The belief that the self cannot be genuinely sovereign is also emphasised by Käte Meyer-Drawe (2000, p 20), drawing on Plessner. This is because the self constitutes itself through 'masquerades', in a 'mirror game of subject, co-subject and thing-world whose pathological boundaries are marked by restless self-identity and complete objectivity'. The view that there is 'no authentic core to the self' (Meyer-Drawe, 2000, p 136) refers to a tradition within which Plessner (2003 [1967], p 310) also stands when he states that '"persona" means mask'. By viewing a human as 'an actor playing themselves' (Plessner, 2003 [1967], p 311), he returns to the Roman understanding of *persona*, which has little, if anything, to do with 'true' elements. For Plessner, this is not about protecting something that is 'authentic'. Rather, it is about a person's worth and integrity, shown *in the variety of ways to depict the situation*, and in the impossibility of defining it. It is possible to speak of humiliation (in the sense of the 'production' of shame) in this context if the social game's capabilities for simultaneously requiring and creating distance from oneself and Others are somehow eradicated – such as through reducing the person to a particular state of 'being like that'. For Plessner, this kind of pinning-down cannot only be imagined with regard to being exposed to the look. It can also be envisaged with regard to social situations within which the opportunity to depict oneself differently, to play with masks, is prohibited (Magyar-Haas, 2014, 2020).

Plessner's theory is similar to well-known approaches from the field of role theory, and vice versa: approaches from the field of role theory are not far removed from the considerations of mask theory. Consequently, it is not surprising that Erving Goffman prefaced his now-canonical study, *The Presentation of Self in Everyday Life* (1959), with a 1922 quote from George Santayana that seems to praise both masks and symbolism at once: 'Masks are arrested expressions and admirable echoes of feeling, at once faithful, discreet, and superlative ....' It is common for analyses of masks to focus on the face. As a result, the relevance of masks in a social environment is grounded in protecting the face, or indeed, in 'saving face'. Even for Plessner, masks and public roles play a kind of 'protective function'. Ultimately, for Plessner, the face is shaped by its 'front-facing openness to the outside world and its inward-facing concealment' (Plessner, 2003 [1941], p 251). For him, the face is 'the interface and mediator of the self to the Other, of the inside to the outside' (Plessner, 2003 [1941], p 250), the 'actual surface of the mirror', the 'sounding board of mental agitation' – and thus, shame (Plessner, 2003 [1941], p 258). Given that the face can disclose 'too much' about a person, social masks and roles are required to protect a person's integrity and value (see Magyar-Haas, 2020).

The characteristic problem, or paradox, of shame comes to a head in this embodied constitutiveness of the self: although shame is associated with the desire to hide, make oneself invisible, 'sink into the ground', it can also express itself visibly on a person's face. Thus, shame clearly marks out the boundaries of the person in that these boundaries explicitly reveal themselves when shame is experienced. Drawing on Plessner, the educational philosopher Micha Brumlik (2002, p 76) emphasises the proximity of the feeling of shame to human embodiment: the feeling may not reveal itself in embodied forms of expression. Instead 'a person's own body or a stranger's body, ... both in terms of its existence and its social, symbolic boundaries, can be a trigger for shame'. In line with this, Brumlik (2002, p 76) views shame as 'the reaction to the breaching of the boundary that is or is drawn by the human body', with a person's faith in the integrity of the self being shaken by this. While Brumlik (2002, p 77) states that the feeling of shame bears witness to exposedness in front of the Other, shame for Meyer-Drawe (2009, p 48) represents 'this fragility of our existence in interactions with Others'.

In light of the perspectives that have been depicted, it would be possible to speak of *double* exposure: if, in line with Sartre, the self is exposed to the Other's look in the Other's presence (even if this presence is merely symbolic), being objectified and humiliated by it, the self (taking into account the approaches followed by Plessner, Goffman, Brumlik and Meyer-Drawe, which systematically take account of people's embodiment and sociality) is once again exposed to the Other's look as a result of blushes and the physical manifestations of shame.

The shamed subjects of social expectations and pedagogical norms

According to the previous depictions, the intrinsically different self is a prerequisite for the feeling of shame.[4] However, the grounds for feeling shame are also connected to internalised norms and social situations of being observed and judged: people are ashamed in front of (imagined) Others when they breach a norm that is carried over from society to the self and recognised by the self. This section will explore social norms and normalisations that are relevant for the context of social work. As part of this, it will reconstruct the extent to which these might trigger shame in addressees of social work.

Pedagogy explicitly works with the gap between 'is' and 'ought to be'. A normative focus is as inherent to pedagogy as social work's social 'mandate' is explicitly normative. Both are embedded in socio-political discourses and acts which influence both the professions' areas of activity and the disciplines themselves, in terms of their normative approach. The socio-political changes that begun in the late 1990s, whether in the form of the Personal Responsibility and Work Opportunity Reconciliation Act (PRWORA) introduced in the US in 1996, in the shape of New Labour and their Third Way in the UK, or in terms of the Hartz legislation in the Federal Republic of Germany, can be brought together under the concept of the 'social investment state' or the 'activating state' (Dingeldey, 2006; Kessl, 2006; Dahme and Wohlfahrt, 2007). Within the context of the transformations of the social state (see also Chapter 1), it becomes possible to recognise common characteristics of a social policy focused on activation: such as the 'economisation of political rationality, moralisation of individual responsibility' (Casale, 2009, p 60), along with the establishment of 'workfare' policies (Wohlfahrt, nd) and a focus on ability that function on a quid pro quo basis and are associated with more restrictive regulations and sanctions. The primary objective of the 'workfare programme' is to (re)integrate individuals receiving social aid into the job market. This aim alludes to changing people's availability for the job market in so far as it imperatively requires mobility and flexibility, and also anticipates reduced wages and temporary positions. In her analysis of the concept of the activating state, Irene Dingeldey (2006, p 7) asks why and to what ends unemployed individuals 'should be activated ... against the backdrop of persistent mass unemployment in Germany'. Drawing on Achim Trube, she refers to the politically driven 'game of blame-the-victim', which sees 'the victim of the development ... redefined to become the perpetrator who either needs to be re-educated or excluded from a supportive community, without this actually solving the problem of a lack of demand for workers' (Dingeldey, 2006, p 8).

Social work is rooted in these contexts of social policy and employment market policy. It acts within them, or relates to them, just as it is co-regulated and instrumentalised through them, as in the case when 'there is an expectation that social work will also play a role in monitoring and re-integrating unemployed individuals and people who receive social aid' (Dahme and Wohlfahrt, 2007, p 28). (Socio-)pedagogical contexts have a divergent approach to handling these ideals and constructs of a good citizen, viewed as 'good' because they are willing to perform, with these ideals and constructs in turn strongly promoted as norms to be attained. If a boundless myth of feasibility or the attainability of the objective of what 'ought' to be is simultaneously projected into this ideal, the relationships between what 'is' and 'ought to be' are potentially more precarious, and grounds for shame more omnipresent, because failure is almost 'pre-programmed' in these expectations. This goes hand in hand with a feeling of permanent inadequacy (how this phenomenon manifests itself in the context of food banks, see Chapter 4), being held back in the context of continual, international, near-competitive comparisons, as well as localising and pinning people down to a particular state of 'being like that' (not flexible, not willing to perform; see also Sicora's reflections on 'you made a mistake' and 'you are a mistake' in Chapter 9), which may well give rise to shame. The clear statement of how things 'ought to be' in various contexts hardly makes it possible for the 'individual who is to be re-educated' to partake in the social game: rather, the risks of losing face are magnified. The discrepancy between how things 'are' and how they 'ought to be' in the context of social work is problematic in two respects. The first issue arises when the attainment of how things 'ought to be' is used to legitimise social work, and the second comes when social work is subjected to a dual obligation, both in terms of its clients and in terms of social expectations. Social work shows sensitivity towards subjects' dispositions, and yet, at the same time, its objectives of making individuals undertake adjustments to comply with social norms tend towards adapting and assimilating clients of social work into communities revolving around labour and values (Ziegler, 2001, p 11; see also Magyar-Haas, 2009, p 78).

In light of Plessner's philosophy, it would be pertinent to ask how not pinning people down to 'being like that', or defining them in this way, functions within the context of social work. How much space is granted for masks and roles, for the various ways in which 'being like that' can be depicted? The humiliation inherent to the structure then becomes recognisable if a socio-ethical reading of Plessner is deployed to enquire as to the identity of the client that social work addresses (see Magyar-Haas, 2009, pp 88–90). This question relates to issues of *identifying and labelling* individuals: for the social mandate of normalisation to be performed, potential addressees need to be identified as 'clients' on the basis of certain characteristics, with a precise image of their life situation, problems and life plan made transparent, recorded and documented. In this regard, they are made visible and can be 'looked at' by society and the state in a symbolic sense: 'Whereas the trust in science, technology and experts – social workers – has been undermined, audit has increased, and this process is intimately related to our pervasive concerns about risk ... which plays a key role in the "blaming system" and new forms of accountability' (Parton, 1996, p 112). In this regard, 'clients' are constructed as 'passive' entities in two respects: in that they are shown as being inflexible and barely motivated, and in that they are required to adhere to a particular 'type' that can be moulded and activated without any disagreement or stubbornness. In this, it is striking how few programmes and stipulations focusing on policies of activation deal with questions of subversion, or how strongly they believe that they are able to monitor subversion. This reveals that activation programmes of this kind are primarily focused on matters of function and fulfilment, putting their clients first and foremost in the role of the object. Whether and how far subjects act 'actively' only comes into view when they display resistance in the face of socio-political requirements – which is where their power also lies.

It is precisely the phenomenon of shame that provides information as how far public expectations, socially propagated ideas and norms as to what is seen as a 'good' and 'successful' life, as well as the individualisation of non-success, have been internalised – because people would not be ashamed if they did not want to align with the norms in question (Landweer, 1999, p 61). A person affected by a norm only sees it as a norm 'if they realise that this norm is of relevance to others' (Landweer, 1999, p 68). In this regard, it seems easily comprehensible that activating socio-political stipulations could well affect everyone and the norms proclaimed within them could be said to apply to everyone. However, these stipulations are primarily aimed at the clients of social work who have to fulfil them in practice, as well as the professionals who have to assist them in securing the fulfilment of this. The promise of the modern social age, and particularly the significant social promise of the post-war years, that work was the gateway to success and social advancement, has been deconstructed and shown to be a myth multiple times over the past few years – including with demonstrations that economic and social power was concentrated in the hands of a small number of oligarchs (see Neckel, 2013; Nachtwey, 2016). However, on the level of ideology this promise has retained its power, and jobseekers are still required to show their willingness to perform on a structural level. This demand is seen, for example, in section 31(a) of the German Social Code II, paragraph 1. This paragraph provides for sanctions 'in the event of a breach of obligation pursuant to section 31':

> as a first step, unemployment benefit II [shall be reduced] by 30 percent of the standard requirement given under section 20 for an individual fit to work and entitled to receive benefits. After the first repeat of a breach of obligation pursuant to section 31, unemployment benefit II shall be reduced by 60 percent of the standard requirement given under section 20 for an individual fit to work and entitled to receive benefits. Entitlement to unemployment benefit shall fully lapse for every repeated breach of obligation pursuant to section 31.

Humiliation as the reproduction of power

When differentiating between the sources of shame, Micha Hilgers (1996, p 19) discusses the significance of the 'discrepancy between the self and the ideal' and the 'breaching of the boundaries of the self and limits of intimacy', but he also refers to the experience of 'active abasement from outside' as well as 'a person's own dependence on their relationship to Others'. This section demonstrates that this dependency or reliance on Others enables us to recognise the intertwined nature of the relationship between shame and power. On the basis of Plessner's anthropology and theories of power, Norbert

Ricken (2006, p 142) argues that the 'fundamental breaking and brokenness of people' referred to with the term 'withdrawal' 'can be understood as a systematic siting of the problem of power'. Ultimately, Ricken claims that structures of this kind, a genuine reliance on others, are both a condition of power and 'the topic of every power-based action' (Ricken, 2006, p 147). An anthropological reflection worded in this way makes it possible

> to criticise power on two levels: *methodologically*, as a criticism of a way of thinking revolving around theories of identity that ... suggests that the differences that make up people themselves are resolvable ..., and *in terms of content*, as a criticism of the discreditation of reliance and dependence that is increasing in the present day, and is presented within sociality as avoidable and implicitly passed on to others. (Ricken, 2006, p 149, emphasis added)

Every self is genuinely reliant on Others. Relying, or depending, on Others is not an action that evokes shame and triggers humiliation in the sense of breaching boundaries, pinning someone down or limiting the ability to act. Instead, it is the definition or pinning down of people or entire groups with regard to this aspect, which then sees dependence construed as avoidable.

In his study *Crime, Shame and Reintegration*, the criminologist John Braithwaite (1989, p 55) distinguishes between 'reintegrative shaming' and 'disintegrative shaming', in the sense of stigmatisation. The former 'means that expressions of community disapproval, which may range from mild rebuke to degradation ceremonies, are followed by gestures of reacceptance into the community of law-abiding citizens', while the latter, 'in contrast, divides the community by creating a class of outcasts. Much effort is directed at labeling deviance, while little attention is paid to de-labeling' (Braithwaite, 1989, p 55). It is possible to talk of these kinds of stigmatisation (based on exclusion) if people or groups are identified as clients due to certain characteristics associated with the body (such as 'fat' or 'ungroomed' etc) or due to certain behaviours that do not appear to satisfy the norms.

From a historical perspective, divergent and ritualised forms of public humiliation arose that were aimed to 'train' 'shameless' people to feel shame. Depending on the structure of the society in question, they were targeted at prostitutes, people in socially disadvantaged positions, the so-called 'uneducated classes', people receiving social aid and so on. Various shame rituals were intended to inculcate propagated norms.

Analysing Shakespeare's 1604 work *Measure for Measure*, Michael Meyer (2011, pp 97–103) highlighted the extent to which dramas display the 'hushing-up of shame … as a privilege accessible by the powerful' (Meyer, 2011, p 100), along with the extent to which public shaming is based on defamation, and causes neither regret nor shame. It is true that penance can be acted out to gain formal reintegration into society, but again, this neither guarantees that shame will be felt, nor that behaviour associated with negative connotations will be amended (Meyer, 2011, p 101). The shame ritual, a term which is taken to mean public humiliation here, appears to be 'a powerful tool with which to discipline other people' (Meyer, 2011, p 103).

Joel F. Handler and Yeheskel Hasenfeld (2007) explore the shame-inducing character of a politician who views poverty as the consequence of individual (flawed) behaviours, and thereby differentiates between the 'deserving' and the 'undeserving poor', instead of focusing on the structural conditions of poverty (see also Chapter 4). Their research focuses on structural humiliation that results from the individualisation of social problems, and the shifting of responsibility onto individuals or social groups that goes along with this. The incapacity and inability of these individuals and groups sees them be pinned down, labelled – and humiliated.

Further reflections: shame and humiliation, social work and professionalism

Humiliation seems to be inherent to the structure (or context) of social work. Labelling certain people or groups of people as clients or addressees, and thereby engendering them as 'delinquent' or 'somehow deficient', creates a hierarchy and power differential. From a structural perspective, these people and groups of people are rarely given recognition (see Magyar-Haas, 2012). The breaching of people's boundaries, their integrity and values, however, is displayed in actual therapeutic practices labelled as 'pedagogical' that occur in certain in-patient facilities (Magyar-Haas, 2015), as well as in sexualised violence against children and young people in pedagogical contexts (Retkowski, Treibel and Tuider, 2018; see also Chapter 5).

In this regard, humiliation can be seen as the (intentional) instrumentalisation of shame. It targets the personhood of a person (or group of people), attacking their fragility and exposedness. In the event of humiliation, a person is assigned object status, pinned down to a particular behaviour or way of 'being like that'; the actions they could potentially undertake are reduced in scope or inhibited, and their helplessness is laid bare. In this respect, humiliation can (but does not have to) evoke the feeling of shame for the shamed party. Ultimately, it can also trigger anger or rage (see shame/anger loops, Scheff, 2003, p 258).

At the same time, according to Oevermann (1996, p 88), the 'maintenance and safeguarding of an individual's embodied and psycho-social integrity, in the sense of a valid concept of human value' can function as a central criterion of professional activity. Even the framework that social law enacts around social services and facilities in Germany emphasises that they are to contribute 'to ensuring that people live with dignity, and to providing equal conditions within which people, especially young people, can freely develop their personality' (German Social Code I, section 1). From a philosophical perspective, 'discussions of human value [target] an area located prior to any separation between what is and what ought to be; an area in which human existence is viewed as intrinsically valuable' (Haucke, 2003, p 15). In line with this, human existence per se is worthy of recognition, in all its precarity and vulnerability: recognition is not solely deserved for (the attainment of) some kind of 'ought-to' state, such as in the form of the successful, high-performing, independent citizen.

Against this backdrop, it seems almost paradoxical that social work is required explicitly to work with the gap between how everything 'is' and how it 'ought to be': on the one hand, its social mandate is clearly normative, focused towards questions of what 'ought' to occur: adapting its clients' and addressees' ways of life to suit certain ideas of norms and values. On the other, it focuses on guaranteeing human values (and consequently, existence), and on respecting the integrity of the body, including its weakness and inabilities. In terms of the focus on 'how everything is', the objective is to recognise those aspects that seem socially unrecognisable. In terms of the focus on 'how everything ought to be', the aim is to bring about those aspects that, theoretically, do not need to be brought about, as they are already recognisable. An attentive approach to these paradoxes that pays heed to questions of shame calls for the qualities associated with professional staff, professional actions marked by 'respectful uncertainty' (Taylor and White, 2006), and critical reflection on social norms and expectations, as well as research on this and recognition as to how addressees and professionals deal with structures that evoke shame.

Notes

1 Within the chapter I refer to contributions by German academics whose works are available only in German. The quotes from their papers and books have been translated from German into English to the best of my ability.

2 The word 'gaze' is intended to refer to the French 'le regard' which Sartre uses in his work. However, in the English translation of Sartre, 'le regard' is translated as 'the look'. Therefore, in this chapter, 'look' is still retained in Sartre's quotations, although 'gaze' would be closer to the French original.

3 The following is a revised version of a section from the article by Magyar-Haas (2012).

4 This section and the following analyses are based on Magyar-Haas (2012) and have been revised intensively.

References

Braithwaite, J. (1989) *Crime, Shame and Reintegration*, Cambridge: Cambridge University Press.

Brumlik, M. (2002) *Bildung und Glück. Versuch einer Theorie der Tugenden*, Berlin: Philo.

Casale, R. (2009) 'Fit statt fett. Staatliche Erziehungsmaßnahmen in Zeiten der Deregulierung', in B. Grubenmann and J. Oelkers (eds) *Das Soziale in der Pädagogik*, Bad-Heilbrunn: Klinkhardt, pp 53–65.

Dahme, H.-J. and Wohlfahrt, N. (2007) 'Aporien staatlicher Aktivierungsstrategien: Engagementpolitik im Kontext von Wettbewerb, Sozialinvestition und instrumenteller Governance', *Forschungsjournal Neue Soziale Bewegungen*, 20(2): 27–39.

Dingeldey, I. (2006) 'Aktivierender Wohlfahrtsstaat und sozialpolitische Steuerung', *Aus Politik und Zeitgeschichte*, 8–9: 3–9.

Elveton, R. (2007) 'Sartre, Intentionality and Praxis', *Sens [public] International Web Journal*, 1 http://sens-public.org/articles/361/

Frevert, U. (2009) 'Was haben Gefühle in der Geschichte zu suchen?', *Geschichte und Gesellschaft*, 35(2): 183–208.

Goffman, E. (1959) *The Presentation of Self in Everyday Life*, Garden City, NY: Doubleday.

Handler, J. F. and Hasenfeld, Y. (2007) *Blame Welfare, Ignore Poverty and Inequality*, Cambridge: Cambridge University Press.

Haucke, K. (2003) *Das liberale Ethos der Würde. Eine systematisch orientierte Problemgeschichte zu Helmuth Plessners Begriff menschlicher Würde in den Grenzen der Gemeinschaft*, Würzburg: Königshausen & Neumann.

Hilgers, M. (1996) *Scham. Gesichter eines Affekts*, Göttingen: Vandenhoeck & Ruprecht.

Kessl, F. (2006) 'Aktivierungspädagogik statt wohlfahrtsstaatlicher Dienstleistung? Das aktivierungspolitische Re-Arrangement der bundesdeutschen Kinder- und Jugendhilfe', *Zeitschrift für Sozialreform*, 52(2): 217–32.

Landweer, H. (1999) *Scham und Macht. Phänomenologische Untersuchungen zur Sozialität eines Gefühls*, Tübingen: Mohr Siebeck.

Lietzmann, A. (2007) *Theorie der Scham. Eine anthropologische Perspektive auf ein menschliches Charakteristikum*, Hamburg: Kovac.

Magyar-Haas, V. (2009) 'Gemeinschaftskritik – Maske – Würde. Die Relevanz Plessners Ethik für die Soziale Arbeit', in B. Grubenmann and J. Oelkers (eds) *Das Soziale in der Pädagogik*, Bad-Heilbrunn: Klinkhardt, pp 77–96.

Magyar-Haas, V. (2012) 'Beschämende Vorgänge. Verhältnisse von Scham, Macht und Normierung in Kontexten der Sozialpädagogik und Sozialen Arbeit', in S. Andresen and W. Heitmeyer (eds) *Zerstörerische Vorgänge. Missachtung und sexuelle Gewalt gegen Kinder und Jugendliche in Institutionen*, Weinheim: BeltzJuventa, pp 195–214.

Magyar-Haas, V. (2014) 'De-masking as a characteristic of social work?', in J. de Mul (ed) *Plessner's Philosophical Anthropology: Perspectives and Prospects*, Amsterdam: Amsterdam University Press, pp 275–88.

Magyar-Haas, V. (2015) 'Verhaltenstherapeutische Stufenpläne als Instrumente der Beschämung?', in F. Kessl and F. Lorenz (eds) *Wenn pädagogische Fachkräfte bestrafen, belohnen und festhalten: Eine kritische Reflexion verhaltenstherapeutischer Instrumente*, EREV-Reihe: Beiträge zu Theorie und Praxis der Jugendhilfe, 12, pp 48–60.

Magyar-Haas, V. (2020) *Masken-Spiele. Zur Verhandlung von Grenzen in pädagogischen Räumen*, Bielefeld: transcript (in prep.).

Mead, G. H. (1972 [1934]) *Mind, Self, and Society: From the Standpoint of a Social Behaviorist*, Chicago: University of Chicago Press.

Meyer, M. (2011) 'Scham und Schande in der Frühen Neuzeit Englands', in M. Bauks and M.F. (eds) *Zur Kulturgeschichte der Scham*, Hamburg: Meiner, pp 85–103.

Meyer-Drawe, K. (2000) *Illusionen von Autonomie. Diesseits von Ohnmacht und Allmacht des Ich*, Munich: Kirchheim.

Meyer-Drawe, K. (2008) 'Höhlenqualen. Bildungstheoretische Provokationen durch Sokrates und Platon', in R. Rehn and C. Schües (eds) *Bildungsphilosophie. Grundlagen Methoden Perspektiven*, Freiburg and Munich: Karl Alber, pp 36–51.

Meyer-Drawe, K. (2009) 'Am Ursprung des Selbstbewusstseins: Scham', in A. Schäfer and C. Thompson (eds) *Scham*, Paderborn: Schöningh, pp 37–49.

Nachtwey, O. (2016) *Die Abstiegsgesellschaft. Über das Aufbegehren in der regressiven Moderne*, Berlin: Suhrkamp.

Neckel, S. (1991) *Status und Scham. Zur symbolischen Reproduktion sozialer Ungleichheit*, Frankfurt am Main: Campus.

Neckel, S. (2013) '"Refeudalisierung": Systematik und Aktualität eines Begriffs der Habermas'schen Gesellschaftsanalyse', *Leviathan*, 41(1): 39–56.

Oevermann, U. (1996) 'Theoretische Skizze einer revidierten Theorie professionalisierten Handelns', in A. Combe and W. Helsper (eds) *Pädagogische Professionalität. Untersuchungen zum Typus pädagogischen Handelns*, Frankfurt am Main: Suhrkamp, pp 70–182.

Parton, N. (1996) 'Social work, risk and "the blaming system"', in N. Parton (ed) *Social Theory, Social Change and Social Work*, London: Routledge, pp 98–114.

Plessner, H. (2003 [1928]) *Die Stufen des Organischen und der Mensch. Einleitung in die philosophische Anthropologie. Gesammelte Schriften IV*, ed. G. Dux, O. Marquard and E. Ströker, Frankfurt am Main: Suhrkamp.

Plessner, H. (2003 [1941]) 'Lachen und Weinen. Eine Untersuchung der Grenzen menschlichen Verhaltens', in G. Dux, O. Marquard and E. Ströker (eds) *Ausdruck und menschliche Natur. Gesammelte Schriften VII*, Frankfurt am Main: Suhrkamp, pp 201–387.

Plessner, H. (2003 [1967]) 'Der Mensch im Spiel', in G. Dux, O. Marquard and E. Ströker (eds) *Conditio humana. Gesammelte Schriften VIII*, Frankfurt am Main: Suhrkamp, pp 307–13.

Retkowski, A., Treibel, A. and Tuider, E. (eds) (2018) *Handbuch Sexualisierte Gewalt und pädagogische Kontexte. Theorie, Forschung, Praxis*, Weinheim: Beltz.

Ricken, N. (2006) *Die Ordnung der Bildung. Beiträge zu einer Genealogie der Bildung*, Wiesbaden: VS Verlag für Sozialwissenschaften.

Ruhloff, J. (2009) 'Die Scham der Widerlegung', in N. Ricken, H. Röhr, J. Ruhloff and K. Schaller (eds) *Umlernen*, Munich: Fink, pp 47–55.

Sartre, J.-P. (1992 [1943]) *Being and Nothingness: A Phenomenological Essay on Ontology*, New York: Washington Square Press.

Schäfer, A. (2000) 'Scham: Das Problem moralischer Subjektivierung', in S. Abeldt, W. Bauer, G. Heinrichs, T. Knauth, M. Koch, H. Tiedemann and W. Weiße (eds) *"… was es bedeutet, ein verletzbarer Mensch zu sein". Erziehungswissenschaft im Gespräch mit Theologie, Philosophie und Gesellschaftstheorie*, Mainz: Grünewald, pp 221–33.

Schäfer, A. and Thompson, C. (2009) 'Scham: eine Einführung', in A. Schäfer and C. Thompson (eds) *Scham*, Paderborn: Schöningh, pp 7–36.

Scheff, T. J. (2003) 'Shame in self and society', *Symbolic Interaction*, 26(2): 239–62.

Scheler, M. (1957 [1913]) 'Scham und Schamgefühl', in M. Scheler (ed) *Gesammelte Werke Bd. 10. Schriften aus dem Nachlass Bd. 1: Zur Ethik und Erkenntnislehre*, vol 2. Bern: Francke, pp 65–147.

Schorn, A. (1998) 'Scham und Entfremdung', *Journal für Psychologie*, 6(1): 53–8.

Simmel, G. (1983 [1901]) 'Zur Psychologie der Scham' in G. Simmel *Schriften zur Soziologie: Eine Auswahl*, Frankfurt am Main: Suhrkamp, pp 140–50.

Taylor, C. and White, S. (2006) 'Knowledge and reasoning in social work: educating for humane judgement', *British Journal of Social Work*, 36(6): 927–54.

Wohlfahrt, N. (nd) 'Aktivierender Staat: Vom Welfare- zum Workfare-System' https://docplayer.org/25567202-Norbert-wohlfahrt-aktivierender-staat-vom-welfare-zum-workfare-system-1-vorbemerkung.html

Wurmser, L. (1981) *The Mask of Shame*, Baltimore: Johns Hopkins University Press.

Ziegler, H. (2001) 'Prävention: Vom Formen der Guten zum Lenken der Freien', *Widersprüche. Zeitschrift für sozialistische Politik im Bildungs-, Gesundheits- und Sozialbereich*, 21(79): 7–24.

Zwierlein, E. (2011) 'Scham und Menschsein. Zur Anthropologie der Scham bei Max Scheler', in M. Bauks and M. F. Meyer (eds) *Zur Kulturgeschichte der Scham*, Hamburg: Meiner, pp 157–76.

PART II

Experiences of shame: service user perspectives

4

Poverty as an attack on subjectivity: the case of shame

Holger Schoneville

A social work perspective

Poverty has always been an important topic for social work and social policy and its relevance cannot be overestimated. The question therefore does not seem to be whether an analysis of poverty is necessary for social policy as a whole or social work in particular, but on what such an analysis is actually focused and through which theoretical framework it is informed. While the term poverty might seem self-explanatory and associations of what it describes might come to mind quickly, the debate about poverty analysis and theoretical perspectives on poverty reveals a variety of different approaches and perspectives: it can, for example, be analysed in purely economic terms through the description of a single variable, for example the distribution of household incomes. It can also be analysed in a more multidimensional way, by focusing on different parts of a person's living situation (such as employment, housing, education, health and so on). The same is true for the explanation of the phenomenon of poverty and social exclusion: while structuralist approaches are capable of explaining the relevance and embeddedness of the phenomenon for the whole society, praxis analytical perspectives are able to explain the reproduction of inequality in its practical, everyday production of differences. These are just a few examples of perspectives on and explanations of poverty that are extremely informative for social policy. They, and the findings they provide, can be understood as part of the foundation of social work knowledge. But they do not constitute a social work perspective.

A social work perspective needs to be – and this is my argument – able to describe, analyse and explain the meaning of poverty for the individual. At the core of a social work perspective on poverty lie the terms 'subject' and 'subjectivity'. It must be capable of analysing, describing and explaining the meaning of the social structure, which is reproduced in actions and institutions, for the individual and their capability to form meaningful self- and world relationships. With the term subjectivity, not only the promises of modernity, like individual freedom, autonomy and dignity, become part of the account, but also their endangerment and the possibility that the subject could be disrespected.

This is the point at which emotions come into play and where the specific emotion of shame becomes relevant. Part of the term of the subject is that the individual is not simply a rational calculating actor. Those conceptions might be tempting, after all they simplify the analysis immensely – especially if the decision of what is recognised as rational lies in the power of the academic. The term of the subject entails that the individual is one who experiences the world, others and themselves in a variety of ways. While rationality can be one of them, emotions are a central means by which humans make sense of their experience. Shame can be understood as a specific emotion, one in which the vulnerability of the subject becomes visible. It is an attack on subjectivity and the subject, it endangers the self-relationship such as self-esteem and undermines the subject from within. And it is precisely the (possible) endangerment of the subject and its positive self-relationships that makes the exploration of the emotion of shame so valuable to inform a social work perspective.

By these remarks I do not want to state that this is an exclusive perspective for social work; there are obviously other disciplines interested in the relationship between poverty as a social condition within society and the effect it has on the individual. My argument is, while it may be perfectly fine for a sociological or economistic perspective to concentrate, for example, on the precise description of the unequal distribution of income or to analyse the effects of low and very low financial resources regarding the general conditions of life (such as health, education and so on), this would not be enough to form a social work perspective. Such a perspective needs to have an understanding of how the structure of society, the individual position within it and subjectivity are interlinked.

Within this chapter I will try to illustrate the outlined argument, while exploring the connection among poverty, social work and shame. After a few theoretical remarks and considerations, I will provide an example from a research project which I conducted. My main interest in the project was to understand what it means for people to live their life under the conditions of poverty, in one of the richest countries of today's world. I thus conducted interviews with food bank users in different parts of Germany. The aim of this chapter is not to give an account of poverty in Germany, or the specific relationship among social policy issues, social work, poverty and shame. I will, however, through the exploration of the connection of poverty and shame, highlight the importance and potential of a perspective – a perspective that I claim, is a genuine social work perspective – that has the (vulnerable) subject at its core.

The (vulnerable) subject and subjectivity

Within the social work debate, my theoretical position is not without a tradition (for example Winkler, 1988; Sünker, 1989; Scherr, 1997): Michael Winkler for example, in his theory of social pedagogy, claims that the term of the subject is 'the spiritual core of social-pedagogical thinking' (Winkler, 1988, p 98).[1] It, Winkler argues, not only allows one to conceptualise the 'endangerment' of the subject, but also 'to find a purpose for action, in order to overcome conditions, in which the existence as a subject is made impossible' (Winkler, 1988, p 98). Since the early 2000s, he has constantly pointed out that the subject is indeed vulnerable and has highlighted the social phenomena that endanger subjectivity (Winkler, 2003, 2004, 2010).

Within this debate, the subject and subjectivity are always to be understood as intersubjective. Subjectivity, as the relationship that individuals are able to form towards the world, others and themselves, is not created in a vacuum. Individuals do not develop images of social norms and values or themselves in solitude. Subjectivity and the subject are only created in society and through the recognition of others. While the term 'identity' points towards the narrative explanation that one has about oneself, the term 'subject' goes beyond the self-explanation and captures the individual's relationship to itself as well as the social embeddedness in society, which becomes part of the individual. This theoretical position highlights, therefore, as Alfred Schäfer and Christiane Thompson (2010, p 9) point out, a decentration of the autonomous subject.

There are different theoretical considerations that aim to conceptualise the terms of the subject and subjectivity. One of the most prominent accounts has been published by Axel Honneth (1995) in his recognition theory. A concept that has seen some attention within the social work debate in the last years (Schoneville, 2012; 2020; Schoneville and Thole, 2009; Garrett, 2009; Webb, 2010; Houston, 2016; Frost, 2016).

Drawing heavily on Hegelian thought, Honneth (1995, pp 92–130) claims that the subject and subjectivity are part of a social 'struggle for recognition', and shows that the self-relationship, or 'practical relation-to-self' as he calls it (in terms of self-confidence, self-respect, self-esteem), is based on the specific embeddedness in society and the specific experiences individuals have. Honneth argues that humans can experience recognition in intersubjective relationships with others and that it is only through recognition by others that humans can relate to themselves in a positive way. He conceptualises three different spheres and modes of recognition: firstly, he claims that the knowledge that one is able to control one's own body rather than be controlled by others, requires a recognition of others' physical integrity. Only if such experiences of recognition have been made will individuals be able to form basic self-confidence. The individuals will, secondly, only be capable of understanding themselves as someone who is equal within the sphere of the democratic and constitutional state, if they have experienced recognition as someone who is equal – and has equal rights – by others. Self-respect and the knowledge of individual rights are based on a recognition of the moral responsibility of others. Thirdly, the experience of being a valued member of society depends on a recognition of one's individual capacity, traits and abilities. Only through recognition of its individual achievements as valuable, will the individual be capable of forming self-esteem.

While the formation of a 'practical relation-to-self', in the form of self-confidence, self-respect, self-esteem, might sound very harmonious so far, it has to be considered that it is also possible that subjects' needs and emotions, moral responsibility, or their traits and abilities don't get recognised. In fact, in an abundance of cases the absence of acts of recognition can be observed. This is the reason why Honneth (1995, pp 131–9) conceptualises experiences of disrespect as the opposite of the different forms of recognition. While the experience of recognition enables humans to build positive self-relationships, experiences of disrespect attack those and endanger them.

This is also the reason why Honneth's recognition theory is misunderstood if only seen as a model of positive identity formation. It should instead also be read as a theory of social conflicts. Within these conflicts, individuals and/or social groups engage in social struggles for recognition. The starting point is always the given structure of the society, which is formed and sustained through power. For Honneth, these struggles are motivated by an individual's experiences of disrespect regarding their abilities and efforts to gain recognition within the given order. Disrespect may be experienced as silent individual suffering, but if individuals are able to understand their own experiences of disrespect as a form of social injustice, they may aim to fight against this injustice by entering a social struggle for recognition. These efforts can either mean that they try to gain recognition within the current social order or they try to change the social structure into one in which recognition can be gained. While the first fundamentally accepts the given order, struggles for recognition of the second kind claim that the root of the experienced injustice is the social order, which is mirrored in an order of recognition, itself. They therefore aim to change the order of recognition and therefore the social order as a whole. Because struggles for recognition attempt to fundamentally change the order of society as a whole, they always have a collective rather than a purely individualistic dimension – this is the reason why Honneth stresses the importance of social movements.

A social work perspective that takes these conceptualisations seriously and understands, analyses and describes the social world of its (potential) users in such terms, is able to gain an understanding of the complex connection of social structure and subjective experiences. It leads to an understanding of how and why objective realities – like the lack of financial resources or unemployment – of (potential) social work users have consequences not only with regard to their life opportunities, but also in the way they experience themselves in relation to specific others and society in general. It may also enable a critical reflection of the social work profession itself. In cases in which social work tends to individualise social problems and accepts the social order as a given it may provide an important reminder that the injustice which some (potential) social work users experience is rooted in the order of society itself. In this view, very selective individualistic interventions may prove to be a part of the problem, rather than actual support to overcome the problematic living circumstances.

Shame and poverty

A theoretical perspective that has the (vulnerable) subject at its core also highlights the importance of emotions. In his classic study, Sighard Neckel (1991, p 16) suggests a simple definition: 'In emotions, the experienced reality is directly endowed with a certain meaning.' Emotions are, at least partly, pre-rational and part of the bodily experiences of the world. Shame, Neckel carries on, can be understood as a specific emotion: 'Shame is the feeling, to have lost self-respect in the experienced reality.' While Honneth conceptualises experiences of disrespect as the opposite of recognition, it seems to make sense to argue that the feeling of shame can be understood as a possible emotional reflection of certain experiences of disrespect.

While the mainstream of poverty analysis is very much focused on quantifiable variables that provide a general picture of poverty's effect, there is also a debate that stresses the importance of a more comprehensive approach, which includes the subjective experience of poverty. An important contribution within recent years has been made by a number of scholars, who point out the importance of shame in connection with poverty and anti-poverty measures within social policy (Walker, 2014; Chase and Bantebya-Kyomuhendo, 2014; Gubrium et al, 2014). Analysing a number of case studies in different countries, they point out in which ways shame is connected with poverty and measures to fight or alleviate it. Even though the ways in which poverty and shame are connected varies, the studies are able to show that the connection itself is an overarching feature. They highlight that not only poverty itself is a reason for shame, but that often anti-poverty policies become a reason why people feel ashamed. Robert Walker (2014, pp 49–66) underlines that poverty and anti-poverty measures are often connected to stigmatisation. In his conceptualisation poverty (and measures against it), stigma and shame build a nexus.

That shame is an emotion that serves a social function is hardly disputed. Thomas Scheff (1988) pointed out that shame plays a crucial role in order to establish conformity towards social norms. And Neckel (1991, p 193, see also the chapter by Neckel), in his study, furthermore points towards the structural function of shame as part of the symbolic reproduction of social inequality: 'Shame in modern societies has a function in the social stratification and is to be understood as a lasting phenomenon of the symbolic reproduction of social inequality.' In this view the reproduction of social inequality is not only something formal or structural, but is mirrored in emotions. If social inequality is not reduced to the unequal distribution of financial resources and material goods, but is also related to the stratification of social status within the hierarchical order of society and a question of power within the hierarchy, the concept of inferiority becomes an important topic. Poverty is part of the reproduction of inequality and, according to Neckel, it is important to ask in which ways people who live in poverty experience inferiority and in which emotions this is mirrored.

Poverty and social support within food banks: an empirical exploration

Within this section I will try to illustrate the highlighted arguments by providing an insight into an empirical project that focused on the question of what it means for people to be poor and to rely on the support of a food bank in Germany.

The project itself understood poverty and social exclusion not as places outside of 'the social': people who are affected by processes of social exclusion have not fallen out of the orbit of society, they don't live their lives in social black holes. Poverty has to be understood as a specific area within society. The specific situation of people affected by poverty is that they are excluded from certain parts of society (eg the labour market) while included in other parts – like the system of social work or as users of charitable organisations. Only if we analyse the tense social space that is created by processes of exclusion and processes of secondary integration at the same time can we describe the social situation of people 'in poverty' in an adequate way. The way in which this space is formed relies heavily on the way in which the welfare arrangement itself is constructed. The welfare arrangement as a whole and the institutions within it can therefore be understood as entities which regulate social relationships.

In recent years, forms of social support that realise help beyond the welfare state and on the basis of volunteering have increased significantly in both quantitative and qualitative terms. Current estimates assume that around 1.5 million users regularly make use of one of the more than nine hundred food banks in Germany. There are also similar local and superregional initiatives that provide food or clothing, furniture and other goods, and services of daily life. These initiatives can be understood as part of a new form of charitable poverty relief that we call 'new charity economy' (Kessl, 2015; Kessl et al, 2020; Schoneville, 2018).

An essential feature of the new charity economy as a whole and food banks in particular is that they provide support beyond the welfare state and that the help is based on charitable acts of giving. Food banks can be understood as a symbol for the transformation of welfare (state) arrangements (Schoneville, 2018). They mark a different way of addressing poverty issues within society: they neither aim to fight – nor are they capable of fighting – poverty, but merely alleviate the consequences. The support within food banks is not based on equal rights as citizens, but is a form of almsgiving – a charitable act. The role that the support within these cases plays fundamentally differs from the rights-based approach within modern welfare states.

That the usage of food banks is associated with emotions of shame is relatively well documented within a variety of different research projects within Europe (Schoneville, 2013, 2017a, 2017b; van der Horst et al, 2014; Garthwite, 2015).

Methodology

In order to explore the meaning of poverty for those who use a food bank – not only in a formal way, but to take the subjective experience of poverty into account – I conducted narrative-biographical interviews (Schütze, 1977, 1983, 1987; Glinka, 1998, 2009) with users of food banks. These interviews can be understood as narrative identity constructions (Lucius-Hoene and Deppermann, 2004a, 2004b), in which the interviewees not only describe the world they live in and put themselves in relation to others, but also construct a narrative of themselves – their narrative identity.

Within the analysis of these narrative construction of identity, it became clear that one topic, or, to be more specific, one emotion is repeatedly addressed: the emotion of shame. Be it in the form of 'I am ashamed' or in the form 'I am not ashamed', the thematisation of the emotion of shame is a central and connecting element (Schoneville, 2016; 2013).

In the next two sections, I would like to illustrate how the topic of shame is embedded within the narrative descriptions of the interviews.

Social exclusion as loss of status

The first case is that of Salim Özkaya,[2] who is a father of two and used to work as a firefighter. After a difficult break up with his former wife, he stopped working to look after his children. Within the interview he states how the mixture of unemployment, obligations within the family, and debt from a house that he bought with his former wife, led him to apply for social benefits and later to use food banks. In the following passage he describes how he felt regarding the usage of social benefits.

> [U]nemployment benefits that was for us the bottom bottom rung and that I myself got into that situation that was something I really felt ashamed of.

Within this short quote, Salim Özkaya describes how he and his former colleagues saw unemployment benefits and people who depend on them. With the image of the 'bottom rung' he positions the group socially within the hierarchical order of society. At the same time, he attaches a negative attribute to this position and refers to social and moral stigmatisation. The description shows that he himself shared these views. A bit later in the interview he describes that he and his colleagues from work made jokes about people who are reliant on social support such as unemployment benefits. Only with the backdrop of these views can it be fully understood what it means for Salim Özkaya to be in a situation in which he needed support. For him, it means not only a form of social decline, but the experience of inferiority and exposure to stigmatisation. The stigmatisation is especially significant for him, because he himself shared the views and normative judgement behind it. The values and norms on which the stigmatising judgement are based are not only shared socially, but are part of himself. He sees himself today as confronted with his own views and judgements.

On several occasions during the interview he pointed out what it means for him to be unemployed. Here he describes the consequences it had on his participation within his local community:

> Because everyone knew you as a fire fighter. You really were regarded as someone. You went to the curling competition [a local sports competition] every year. You always helped setting up the Christmas party. And you really were regarded in the whole community and city. You really were considered as a normal citizen.

At the beginning of this narrative construction Salim Özkaya refers to the visibility, social recognition and the social status that were linked to his former job and his activities as a volunteer within the local community. His professional position and his engagement both meant that he was respected as a valued member. He furthermore points to the concept of a 'citizen', referring therefore to the recognition that he gained as someone who has equal rights among other equals.

Directly following the previous quote, he describes what it meant for him to become unemployed within this context:

> And then I really felt ashamed to say that I am on unemployment benefits.

Salim Özkaya presents the public statement that he is unemployed and a recipient of benefits as a confession. Within the confession he publicly admits that he does not have the same social position, but is in need of unemployment benefits. He points out that making this public was associated with feelings of shame. The way in which he formulates his statement shows how the social position and role 'unemployment benefit recipient' became part of his narrative construction of identity.

Within the narration he becomes a benefit recipient. While his former professional occupation was at the core of his narrative construction of identity, it now gets replaced by the role of a benefit recipient. While the former social status through work and his social activities were the foundations for his constellation of recognition, the new situation not only excludes him from these but the new status and its inferiority also give rise to feelings of shame.

For Salim Özkaya this meant, as the following statement shows, a fundamental change in his social life and his self-concept:

> Somehow everything got lost. I did not visit any friends any more. I did not participate in any form anymore, because I felt ashamed that I was nothing.

The case of Salim Özkaya shows that to be unemployed and to rely on benefits means the loss of a respectable position within the social order of recognition – he himself puts this as 'somehow everything got lost' and 'I was nothing'. The combination of the loss of his old social position together with his new status – unemployment benefit recipient – means stigmatisation and loss of face within his social networks. These societal relationships find an emotional response in the expression of shame and lead to a withdrawal from his social connection within the community of the village as well his friendships.

Exclusion as loss of control over one's own life

The second case I would like to introduce is that of Petra Gräfe; she was 52 at the time of the interview. She was born in a small city in a rural part of north Germany and had lived there all her life. Within the narrative opening of the interview she unfolds her biography and constructs her narrative identity within the context of work. Within this it becomes clear that she not only understands employment as a biographical normality, but also as an ideal – the foundation of her self-image and self-worth – she draws an image of herself as a worker. After an apprenticeship, she worked for twenty years as a typesetter in a printing firm within the small city. But after a change in the ownership of the company, the whole business was restructured and in 1998 she was given notice due to the changing operating conditions of the business. After she was made redundant, she struggled to find a job within the same sector, which has been deeply affected by technical transformation. And when she finally found new employment, she was one of the first who was let go when the profits of the company went down.

Within the interview she describes the loss of her job as something completely unexpected and as a shock. The interview shows that her biographical self-concept as a worker was fundamentally damaged by the experience. In the description of her experience of being unemployed it becomes clear that she felt superfluous and dispensable. At the same time, her father fell ill and she – her mother having died the year before – cared for him until he died. A short time later, she describes in the interview a fight with her stepbrother over inheritance, which, in particular, included the house she lived in with her parents. The combination of these issues – her unemployment, the death of her parents, the struggle over the inheritance and the insecurity regarding her home – she describes as the reasons why she increasingly secluded herself and at one point stopped leaving the house entirely. She describes here the reason for her self-exclusion:

> No, I mean, that was a slow and subtle process, that one more and more isolated oneself from the outside world. I did not know how to. I didn't have anyone who I could have asked for help. No relatives anymore. And friends or acquaintances one would not like to ask because one is so ashamed of it somehow.

Petra Gräfe reacted in a similar way to Salim Özkaya, with isolation from social networks, but in her case this had more extreme consequences. Towards the end she didn't leave her house anymore and when she did, she left it only in the night, in order to avoid being seen. She stopped opening the mail, including bills that were send to her, and therefore her bank account became overdrawn. She had, as she commented in her interview, completely lost control. She experiences this time with a mixture of excessive demand and stress combined with the feeling of shame. At one point, because she didn't pay any bills, the supplier cut off her electricity for fourteen days. She also explains that during this time she lacked the will to live any longer. She mentions that she ate only very little and at one point stopped eating and drinking for several days, resulting in the loss of 25 kilogrammes. In her narration she says that the reason was that she didn't have any food in the house and had neither the financial resources to buy new food nor the mental strength and energy to go and get some. In her description it becomes clear that the whole time was immensely demanding. The difficulty is mirrored in the way Petra Gräfe presents this part of her life in the interview: multiple times she interrupts her own narration and mentions that she is still ashamed to even talk about the time and what happened to her.

The case of Petra Gräfe shows how different problems can accumulate and can become a trajectory that the individual can't escape. The combination of unemployment, the death of her parents and the fight over the house led to an almost complete loss of control over her own life. The loss of control and the extensive isolation from social networks then led to further problems.

Help as support and shame

The case of Petra Gräfe also shows that the food banks not only provide a specific form of support but can also be shaming. At different times within the interview Petra Gräfe points out that the feeling of shame was directly related to the form and way in which she received help but also to her general dependence on support.

She also pointed out that the reason why she didn't try to get help was, firstly, that she felt completely unable to act and, secondly, that feelings of shame in particular hindered her. Only when she stopped paying her bills and her electricity was cut off for several days was a local support team was notified; social workers then reached out, came to her house and gave her support. Through the help of the social worker she got to hear about a debt advice service, which she then used to sort out her financial situation. Her description in the interview shows that the acknowledgment to herself and others, that she was someone who wasn't able to deal with her everyday life and who needed help gave rise to feelings of shame.

Her first contact with the local food bank came about when she got referred, as part of a local job centre scheme, to work there in a so-called 1€ job – a scheme that is officially called Working Opportunities with Additional Cost Compensation and in which unemployed people work in some sort of social organisation and receive €1 per hour. It was only then that she started to consider receiving food from the food bank herself. Before her work there, she knew about food banks only from the newspapers. Within the interview, she described that before her work there she would have not wanted any contact with the food bank, because she saw it as a social place at the end of the line. She wanted to avoid the social positioning and the social stigmatisation that she associated with the food bank. Only after she had worked there for several weeks did she start to use the food bank herself. She here describes her (former) perception of food banks:

> [B]ut food banks are really the endpoint for yourself, that is reached when you have to buy there. Also, for oneself maybe, that one just feels ashamed for it, you know ...

The food bank and the support that is provided there is portrayed here as a biographical end point. Its place within the hierarchical social order is also seen as at the bottom of society. The acceptance one has to rely on such support is therefore also placed within a societal relation, one that Petra Gräfe described as problematic for her.

The description of support through the food bank is described by Petra Gräfe within a contradictory structure: while she points out that she would have not been able to free herself from her former living circumstances without the help of others, she also describes at length that to rely on others and to acknowledge that she was in need of help meant that she felt shame. The food bank, as an institution and as a social place within society, is a constant reminder that she relies on others for her food. The food bank therefore became a place at which she is constantly confronted with feelings of shame.

Whether she will continue to use the food bank after her work placement comes to an end, is a question that she answered very reluctantly. She stresses that the support of the food bank does help financially, but that she does not know whether she could bring herself to stand in the queue in front of the food bank. She points out that her usage is currently invisible to outsiders, because she can use the food bank during a work break. When she doesn't work there anymore it will become publicly visible that she is a user of the food bank. Her description shows that even though she got to know the food bank while working there, public usage would mean being publicly labelled as a food bank user. Even though she worked there, this label would be a form of stigmatisation which comes with feelings of shame.

> [Y]es, that is (laugh) if one than really lines up in the queue as a customer, that is a problem. I mean, now it is really nice. While one works there, one can just buy things without being in the waiting area. And, yes, that is the question then. Basically, one should do it. I mean, why (breathes deep in and out). Yes, that is again, because it is public again, that is. I mean, that one buys there, I mean at the moment that is just between us and no one else witnesses it, because it is in the lunch break ...

Conclusion: poverty as an attack on subjectivity

The interviews reveal several contradictions: to be poor not only consists of a lack of economic resources, but, for the individuals, their own expectations of how they should be and their experience of how they are contradict each other. These contradictions result in the emotion of shame. This feeling originates in the fact that they are unemployed, that they are excluded from standards of social consumption as well as their contested parental responsibility. Part of it is also that they have to go to a job centre to apply for unemployment benefits, as well being provided with groceries at the local food bank. In these situations, the fundamental contradiction between normative expectations – which they share – and their life situations becomes obvious. That this happens in public has a particular effect: it is the gaze of others that makes them publicly poor, unemployed and excluded. In the corridors of the job centre and in the queue in front of the food bank, they are exposed to the gaze of others – the otherwise private life situation becomes public.

The structural embedding within the society, the specific way of their integration, means that they can't see themselves as an 'equal among equals', not as 'citizens', not as 'good mothers' and not as 'normal people'. Not only because they are excluded from certain parts of the society, but because of the new forms of integration. These forms of integration are part of political regulations and are (at least partly) created through the formation of the welfare (state) arrangement, in which poverty is addressed in certain forms and not in others. The way in which they are addressed creates relationships in which people who are poor, unemployed and who rely on support for fundamental goods face constant attacks on their subjectivity.

In terms of the conceptualisation of a social work perspective on poverty, these empirical findings illustrate what we can gain if the focus is on (vulnerable) subjects and the ways in which the specific social reality affects the individuals' relationship to themselves, others and the social order. It allows to understand the social and subjective meaning of poverty in the reality of everyday lives and shows the ways in which individuals create meaning and how social situations lead to subjective suffering.

Notes
[1] My own translation from the German original.
[2] The names and places have been changed to provide anonymity.

References

Chase, E. and Bantebya-Kyomuhendo, G. (2014) *Poverty and Shame: Global Experiences*, Oxford: Oxford University Press.

Frost, L. (2016) 'Exploring the concepts of recognition and shame for social work', *Journal of Social Work Practice*, 30(4): 1–16.

Garrett, P. M. (2009) 'Recognizing the limitations of the political theory of recognition: Axel Honneth, Nancy Fraser and social work', *British Journal of Social Work*, 40(5): 1517–33.

Garthwite, K. (2015) *Hunger Pains: Life Inside Foodbank Britain*, Bristol: Policy Press.

Glinka, H.-J. (1998) *Das narrative Interview. Eine Einführung für Sozialpädaogen*, Weinheim and Munich: Juventa Verlag.

Glinka, H.-J. (2009) *Das narrative Interview in seinen zentralen Analyseschritten*, Munich: DGVT Deutsche Gesellschaft für Verhaltenstherapie.

Gubrium, E. K., Pellissery, S. and Lødemel, I. (2014) *The Shame of It: Global Perspectives on Anti-Poverty Policies*, Bristol: Policy Press.

Honneth, A. (1995) *The Struggle for Recognition: The Moral Grammar of Social Conflicts*, Cambridge, MA: MIT Press.

Houston, S. (2016) 'Empowering the "shamed" self: recognition and critical social work', *Journal of Social Work*, 16(1): 3–21.

Kessl, F. (2015) 'Charity economy: a symbol of a fundamental shift in Europe', *Tidsskrift for Socialpaedagogik*, 1: 47–52.

Kessl, F., Lorenz, S. and Schoneville, H. (2020) 'Social exclusion and food assistance in Germany', in H. Lambie-Mumford and T. Silvasti (eds), *The Rise of Food Charity in Europe*, Bristol: Policy Press, pp 49–78.

Lucius-Hoene, G. and Deppermann, A. (2004a) 'Narrative Identitäten und Positionierung', *Gesprächsforschung: Online-Zeitschrift zur verbalen Interaktion*, 5: 166–83.

Lucius-Hoene, G. and Deppermann, A. (2004b) *Rekonstruktion narrativer Identität. Ein Arbeitsbuch zur Analyse narrativer Interviews*, Wiesbaden: VS Verlag für Sozialwissenschaften.

Neckel, S. (1991) *Status und Scham. Zur symbolischen Reproduktion sozialer Ungleichheit*, Frankfurt and New York: Campus.

Schäfer, A. and Thompson, C. (2010) 'Anerkennung: Eine Einleitung', in A. Schäfer and C. Thompson (eds), *Anerkennung*, Paderborn: Ferdinand Schöningh, pp 7–33.

Scheff, T. J. (1988) 'Shame and conformity: the deference-emotion system', *American Sociological Review*, 53(3): 395–406.

Scherr, A. (1997) *Subjektorientierte Jugendarbeit*, Weinheim and Munich: Juventa Verlag.

Schoneville, H. (2012) 'Soziale Anerkennung', in W. Thole, D. Höblich and S. Ahmed (eds), *Taschenwörterbuch Soziale Arbeit*, Stuttgart: UTB.

Schoneville, H. (2013) 'Armut und Ausgrenzung als Beschämung und Missachtung', *Soziale Passagen. Journal für Empirie und Theorie sozialer Arbeit*, 5(1): 17–35.

Schoneville, H. (2017a) 'Armut als soziale Wirklichkeit: Angriffe auf die Subjektivität. Zur Bedeutung von Arbeitslosigkeit, Armut und Ausgrenzung für das Subjekt', in S. Kreher and F. Welti (eds), *Soziale Rechte und gesellschaftliche Wirklichkeiten*, Kassel: Kassel University Press, pp 86–105.

Schoneville, H. (2017b) 'Armut und Schamgefühl. Emotionaler Ausdruck gesellschaftlicher Teilhabe unter den Bedingungen von Ausgrenzung', *Sozialmagazin. Die Zeitschrift für Soziale Arbeit*, 8: 31–9.

Schoneville, H. (2018) 'Poverty and the transformation of the welfare (state) arrangement: food banks and the charity economy in Germany', *Social Work & Society. International Online Journal*, 16(2): 1–9.

Schoneville, H. (2020) 'Die (fehlende) Anerkennung des Subjekts', in P. Cloos, B. Lochner and H. Schoneville (eds) *Soziale Arbeit als Projekt: Konturierungen von Disziplin und Profession*, Wiesbaden: Springer Fachmedien Wiesbaden, pp 107–18.

Schoneville, H. and Thole, W. (2009) 'Anerkennung: ein unterschätzter Begriff in der Sozialen Arbeit?', *Soziale Passagen. Journal für Empirie und Theorie sozialer Arbeit*, 1(2): 133–43.

Schütze, F. (1977) *Die Technik des narrativen Interviews in Interaktionsfeldstudien: dargestellt an einem Projekt zur Erforschung von kommunalen Machtstrukturen*, Bielefeld: Universität Bielefeld.

Schütze, F. (1983) 'Biographieforschung und narratives Interview', *Neue Praxis*, 13(3): 283–93.

Schütze, F. (1987) *Das narrative Interview in Interaktionsfeldstudien 1; Studienbrief für die Fernuniversität Hagen*, Hagen: Fernuniversität Hagen.

Sünker, H. (1989) *Bildung, Alltag und Subjektivität: Elemente zu einer Theorie der Sozialpädagogik*, Weinheim: Deutscher Studienverlag.

Van der Horst, H., Pascucci, S. and Bol, W. (2014) 'The "dark side" of food banks? Exploring emotional responses of food bank receivers in the Netherlands', *British Food Journal*, 116(9): 1506–20.

Walker, R. (2014) *The Shame of Poverty*, Oxford: Oxford University Press.

Webb, S. A. (2010) '(Re)assembling the left: the politics of redistribution and recognition in social work', *British Journal of Social Work*, 40(8): 2364–79.

Winkler, M. (1988) *Eine Theorie der Sozialpädagogik*, Stuttgart: Klett-Cotta.

Winkler, M. (2003) 'Bildung, Subjektivität und Sozialpädagogik', *Zeitschrift für Sozialpädagogik*, 1(3): 271–95.

Winkler, M. (2004) 'Das gefährdete Subjekt. Grundlagentheoretische Überlegungen zur Sozialpädagogik', *Pädagogischer Blick*, 12(1): 34–52.

Winkler, M. (2010) 'Freiheit/Zwang/Objektivität/Leere/Subjektivität/Abrichtung', *Sozialwissenschaftliche Literatur Rundschau*, 33(60): 97–114.

5

Interactions of shame: violence against children in residential care

Marie Demant and Friederike Lorenz

Introduction

Shame in conjunction with social norms is a powerful structural framing in social work. In our chapter we focus on interactions of shame and violence in residential care. These considerations are placed in the context of an increasing international debate on violence against children in pedagogical institutions. Commissions on violence against children show the dimensions of injustice in the history of residential care institutions in different countries (Andresen, 2015; Wright, 2017). At the same time, contemporary cases of staff violence in residential care are disclosed. Obviously, violence against children by professionals is not a historical, overcome issue, but rather a continuous one. We argue that violence, as well as its concealment and legitimisation, is connected with *shame* and *shaming practices* against the background of powerful *concepts* of how children *should be*. Therefore, we ask how shame is *framing* systematic violence against children and focus on its silencing and its disclosure.

Initially, we aim to clarify the terms *violence* and *shame* and why we think that violence against children and shame are linked by concepts on children in educational contexts. Systematic *violence against children* can be understood as a continuum which includes different forms and temporary dimensions of violence (Andresen and Demant, 2017). Under this term, we differentiate between the actions of adults against children which cause harm and those which are not in the interest of the child's subjective development. Violence is characterised by an instrumental use of power resources (see Arendt, 1970) that adults have in educational settings like residential care, such as physical superiority, material resources or the power to interpret children's behaviour in reports (Wolf, 2007). Different forms of violence against children have in common that adults can legitimate them by referring to widely recognised concepts of children's behaviour. Normative concepts of the 'obedient' 'functioning' child enable the shaming of children, the undermining of their resistance and the concealment and justification of violence against them. Such concepts not only work on a discursive level, they can also be materialised in pedagogical group concepts in residential care.

What makes the individual adapt to normative concepts is the emotion *shame*, which can be understood as an effective form of social control and disciplining. Shaming is a social technique to degrade others (see Neckel, 2009, see also Chapter 2). Shame is thereby based on the internalisation of social norms and the emotions of the degraded other because shame confronts the individual with its deviation from recognised concepts, that is, how one *should* be. For the analysed fields – sexual and physical violence against children in families and residential care – it is relevant to pay attention to the *physical dimension of shame* (see English, 1975). People do not only feel shame physically; shaming practices are also often directed at the body by means of judging, punishing and controlling it (see also Chapter 3). Foucault's lectures on governmentality help to understand these different dimensions of power techniques. Within this perspective, the construction of economic and rational subjects is necessary in order to establish the modern art of governing. Foucault pointed out that, even while governing through subjectivation and self-control, disciplinary governing techniques that directly address the body are still effective (see Foucault, 1991, p 102). Thus, in the context of violence against children with disabilities, shame can be tied to body attributes and body appearance against the background of *normative body and behaviour concepts*. In the context of sexual violence, it is important to consider gender-related forms of shaming *alleged sexual behaviour*. They are based on ingrained 'beliefs that women's behavior provokes sexual violence' (Fairbairn, 2015, p 242). Current practices of 'slut-shaming' (labelling girls and women implicitly and explicitly as sluts) (Crenshaw, 1991; Tanenbaum, 2015) are related to historical practices in which girls' and young women's bodies were judged, examined and controlled (Mason and Fattore, 2017). Our analysis also hints at the downplaying or criminalisation of the effects of sexualisation towards boys. Boys are seen as naturally sexually active and aggressive, rather than being affected by child sexual abuse and other forms of violence (Schlingmann, 2018).

In the following we discuss how shame can function as a frame of violence against children in residential care. Firstly, we research the impact of residential care in the biographies of adult survivors of child sexual abuse in the past. Testimonies of survivors, who reported at the

Independent Inquiry into Child Sexual Abuse in Germany, provide us with a historical perspective.[1] The contemporary perspective is, secondly, based on a research project on systematic staff violence in residential care for children with disabilities. The connection between the two contexts are *concepts* which enable parents and professionals in residential care to shame children and to legitimise abuse and maltreatment. These concepts on how children should or should not be are the normative frame in which shame practices can take place and lead to the concealment of violence and the silencing children.

Both perspectives indicate how young people experience shame and humiliation as 'part of structural inequalities' (Mason and Fattore, 2017, p 151) in institutions. Furthermore, they show the negative impact these practices have on children and adolescents in situations of dependency, and when seeking help and disclosure.

Historical perspective: reports of adult survivors of sexual violence in Germany

The following findings of shaming practices related to child sexual abuse in families are based on the reports of adult survivors. These reports have been gathered by the Independent Inquiry into Child Sexual Abuse in Germany in confidential hearings with survivors in 2016 and 2017. In the study, violence in the family context and its structural characteristics were analysed.[2] It is based on a qualitative content analysis of a sample of twenty transcripts of reports from men and women given in confidential hearings. The reports in the sample cover childhood experiences of violence between the 1950s and the 1990s.

In the analysed biographical reports, shame and shaming practices are key factors, as children and adolescent survivors had been defined by and exposed to arbitrary, exploitative and disciplining violence – perpetrated mostly by men, but also by women. Some survivors explicitly described feelings of shame, while others referred to it implicitly. But all survivors described experiences of humiliation and belittlement, with negative effects on their feelings of self-worth. Shaming practices overall presented barriers for children's agency, social connection, voice, and their ability to reach out and receive help. Institutions and professionals appeared in two forms in their childhood and youth: in factual experiences and as a threat. Many survivors reported threats from adults to exclude them from the family or institutionalise them into psychiatry or residential care, often as part of disciplinary punishment. This section therefore focuses on double and multiple experiences of shaming practices in the family, as well as in institutional contexts. According to the experiences of survivors, attributions and judgements in the different areas were rooted in and legitimated by similar specific gender and childhood-related concepts. To present results, we use three examples to describe experiences with shaming in institutions related to familial child sexual abuse. The discussion will take up patterns in shaming, particularly the concept of inappropriate sexual behaviour. Therewith, this section places emphasis on how institutions – and helping contexts – weakened children by adding new forms of shaming to the families' (and societies') shaming practices. Hence, the analysis problematises adults' power to label children and youth based on implicit and explicit concepts in social work, pedagogy and education. The historical relevance of the survivor testimonies and the situatedness of the study in the field of educational sciences make two aspects important. The first is characteristic of the independent inquiry in Germany, which was a forerunner in including the testimonies of survivors of child sexual abuse in families; former ones had mainly analysed institutional, clerical and educational contexts. The second aspect is the need to address the responsibility of educational sciences to acknowledge failures, to question the legitimations of exercising power in education, to re-evaluate concepts and to be accountable.

Experiences with multiple-shaming in reports of survivors of child sexual abuse

This section pursues the question regarding how and why shaming in families and institutional contexts are correlated. It reifies general results of the previously described study with a short analysis of chosen examples. While being individual, they exemplify structural similarities in experiences with violence and shame. Two main results of the study concerning shame are relevant here: firstly, shaming practices by perpetrators and other family members emerged as a structural characteristic of child sexual abuse in the family. Secondly, many children additionally experienced being shamed in institutional settings and by professionals, for example when they reached for help or disclosed being abused. In this section, we focus on the attributions and humiliating practices by adults in the family and in institutions. Shaming attributions and practices were reconstructed from childhood reports based on one or several concepts. Children and adolescents were constructed as: (1) bad or wicked, thus needing to be disciplined and punished; (2) students who had to adapt to rules in the family, school or institution; (3) lying, crazy, maladjusted or ill, thus needing to be treated psychologically or medically; and (4) sexually precocious and/or sexually appealing and therefore lying about the abuse or responsible for it.

As mentioned, the reports of the survivors about their former childhood are descriptions of a vast number of situations of humiliation. Children even experienced being debased and shamed structurally or verbally when physical violence was absent. Additionally, perpetrators gained power by shaming, since it enabled them to position themselves on the seemingly right side of morality and normality. In their biographical reports, survivors described the emotional effects this had on them as children and how they experienced power and hierarchy through shaming. The particularity of individual memories about childhood has to be taken into account when drawing results. Also, the different timespans and contexts in which survivors grew up require differentiation. With regard to these differences, there remain indices to take shaming practices seriously as a systematic form of injustice against children and adolescents.

Along with two examples, we want to show how shaming becomes effective. In the first example, a survivor reported being sexually abused by her stepfather when she was a girl. Her mother found her hidden diary in which she had written about it. In the following quotes, she describes her mother's, the perpetrator's and her aunt's reactions: all accused her of telling lies:

> Shortly after my stepfather came in again, he really gave me shit and said that 'I should not believe that anybody would believe me and what the little slut in me was thinking, and I shouldn't have said something.' ... And after that my mother, after he had been out of the room, my mother spoke to me again. Something about 'I should stop telling such dirty lies and how I got the idea to tell such dirty lies anyway and I was a little slut and so on.' And then it really went on for a half year each time the others [the two aunts] visited, they regularly really picked me apart, how I always call it with many adults, and said 'I should really stop telling dirty lies and dare not talk about it to anyone and how I got the idea to say and write such defamations.'[3] (Independent Inquiry into Child Sexual Abuse, 2016)

At some point in her childhood, the youth welfare service got involved, although her mother had 'drilled' into her 'what happens at home stays at home'. The perpetrator and her mother had also made her fear that she or another sibling would be sent to a residential home. She guesses a young teacher might have reported something to the youth welfare services. But the social worker whom she liked ended her involvement after a year. At the end of that year, she sent the girl to residential care for six weeks so that she could gain some weight, an important step in her recovery. Her little brother was sent with her to cure an illness he had. In the residential home, an incident that was similar to the previous situations occurred:

> I noticed directly the first evening that I was actually helplessly at the mercy of the residential home because this specific children's residential home was run by nuns back then and of course they separated girls and boys. That was okay at the beginning. But then my little brother back then stood there, he was five, stood there, and the first evening ... I will never forget, the first evening they had milk-soup with noodles. And he had spilt the soup and stood there crying and called for me. And I jumped up and wanted to help, and at the table was one of the sisters, which immediately held me back from going to where I wanted to go. And I said to her: 'I want to go to my brother.' Then she just said: 'Stop telling dirty lies, that's not your brother, he has a different name than you!' And there, for the first time, I became aware what that actually meant, (laughing) ... meaning siblings and half-siblings. And I stood there again and couldn't help my brother. And for me, that was amongst ... amongst the worst things ... that feeling of helplessness again. (Independent Inquiry into Child Sexual Abuse, 2016)

There are a few aspects which become visible in the story of this survivor. Firstly, the pain of being humiliated by the family is not only experienced repeatedly for half a year; it also endures through the nun in the residential home who contributes to her feeling of helplessness. In retrospect, the survivor describes having to navigate her emotions alone since her adult caregivers were abusive and degrading towards her. A central aspect is also that the shaming damaged her sense of self-agency. She reports how she had to act carefully, for example, when she wrote about the abuse, but hid her diary. This is also an act of self-defence. In the residential home, she actively takes responsibility by standing up from the table to get to her brother and speaking to the nun. By remembering the shaming in her family and by the nun reacting as she did in this situation, her sense that the rules are played out against her self-agency is enforced; for example, her mother's rule 'what happens at home stays at home' and the perpetrator's rule to 'not tell anyone'. The gender separation in the children's residential home is associated with ideas according to which girls and boys could be potentially sexually dangerous towards each other. Normative ideas regarding who can be classed as a sibling and who not refer to normative family concepts. Even when not mentioned explicitly, we can guess the effects of shame from her descriptions of how she became silent and experienced these situations as being 'amongst the worst things'. It is important to note that a teacher and a social worker had been involved, both of whom potentially might have helped her. She hints at being silenced and isolated by saying that the social worker 'didn't stand a chance' to get to her.

The second example is about a woman who survived being imprisoned in a closed residential care home in the former German Democratic Republic (GDR). An expert report for the inquiry, written by Sachse, Knorr and Baumgart (2017), describes how the concept of internalisation of 'discipline' by external coercion in children shaped the continuous violence towards them as part of their pedagogy. Adolescents who didn't function were sent to closed residential care facilities in order to 'restart' the process of external coercion. The subject here had experienced sexual assaults from her father and, after trying to get away from home, was sent to and moved between several residential care institutions. In a closed facility, she was raped by the director. This example shows how shaming practices can become part of conceptualised violence: in order to enforce 'discipline', the bodies and identities of the juveniles were systematically positioned as being shameful:

> There I was in the closed juvenile detention center for the second time. Well, and then everything was stricter, everything tougher, everything more extreme because I was a reoffender. ... Because I always escaped. ... Well, yes ... before that, nothing actually, nothing shocked me anymore. It was ... yes, I knew penalties in that sense before. And since I was in detention at that time, I got a nightly visit on my birthday. So. ... and ... He abused me, the director. ... Two days later, I then ... I had a ... a ... yes, I don't wanna say good rapport, but I had ... the feeling that he was a humane youth care worker. I wanted

to talk to the youth care worker about it, yes, the fact that
Mr. [name of the director] had been coming to me that
night. And because of the lies, or whatever, I got two further
days' prolongation in detention. (Independent Inquiry into
Child Sexual Abuse, 2017)

In this report, it becomes particularly apparent how and why children
and adolescents develop strategies of defence and survival against
violence and silencing. The interviewed person twice disclosed sexual
assault by her father to the youth welfare services. Since she was not
taken seriously, she became a 'criminal' who was trying to get away
from home. After being punished repeatedly, she had the strength to
tell someone and to no longer stay silent about being raped by the
director, for which she was again criminalised. 'From this moment
forth, I only functioned', she said when she described her survival
in the residential care system. After being released, she tried to flee
to West Germany and was sent into custody for a short period of
time. But the authorities didn't mention the flight from the GDR: 'In
my sentence, it says: "Because of criminal acts, a-social behavior and
criminal acts." Really? They have – theoretically speaking – persisted
with the whole parody. … I could have gotten rehabilitation possibly
for fleeing to West Germany.' By telling of her experiences of violence
and injustice in the Independent Inquiry into Child Sexual Abuse, as
well as about her resistance, she restores her sense of self-agency, which
had been erased in the shaming narratives of the authorities.

Family members, professionals and institutions: contributing to the belittlement of children

Regarding the historical perspective, we discuss the concepts that had
an effect on the cases of the two survivors. The first thesis is that
shame leads to silence and isolation not because victims stay silent,
but because shame is a tool to delegitimise and silence victims. The
second thesis is that shaming practices and their underlying concepts
are of relevance to trace historical changes, as well as continuities, in
residential care; an example would be the historic labelling adolescents
who disclosed experiences of violence as liars. Both cases show how
shaming practices in social work institutions were unfolded when
children sent signals for help or during the disclosure of sexual abuse.
Perpetrators shamed based on gender stereotypes and pedagogical
concepts. They thus influenced the self-perception of the child and
his/her behaviour and also how teachers or social workers reacted

towards the child and his/her behaviour. Furthermore, they could show the child that he/she would not be taken seriously by others or would not be supported or protected.

The attributing concepts described in this section reflect historical constructions around the nature of children (and women) and the legitimising practices of their exploitation and oppression. Historically, these constructions have been exercised towards children (and other minority groups) in institutions, as well as in the structure of families.

The two exemplary cases show how shaming became effective because perpetrators, families and institutions used similar stigmatising labels and narratives for children. Shaming attributes defined children's behaviour as the problem, ignored symptoms and signs of violence and delegitimised children's signals for help. Shaming practices against children in the power relations of families functioned as perpetrator strategies. Many survivors experienced situations in which perpetrators made them feel ashamed and guilty by boundary crossing, ignoring their limits and feelings, laughing at their pain. The connection between silence and shame was enforced by perpetrators telling children that they have to keep the assaults and sexualised interactions secret. Such strategies were stabilised by structures and legitimations that enabled adults (especially men) to shame children (especially girls). Shaming in institutions in situations of disclosure and when seeking help was relevant for children who experienced sexual abuse within their families. Many of them told the commission that teachers or social workers could have helped them if they had been more critical towards the parents and if they had taken the children seriously. That the shaming attributions stuck with the children was an effect of perpetrators' strategies, but also a result of family members or professionals avoiding acknowledging the reality of violence towards the children and their responsibility to intervene.

In the reports of the survivors, four concepts turn out to be particularly relevant for the shaming of children in the context of sexual violence. The concept (1) of children as 'bad', especially in an educational sense, basically legitimised disciplinary practices and punishment. In many families and institutions, children additionally experienced emotional abuse when being told that they were 'bad children', constantly ignored at school or if they had to be rigidly obedient all the time. Additionally, many children experienced that (2) they had to adapt to the rules set by family members and perpetrators or by professionals in institutional structures. Most of the survivors experienced heteronomy on an everyday basis in the family and in school, social work and forms of counselling when they were children. Therefore, children learned that they had to do what adults wanted them to, which made it easier for perpetrators to manipulate and control them. Perpetrators could adapt the fact that children wanted or needed to satisfy the expectations of their family members or other adults. Children were also often measured by a rules-based system and not asked about their general well-being. Many survivors reported how their voice was silenced because they were perceived as (3) lying, maladjusted or not trustworthy for other reasons. Voice and agency were only accepted in frames of legal, normal and adequate behaviour. Another powerful concept constructed by perpetrators and professionals around children was the idea of (4) sexually precocious girls and young women. This last concept not only contains all previously mentioned concepts about children and childhood, but also connects them with gender and sexuality. In a broader view, the inquiry hearings contain repeated descriptions of how perpetrators used the act of defining the feelings of mostly girls, but also boys, as sexually active and as wanting sexual interaction. Survivors reported how perpetrators told them that they were sexually appealing and alleged a sexual drive. In some report, survivors described how perpetrators talked to them in specific ways in order to persuade them that they enjoyed the violence. Some women described having been additionally labelled as 'sexually precocious' or 'Lolita' by their social environments. The role assignment and manipulation on behalf of the perpetrator and societal prejudice co-constructed the shaming attributes, making it easier for professionals to react indifferently, abusively or with punishment towards girls and young women.

These factors are useful for understanding the impact of shaming in the context of professionals' reactions to child sexual abuse in the family. In contrast, it is necessary to take positive and empowering experiences in institutional settings into account. According to the study, it made a fundamental difference if children had contact with one relative, family friend, teacher or social worker who valued them properly. It was the absence of appreciation especially which made it harder for children to access help and affected them negatively.

Contemporary perspective: shame-based concepts as a frame of staff violence in residential care

We continue with a contemporary perspective on violence against children and the meaning of shame in this context. Nowadays, violence in education is illegal in Germany. However, besides the ongoing problem of child maltreatment and abuse in family contexts, repeated cases of staff violence in residential care continue to be disclosed. One similarity of all cases in the 2010s which draws public attention was that they stemmed from residential groups which worked according to *behaviouristic concepts*. Such concepts are based on token systems of reward and punishment in order to *change children's behaviour* and to adjust it to normative expectations. In his study *Asylums* (1961), Erving Goffman described how institutions with mandatory therapy can set an *ideal model of behaviour* as a blanket orientation for all patients. According to this behaviour model, patients are constantly being reminded of their personal failure (see Goffman, 2014 [1961]). Such concepts, which aim for ideal behaviour expectations by using reward and punishment systems, can be interpreted as *shame-based concepts*.

Against the background of a case study on child maltreatment in residential care for children with disabilities, we aim to show how a shame-based concept has framed systematic staff violence. Therefore, we will: (1) introduce the case study and its main results; (2) explain why the group concept can be considered as a shame-based one and how its logic was implemented in the written team documentation; and finally (3) mention examples of how shame framed the legitimation of the systematic violence and how shaming practices hindered its disclosure.

Case study on systematic staff violence

This qualitative study focuses on a case of systematic staff violence by a pedagogical team in a residential care home for young people with disabilities. The respective team was responsible for two residential groups, one with five and one with ten children, who were classified by professionals as extremely challenging. Most of the children had multiple diagnoses and were not able to verbalise themselves comprehensively. Under the veil of a behavioural concept called 'IntraActPlus', the young people were maltreated and humiliated daily over the course of at least three years. Because the team videotaped the daily life in the group, some of the violent practices were well documented. They include, for example, verbal humiliation, withholding food, making it compulsory to sit on a chair for hours at a time, holding tight under duress, being isolated in a room and other forms of physical maltreatment. There were also specific violent practices which the team developed for single residents, as, for example, the so-called 'carpet round' – a power demonstration during which a girl was pushed from a chair several times by a number of team members.

After a first disclosure in May 2008 initiated by three team members, and after a final disclosure in August 2009 that was initiated by one of the victims, the extent of the violence was gradually disclosed. This resulted in the organisation's self-indictment and criminal investigations. In a qualitative study (2013–16, University of Duisburg-Essen), the case was analysed on the basis of sixteen narrative and four expert interviews with former and current staff members and the public authorities, as well as by a document analysis of the group concept and the team's documentation (see Kessl and Lorenz, 2016).

The case begs the question regarding how it was possible to conceal the systematic violence that took place over a period of at least three years in a contemporary social work organisation. Data analysis shows the specific possibilities of *legitimation* in such a professional context. Among the team, violent actions were reinterpreted as a healing 'therapy' in the interests of the children, who were labelled as being 'very difficult'. To the rest of the organisation, the parents and the public, the therapy was presented as a modern, effective behavioural method which would normalise the children and prevent them from permanent residence in a psychiatric unit and/or having to take medication: behind this, all the while the violent implementation remained concealed (see Lorenz and Wittfeld, 2019). Data analysis reveals that the professionals did not have to elaborate a specific concealing strategy to keep the daily maltreatment of the children secret. Rather, silence about staff violence could be realised *in the existing daily routines and structures of the organisation*. Embedded in an institutionalised social work context, professionals have the power to define, describe and explain their practices by using their institutional status, as well as pedagogical terminology, to reinterpret their actions in a legitimate way. For example, fixation over hours by holding could be documented as a positive 'relationship offer' (team documentation). In the daily documentation, the team drew up a consistent, professional *self-narration* (see Hall, Sarangi and Slembrouck, 1997) and the violence thus became almost invisible. The writing pedagogues presented and confirmed themselves as a competent, successful team, working according to an innovative therapy, while the young people in the group were outlined as difficult, challenging, dangerous and in need of therapy (Lorenz and Wittfeld, 2019).

A shame-based concept and practice

Altogether, the study's results indicate how the group's concept functioned as the main legitimation of the violence. The team's goal, formulated in the concept, was to fundamentally change the children against the background of the behavioural approach called 'IntraActPlus'. This approach sets an ideal behavioural model. It includes blanket normative behaviour expectations and several ideas regarding how children should learn, maintain eye contact, enjoy body contact and make positive facial expressions (see Jansen and Streit, 2006). The group concept thus proposes two main goals: firstly, to intervene and influence the young people's behaviour by means of immediate reward and punishment and, secondly, to train them to enjoy body contact by treating them with a so-called body-orientated interaction therapy (KIT).

With these goals and methods in mind, every moment of everyday life in the group became part of behavioural training and therapy. The group concept recommended constant interventions in the behaviour of the children in order to optimise this according to normative ideas of self-control: 'Any moment of learning in which one thinks or feels negatively and in which relearning is avoided means training unfavourable self-control' (Group concept). According to the concept, the therapeutic goal for the children was to reduce 'power and avoidance' and develop 'behaviour control' in order to achieve new 'overall goals'. Thus, any self-expression of the children could be reinterpreted as problematic 'power and avoidance', while the use of power by the teachers was regarded as therapeutic action. Team members could legitimise their punitive practices via the group concept as it is based on a reward and punishment logic and explicitly demands a reassessment of punishment: 'We have to learn to see reward and punishment completely devoid of value' (Group concept).

Against the background of this concept, two elements from the IntraActPlus approach were implemented in specific violent forms in the daily life of the group:

1. A strict token system of punishments and awards based on symbolic figures ('blocks'). Every child received a limited number of blocks which were taken away one by one for behaviour considered wrong by the professionals. After losing all blocks, the children were punished. These punishments included different forms of maltreatment.

2. So-called body-orientated interaction therapy (KIT): KIT was carried out by forcing the children to maintain body contact for hours with a few adults, in combination with different forms of maltreatment.

A shame-based theoretical perspective reveals how the concept is based on argumentations and methods which result in shaming children for *how they are*. Consequently, the team's violent attempts to change the children were directed against their physicality, their movements, their facial expressions or the noises they made in connection with their disabilities. With the main goal to normalise the children and to fundamentally change their behaviour, the group concept constructed a strong difference between *how children are* and *how they should be*. The young people were reduced against the background of sweeping behaviour expectations. Disabilities and impairments, as well as the individual needs and desires of the children and their biography and social situation, were either ignored or treated as something deficient to overcome. This absolute nature of the concept finally becomes clear through the fact that, according to the group concept, the parents should also be involved in the alleged therapy in order not to leave any uncontrolled 'niches' for the children:

> On the one hand, the child experiences a secure structure between the facility or therapist and the family and, at the same time, it has no niches to stably maintain misbehavior. (Group concept)

This focus on any uncontrolled 'niche' and any deviation from ideas of normality, as well as the disciplining techniques for intervention in the children's behaviour, qualifies the group concept as a *shame-based concept* (see Lorenz et al, 2018).

Shaming practices framed systematic violence and hindered its disclosure

The reconstruction of the case shows how shame and shaming practices framed the violence in the group and hindered their disclosure. We would like to highlight three different dimensions.

Moral degradation of residents

The residents of the groups were morally degraded (Cremer-Schäfer and Steinert, 2000) on a range of attributions, which can be described as ranging from 'innocent but difficult', to 'innocent but dangerous', to 'dangerous, unpredictable and unreliable' (see also Goffman, 2014 [1961]). Such degradations formed the basis from which the concept and the alleged therapy could be legitimised vis-à-vis various actors. The team members reinterpreted their violent interventions as a form of self-defence and justified their methods due to the 'difficulty' of the children. On top of that, the behavioural concept enabled the team to promise to the public authority, as well as to the management and colleagues of the organisation, that they would change and adapt the residents of the group. Even though the public home supervision had doubts about the 'unusual' concept and its methods, they allowed it in order to establish a specialised setting for 'difficult' children because such settings were (and are) demanded in the field of residential care. Finally, the team made promises to the parents that their children would be normalised by the therapy. In so doing, the disabilities of the children were presented as issues to be overcome.

Part of the violence: practices of humiliation

The violent practices of the team can be described as a permanent daily power demonstration to break the children's will. The team demonstrated superiority to the children and showed them that they had no other option than to adjust. Verbal shaming and humiliation enabled the team to convey to the children their inferiority. The following sequence from the team's documentation is a clear example of how violent interventions dominated the professionals' logic of action and daily life in the groups:

> Manuel was allowed to sit mostly on the chair yesterday. He was constantly losing his blocks and was extended again and again for half an hour. Towards evening, it got better and he was finally allowed to eat. After dinner, he should ... go straight to bed. He did not do it. So he had to sit again on the chair and lost his blocks three times in a row, so he had to sit on the chair until 10:30 pm. (Team's documentation)

With such sequences, the team's documentation testifies a shameful structure in which the children were constantly confronted with their deviations from behavioural expectations and violently sanctioned for them. Shame was often carried out by humiliating punishment practices visible to other children and employees in the group, as this quote shows. The description of hours of forced sitting as something that 'was allowed' is a typical team-internal code by which such punishment practices were euphemistically reinterpreted.

Shaming the victim during disclosure

Most of the young people in the group could not articulate comprehensively. The only resident who was able to verbalise himself was a boy who was also the most morally degraded by the team. In the facility, he was looked upon as if he were an unreliable person and a sexual offender. It was argued that his words could not be trusted. After the first disclosure he made, the team discussed and planned in the documentation what to do if he were to say 'something' to his mother during his weekend visits at home. The manager of the concerned part of the facility gave the order that whenever the boy spoke about his experiences in the group, it should be reported to her. In the year after the first disclosure, no one systematically questioned the boy about his experience in the group; meanwhile, his image as a 'liar' and offender was yet more firmly further established. Finally, on a walk with a teacher during a change into a new group in the facility, the boy spoke about his violent experiences in the former group. In the interview, the teacher said that he had the impression that the boy had already spoken to other employees about his experiences before. But this time his words were documented and reported to the new overall managers of the institution, which led to a comprehensive disclosure more than a year after the first disclosure. This shows how shaming attributions against children can hinder processes of disclosure.

Conclusion

This chapter has presented results from two studies on violence against children with distinct research material and different underlying research questions. By contrasting these, we could find similarities in shaming practices in relation to violence against children in residential care settings. Parallels could be found across completely different settings and temporal phases, such as the 'belittlement' of children and adolescents in care, indicating continuities in the interrelation of power abuse and violence in social work and shaming practices. At the same time, our analysis shows how the pedagogical implementation of concepts that enable shaming practices differs. A further distinction can be drawn from the different timespans. The shaming attributions which survivors of sexual abuse in families and institutions remembered in the first study were mostly shaped by authoritarian and gender-stereotypical concepts in society and education (Koch, 2012). In the second study, the behavioural concept took up modern ideas of individual improvement and legitimated violent technologies, as the 'improvement' of behaviour was connected to disabilities. These differences are in line with works that suggest a structural connection between social control and shame, but emphasise the historic-specific modifications of the ways and forms in which shaming is expressed and internalised (Neckel, 1991; Schäfer and Thompson, 2009, Stearn, 2016; Mason and Fattore, 2017).

Altogether, the two perspectives point out how shame frames violence. Even though both analysed fields are from different periods of time and different contexts, how shame co-enables the practise and legitimisation of violence and hinders its disclosure becomes clear.

The results presented here can be read as documentation for the internalisation of shame through experiences of violence in childhood. As such, they are a reminder of non-individual factors that relate to inner feelings of shame. Here, we have briefly contextualised why we emphasise the role of disciplinary violence and normative discourses in feelings of shame. There are good reasons for introducing the ideal of modern sovereignty into the analysis of shame (Schäfer and Thompson, 2009). Since individuals internalise the techniques and ideals of the Homo economicus, they feel ashamed when they fail in being autonomous subjects. Thus, the controlling function of shame shifts to the inner adaption of norms.

Our argument is that, in society as a whole, violent or disciplinary practices as power techniques are necessary to (re)produce feelings of shame which affect (self-)control. In other words, experiences of the violation of boundaries and belittlement in the context of sexual violence are factors in socialising shame into patriarchal and other hierarchical patterns. By simultaneously shaming children as bad, crazy or sexualised, parents, for example, referred to their power over them – their right to discipline them and their potential to report them to social services. But our research also reveals examples of professionals in residential care who misused their authority by threatening to confine children. Therefore, shaming has to be addressed by the discipline of social work, not as something of the past or found in singular cases, but as a structure of power for which professionals are responsible.

Questions which are derived from these results are concerned with how social workers treat children. How do we protect children from being shamed? Do we aim to change the behaviours of silent, noisy, passive, aggressive, sexually outspoken and troublemaking children, and if so, how? A focus on functioning and healing for education, work and therapy hinder rather than help children who have experienced or are experiencing sexual abuse, maltreatment and other forms of violence. More importantly, children and adolescents need to be given access to agency as a fundamental right, independent of their behaviour.

Notes

[1]   For further information see the English website of the inquiry: https://www. aufarbeitungskommission.de/english-information/.

[2]   The study was one of four accompanying research projects of the inquiry led by commission members. It was conducted in the working group of Sabine Andresen (member and chairperson of the inquiry) at the Institute for Educational Sciences at the Goethe University in Frankfurt. One part of the education-scientific theoretical framework is family theory. The other refers to the emerging field of empirical and theoretical investigations on the need for inquiries into child sexual abuse (Rassenhofer et al, 2013; Andresen, 2015), the impact of inquiries (Wright, 2017) and the topic of acknowledgment for survivors (Kavemann et al, 2016). The framework expands contexts and relations which are relevant to the intra-familial violence by looking at the fields of pedagogy, medicine and social work.

[3]   All quotes from data material are my own translations from German to English.

References

Andresen, S. (2015) 'Das Schweigen brechen. Kindesmissbrauch: Voraussetzungen für eine persönliche, öffentliche und wissenschaftliche Aufarbeitung', in M. Geiss and V. Magyar-Haas (eds) *Zum Schweigen. Macht/Ohnmacht in Erziehung und Bildung*, Weilerswist-Metternich: Velbrück, pp 127–45.

Andresen S. and Demant, M. (2017) 'Worin liegt die Verantwortung der Erziehungswissenschaft? Ein Diskussionsbeitrag zur Aufarbeitung sexualisierter Gewalt', *Erziehungswissenschaft*, 54(28): 39–49.

Arendt, H. (1970) *Macht und Gewalt*, Munich: Piper Verlag.

Cremer-Schäfer, H. and Steinert, H. (2000) 'Soziale Ausschließung und Ausschließungs-Theorien: Schwierige Verhältnisse', in: H. Peters (ed) *Soziale Kontrolle – Zum Problem der Nonkonformität in der Gesellschaft*, Leske + Budrich: Opladen, pp 43–64.

Crenshaw, K. (1991) 'Mapping the margins: intersectionality identity politics, and violence against women of color', *Stanford Law Review*, 43: 1241–99.

English, F. (1975) 'Shame and social control', *Transactional Analysis Journal*, 5(1): 24–8.

Fairbairn, J. (2015) 'Rape threats and revenge porn: defining sexual violence in the digital age', in J. Bailey and V. Steeves (eds) *Putting Technology, Theory and Policy into Dialogue with Girls' and Young Women's Voices*, Ottawa: University of Ottawa Press, pp 229–51.

Foucault, M. (1991) 'Governmentality', in G. Burchel, C. Gordon and P. Miller (eds) *The Foucault Effect: Studies in Governmentality*, Chicago: University of Chicago Press, pp 87–104.

Goffman, E. (2014 [1961]) *Asyle: Über die soziale Situation psychiatrischer Patienten und andere Insassen*, Berlin: Suhrkamp.

Hall, C., Sarangi, S. and Slembrouck, S. (1997) 'Silent and silenced voices: interactional construction of audience in social work talk', in A. Jaworski (ed) *Silence: Interdisciplinary Perspectives*, Berlin and New York: Mouton de Gruyter, pp 181–211.

Independent Inquiry into Child Sexual Abuse (2016) 'Transcript of confidential hearing no. 19', Frankfurt and Berlin.

Independent Inquiry into Child Sexual Abuse (2017) 'Transcript of confidential hearing no.7', Frankfurt and Berlin.

Jansen, F. and Streit, U. (2006) *Positiv lernen*, Heidelberg: Springer Medizin.

Kavemann, B., Rothkegel, S., Graf-van Kesteren, A. and Nagel, B. (2016) *Erinnern, Schweigen und Sprechen nach sexueller Gewalt in der Kindheit. Ergebnisse einer Interviewstudie mit Frauen und Männern, die als Kind sexuelle Gewalt erlebt haben*, Wiesbaden: Springer VS.

Kessl, F. and Lorenz, F. (2016) 'Gewaltförmige Konstellationen in den stationären Hilfen: eine Fallstudie', *EREV-Schriftenreihe*, 16.

Koch, C. (2012) 'Das Kind als Feind, das Kind als Freund. Was haben nationalsozialistisches Erziehungserbe und pädophile Ideologie mit der gegenwärtigen Missbrauchsdebatte zu tun?', in S. Andresen and W. Heitmeyer (eds) *Zerstörerische Vorgänge. Missachtung und sexueller Gewalt gegen Kinder und Jugendliche in Institutionen*. Weinheim und Basel: Beltz Juventa, pp 228–42.

Lorenz, F., Magyar-Haas, V., Neckel, S. and Schoneville, H. (2018) 'Scham in Hilfekontexten: zur Beschämung der Bedürftigkeit', in Kommission Sozialpädagogik (ed) *Wa(h)re Gefühle: sozialpädagogische Emotionsarbeit im wohlfahrtsstaatlichen Kontext*, Weinheim: Belz Juventa, pp 216–32.

Lorenz, F. and Wittfeld, M. (2019) 'Violence against children with disabilities committed by staff in residential care', in S. Popovic, G. Crous, N. Tarshish, L. Van Erwegen and F. Lorenz (eds) *Child Maltreatment and Well-Being: Contemporary Issues, Research, and Practice. Conference Proceedings*, Rijeka: University of Rijeka, pp 9–17.

Mason, J. and Fattore, T. (2017) 'Shame, social orders and the governing of women and girls through institutions in New South Wales', *Emotions: History, Culture, Society*, 1(2): 131–54.

Neckel, S. (1991) *Status und Scham. Zur symbolischen Reproduktion sozialer Ungleichheit*, Frankfurt am Main: Campus.

Neckel, S. (2009) 'Soziologie der Scham', in A. Schäfer and C. Thompson (eds) *Scham*, Paderborn: Schöningh, pp 103–18.

Rassenhofer, M., Spröber, N., Schneider, T. and Fegert, J. M. (2013) 'Listening to victims: use of a critical incident reporting system to enable adult victims of childhood sexual abuse to participate in a political reappraisal process in Germany', *Child Abuse & Neglect*, 37(9): 653–63.

Sachse, C., Knorr, S., and Baumgart, B. (2017) 'Historische, rechtliche und psychologische Hintergründe des sexuellen Missbrauchs an Kindern und Jugendlichen in der DDR', Berlin: Independent Inquiry into Child Sexual Abuse.

Schäfer, A. and Thompson, C. (2009) *Scham*. Paderborn: F. Schöningh.

Schlingmann, T. (2018) 'Genderaspekte sexualisierter Gewalt gegen Jungen', in A. Retkowski, A. Treibel and E. Tuider (eds) *Handbuch sexualisierte Gewalt und pädagogische Kontexte. Theorie, Forschung, Praxis*, Weinheim: Beltz Juventa, pp 261–9.

Stearn, P. N. (2016) 'Shame, and a challenge for emotions history', *Emotions Review*, 8(3): 197–206.

Tanenbaum, L. (2015) *I Am Not a Slut: Slut-Shaming in the Age of the Internet*. New York: Harper Perennial.

Wolf, K. (2007) 'Zur Notwendigkeit des Machtüberhangs in der Erziehung', in B. Kraus and W. Krieger (eds) *Macht in der Sozialen Arbeit*, Lage: Jacobs, pp 103–41.

Wright, K. (2017) 'Remaking collective knowledge: an analysis of the complex and multiple effects of inquiries into historical institutional child abuse', *Child Abuse & Neglect*, 74: 10–22.

6

Emotional labour in social work practice and the production of shame

Carsten Schröder

Introduction

The subject of this chapter is the emotional labour of practitioners in the field of residential care. It focuses on the creation of an emotional atmosphere in the interaction between professionals and service users. The chapter examines the hypothesis that by creating an emotional atmosphere, practitioners try to engender either positive or negative emotions in service users, based on the definition of a given situation by professionals. This way of looking at emotional labour is discussed in the light of ethnographic data from a study by the author, with a focus on the creation of a shaming atmosphere in interactions between practitioners and service users in the field of residential care. In this context, the emotional labour of practitioners is understood as a way to produce an emotional atmosphere in interactions with service users that is used to create potential spaces for learning and development, but also comprises processes of normative regulation aimed at influencing the behaviour of the latter (Schröder, 2017). Central to these processes is the question of how practitioners use emotional labour to produce a shaming atmosphere and thus draw service users into negative emotional trajectories of shame or guilt. The aim is to show that emotional labour is a powerful tool for producing conformity with normative expectations in service users, expectations that are both institutional and defined by the practitioner. On the one hand, working with one's own emotions and those of others can be an opportunity to open up potential spaces for the development of the subject, something which points to the emancipatory element of emotional labour. On the other hand, it also has an instrumental aspect insofar as work on and with the emotions of service users is used as a means to produce conformity with expectations. The theoretical discussion thus examines the dialectically structured relation of emotional labour in professional social work settings as an oscillation between emancipation and social control.[1] The chapter is subdivided as follows: to begin with, the significance of emotions in professional interactions is explored in detail in order to show that professional interactions in social work necessarily require work on one's own emotions and those of others. This is followed by a discussion of shame and shaming in social interactions, before using empirical analysis to examine the negative emotional trajectories of being shamed. The function of emotional labour in an educative relation is discussed next. The last section explores professional perspectives on dealing with shame and shaming.

Social work and emotional labour

In the social formations of capitalist democracy, social work in practice is always linked to social policy, due to the fact that it is embedded in the regulatory context of the welfare state. In this regard, the activities undertaken by social workers have a function that is defined both by reference to society and by reference to the welfare state (see Olk, 1986; Schaarschuch, 1995). This definition has its origins in the individuation of the subject and in the socially created relations of production, relations that are marked by conflicts requiring a societal response to restrictions placed on the life opportunities of individuals and their scope for action (see Hornstein, 1995, p 24). What is at issue here are the constitutive elements of socially produced inequalities, through which

> entire groups are excluded from the opportunities of a society. The systematic creation of poverty, the blocking of educational opportunities, the marginalisation and exclusion of social groups, the production of the 'weight of the world' are some of these mechanisms, which at the same time demand that steps be taken in terms of social policy.[2] (Winkler, 2004, p 86)

Centrifugal social forces of inclusion and exclusion are at work here, which means that not everyone is given the same opportunities to participate in the life of society (see Dewe, 2009, p 93). This implies not only that structures of social inequality take shape in relations of societal production which exclude some people from the chances offered by society, but also that possibilities for developing forms of autonomous living and a self-determined life are under threat – as, for example, in the case of the unemployed, of single parents or of individuals with drug or alcohol dependence (see Sünker, 1995, pp 87ff; Schoneville, 2013; see also Chapter 4).[3] While the professional actions of social workers are embedded in the regulation of the conflictual relation between subject and society (see Wagner, 2013, p 167), they are also characterised by a normative orientation towards social justice as a professional frame of reference (see Sünker, 1995, p 87). Social workers help to deal with the socially created problems of social reproduction processes (see Winkler, 2006, p 67), so that 'both autonomous living and social normality with its intended effect of relieving or defusing social problems and conflicts are categorical reference points for the dialectical mediation between individual and society in social pedagogy' (Wagner, 2013, p 169). In this context, the activities of social workers are embedded in a dialectic of help and control. This demands of practitioners that they 'maintain a constantly threatened equilibrium between the legal claims, needs and interests of clients, on the one hand, and the interests of control pursued by public steering agencies in each given case, on the other' (Böhnisch and Lösch, 1979, p 27).

Acting professionally can thus be reconstructed as support at the interactive level and as socialising control at the structural level (Müller, 2001, p 34). According to Wagner, the modes that categorially define the professional actions of social workers are socialisation and recognition (see Wagner, 2013, p 167). Social workers establish a connection with social relations of production in order to demonstrate socialisation prospects to their client groups (see Winkler, 1988, p 275). The institutions of social work can be understood as sites of socialisation and recognition, where it is possible to define the professional tasks of practitioners as that of establishing a societally defined normality (socialisation) and of opening a potential space for developing *forms of autonomous living* (recognition) (see Sünker, 1995, pp 73ff; Winkler, 1995, p 114; Wagner, 2013, pp 168f).

The discussion that follows intends to show that professional emotional labour is arguably part of what it means to act as a social worker in interactive constellations, and that it is used in the institutional settings of social care and social work in order to establish conditions for the socialisation and individuation of service users. In analytical terms, there are two aspects that will be explored in order to establish the connection between professional actions and emotions: (1) professional action as an interactive process; (2) emotions in professional interactions.

Professional action as an interactive process

The practical context of social work is that of an interactive web of relationships between social workers and service users (Wagner, 2013, p 177). The nature of acting professionally as a social worker, leaving aside administrative and bureaucratic tasks, is thus something that is revealed in particular in the interactive work done in face-to-face encounters within an institutional relation of service provision (see Schaarschuch and Oelerich, 2005, p 13). Dewe et al (2001) develop a concept of professional action which demonstrates that the professionality of practitioners is constituted above all in their interactive relations with service users:

> Professional action presupposes a definable specific focus
> and an identifiable underlying rationale or focal point by
> reference to which it claims validity institutionally and
> in terms of the rationale of the interaction. A definition
> of social work may be helpful here which is formulated
> through processes of dialogue and which focuses on service
> users regaining and increasing their autonomy of action.
> (Dewe et al, 2001, pp 17f)

Professional action is characterised by the fact that through interaction, a new, shared element is generated which may be defined as a cooperative, dialogic and co-productive relation (see Rose and Wulf-Schnabel, 2013, p 100). It is a mark of professional interactions in social work that the initial contact with clients usually involves a discussion of why and in what context service users are availing themselves of the social work service, as well as an interpretation and definition of the day-to-day issues facing them and an interactive development of prospects for a more successful and self-determined daily life (Sünker, 1989; Thiersch, 2009; see Schäfter, 2010; Messmer and Hitzler, 2011, pp 56f). Professional practitioners as co-producers and service users as producers of their own selves focus on a shared perspective in the interactive process (see Schaarschuch, 2006, p 102).[4] Here it is possible to speak of an interactive process of production, since practitioners and service users direct their activities within the working relationship towards a new, shared element. This is because 'what is to be appropriated is defined in actual, joint activities' (Kunstreich, 2005, p 1095). The process of managing and interpreting problems happens intersubjectively and can be conceptualised as a reciprocal and responsive relation of speaking, responding and questioning (see Sünker, 1989). This interaction has an intensely dialogic element. Having said that, it should not be assumed that it is a non-coercive space. On the contrary, the relation between practitioners and service users is structured asymmetrically in terms of power and resources: the *power of the institution* and the *privileged access to knowledge* enjoyed by the practitioner as compared to the users of social work imply an unequal relation in which there can be no question of a symmetrical relationship or of symmetrical communication. In substance, what is at issue in the structural asymmetry of power and resources in interactions between social workers and service users is the question of support and domination or, in other words, of support and control.

Emotions in professional interactions

This section aims to demonstrate that interactions and relations between social workers and service users also have an emotional dimension. In connection with this, emotional labour is understood as an interactive process in which the operations of institutional emotion management are considered in relation to the creation of opportunities for the users of social work to learn and to develop (see Müller, 2011).

According to Dörr and Müller, 'emotions contain messages that tell actors how they are to understand particular relational qualities' (2005, p 235). Emotions are embedded into a particular situation at a given moment in time, where there may be a discrepancy between the emotions of social workers and expectations as to how they are meant to act in that situation. This triggers efforts to manage these feelings (see Müller, 1997, p 216). For example, when scared by a threatening display by a young person, practitioners may in certain situations hide the emotions which frighten them in order to save face as professionals. As a result, both the normative horizon within which feeling happens and the processes of emotion management are of central concern in professional modes of action (see Müller, 1997, p 216). Few would deny that practising as a social worker involves emotional labour. It is a distinguishing feature of professional social work (see Wulf-Schnabel, 2011, p 46). Professional practitioners appear both as a point of human contact and in their role as representatives of an institution (see Gildemeister, 1984). When Thiersch (2009), C. W. Müller (1997) and B. Müller (2011) speak of the cultivation of emotions, this entails the claim that emotions should be considered in relation to professionality. This is evident, for example, in Jan Wulf-Schnabel's statement that '[t]o bring their emotions into their work in a professional manner and to notice and accept the feelings of service users are everyday work requirements for the employees' (2011, p 46). This means that working with and on feelings is a constituent part of what it means to act professionally at work. When feelings such as sympathy, compassion, disagreement and empathy are aroused, practitioners must subsume themselves and their personalities to the institutional setting. Professionality and personality are thus intertwined in everyday working life. In essence, emotional labour describes the professional practice of dealing with emotions in work-related interactive relations between professional actors and their clients (see Dunkel, 1988, p 67):

> As a rule, emotional labour is embedded in specific situations and directed towards an object. It invariably also includes a display of the Self in order to reach a goal, in the context of professional objectives that help define this goal ... It is usually emotions assessed as discordant, commendable, dysfunctional or deviant with regard to the requirements of the situation that become the object of emotional labour. Emotional labour is constituted in the hiatus between 'is' and 'ought' within which practitioners produce and reproduce normative frameworks at the interactive level. Emotional norms concern what someone feels and ought to feel, on the one hand, and what someone interprets another person to be feeling and what that person ought to be feeling, on the other. The processes by which feelings are managed in emotional labour are aimed at the establishment and maintenance of an institutionally defined and interactively produced normality.[5] (Schröder, 2017, pp 252f)

Especially in social work, the type of action that is characteristic for professional interactions means that emotions cannot be reduced to the status of a confounding variable or a side effect (see Dunkel, 1988, p 66). On the contrary, they are central to a professional practice in which an awareness of one's own feelings and those of others is an important aspect of interacting with service users, as is the ability to cope with the emotions that arise in the process (Dörr and Müller, 2005, p 234). This 'is a fundamental precondition if one is to try and make good on the professional claim of entering into a dialogue with those concerned as partners, that is, of enabling them to experience a sense of not speaking into the void when communicating/sharing what they have to say' (Dörr and Müller, 2005, p 234). In shaping their actions in a way that defines itself as professional, social workers invest their expert knowledge and their skills in their work with service users – in the sense of professional advice and counselling, care, mentoring and education. At the same time, they shape an interactive and relational process and bring to it qualities, abilities and skills that belong to them personally, in order to create relations of trust or to appear as a likeable person (see Graßhoff and Schweppe, 2009, p 308; Moesby-Jensen and Nielsen, 2015, p 692). The emotional labour of practitioners in social work relates to the personal development of service users (see Wulf-Schnabel, 2011, p 48). To an extent this view is convincing, given that the professional actions of practitioners are aimed at the emancipation and autonomy of service users or entail changes in their circumstances towards a more successful and self-determined everyday life (see Sünker, 1989; Thiersch, 2009). Even though the emotional labour of social workers relates mainly to the service users, this does not mean that professional actors do not also work on their own emotions. Dörr and Müller argue that the emotional involvement of social workers in interactive relations requires a regulation of their own emotions (see 2005, pp 233f). The interactive process thus has a reciprocal character in that the professional practitioners work both on the feelings of service users and on their own feelings (see Dörr and Müller, 2005, p 234). In essence, professional practice is realised at the level of the interactive process and also entails an awareness of, reflection on and regulation of the practitioner's own feelings (see Dörr and Müller, 2005, pp 233f). In line with the arguments made so far, the core characteristic of emotional labour in social work consists in practitioners managing their own feelings and those of service users with a view to the requirements of their work. It is an inherent part of their professional activities (see Dunkel, 1988, p 67; Hochschild, 1990; Schröder, 2017).

The production of shame in social interactions

The moments when people feel shame or when they are ashamed of something are related to social production and reproduction, since these processes create normative expectations associated with specific demands or expectations that people may fail to meet or in regard to which they perceive themselves as deficient or inadequate (see Neckel, 1991, p 77, see also Chapter 2). In this respect, shame and shaming occupy the space between individual experience and social practice. People in their everyday life thus try at any cost to present themselves so as to appear self-confident, good and 'skilful; in being the way they are, they show that they are in control of themselves, that they are competent and the master of their fate. To be ashamed would mean to fail in this aspiration. Shame would be embarrassing; it is shaming to be ashamed. (Thiersch, 2009, p 161)

Shame and shaming need to be understood as social feelings that involve a person's negative experience under the gaze of others (see Sartre, 2016 [1943], p 495, see also Chapter 3). This situation is accompanied by a sense of having done something wrong, a deficiency for which the person feels responsible. This is accompanied by the devaluing of the self felt when experiencing shame (see Neckel, 1991, p 16). The loss of personal worth that is part of the experience of shame implies losing self-respect in front of others and in one's own estimation (see Neckel, 1991, p 16): in this sense, the experience of shame and of being shamed in the eyes of others reveals a defect or an inadequacy which does not satisfy applicable norms (see Demmerling and Landweer, 2007, p 229). Under the gaze of others, subjects who are ashamed or who are being shamed are drawn into a negative emotional trajectory and perceive themselves as degraded, defective or deficient (see Sartre, 2016 [1943], p 496). In this context, the concept of an emotional trajectory refers to the fact that in experiencing emotions, a path is laid down which affects the potential space for action (see Slaby, 2011, p 38). This negative experience of shame and of being shamed entails a way of being situated in the world that can be described as a feeling that makes the skin burn and the face blush, or as a shrinking in which those affected wish the ground would open and swallow them up. It can also take the form of an aggressive defensiveness that is directed outwards and produced by the shaming looks and disparaging comments of others (see Demmerling and Landweer, 2007, p 220). Read in this way, feelings of shame and of being shamed have their basis in being affected emotionally in a way that involves negative emotional trajectories and that reflects the self-perception of subjects in their relation with themselves and with the world (see Slaby, 2011). Emotions of shame and of being shamed have an intentional relation to the world, since these feelings are invariably linked to an infringement of moral norms (see Demmerling and Landweer, 2007, p 229). This requires an awareness of and interaction with the normative expectations of society that are produced and reproduced in intersubjective relations.

Expectations about when and why a person ought to be ashamed are generated intersubjectively through symbolic reproductions. They are expressed through verbal language, bodily gestures and facial expressions and interpreted in social processes of interaction (see Abels, 2007, pp 44f). In this regard, shame and shaming go beyond subjective experience and can be located in the narratives, discourses and dispositions of social practice, where they are a means for structuring and shaping social interactions: 'By interacting, actors [produce] shared symbols. They look to these symbols for guidance, confirm them by their actions and revise and redefine them. In this way, the meaning of the interaction is continually renegotiated in reciprocal interpretations' (Abels, 2007, pp 44f). What happens in social processes of interaction is that subjects, in their relation to themselves and to the world, act while being aware of the verbal, bodily and symbolic representations of others (see Neckel, 1991, p 31). Shame and shaming are thus founded on a symbolically produced, intersubjectively created and rule-bound system of meaning, which forms the basis for the reproduction of normative expectations and the punishment of infringements and deviations by forms of shunning and personal disparagements (see Landweer, 1999, pp 196f; Abels, 2007, p 46). Underlying this is a process of interpretation which entails a positioning of the self in regard to the situation and to the other person (see Slaby, 2011). Actors interpret their own feelings in a way which involves an observation of the self with regard to their own emotions. In doing so, they look at themselves through the eyes of others in order to be able to tell what their own feelings mean for the social situation (see Gerhards, 1988, p 197). This enables them to use this reflexive perspective to interpret and evaluate their own modes of behaviour. In and through interactive social relations, they develop an awareness of social norms, their inherent dynamics and the expectations these involve (see Neckel, 1991, p 32).

Whereas the feeling of being ashamed is constituted primarily in the way subjects regard themselves in their relation to others, shaming comes from the outside and it is others that expose the shamed person to the humiliations and loss of self-worth it involves. A feature of shaming is that recognition for a person's legitimate claims is denied or withheld in networks of social relations. It is used as a strategic tool in interactions in order to gain the upper hand over another person where there is an unequal balance of power and resources (see Neckel, 1991, p 194). Within interactive relations, shaming situations are thus marked by one person being stronger or weaker than another in an unequal power relation (see Neckel, 1991, p 148). The perception of oneself as the weaker party is based on a self-assessment that includes judgements and categorisations in which the weaker person carries out a 'negative *self*-classification' (Neckel, 1991, p 155, original emphasis). To be the weaker party in a social relation under conditions of structural inequality of power in essence means being poor in power resources (see Neckel, 1991, p 148). Having power means having cultural, symbolic, economic as well as social resources – such as knowledge, money, influence, authority and prestige – at one's disposal in order to 'achieve certain results in accordance with one's own interests' (Neckel, 1991, p 152). A sense of inferiority makes people aware of their own powerlessness, a powerlessness that is coupled with an inability and a lack of resources to make their influence felt in the struggle for recognition. To feel shamed by being the weaker party presupposes the acceptance and validity of norms which are accompanied by a 'moral self-condemnation of one's own inferiority' (Neckel, 1991, p 154). 'Being shamed by inferiority means interpreting the deficit on which the inferiority is based in a way which lays the blame for causing it on oneself and which shares the contempt with which it is met' (Neckel, 1991, p 154). The weaker person feels inferior. This means that while the shaming and the feelings of inferiority and worthlessness which accompany it come from the outside, they are turned inwards by the person who experiences them (see Neckel, 1991, p 155).

The emotional labour of professionals and the trajectory of shame and shaming

The analysis of empirical data from the author's study aims to show that the emotional work of practitioners is used to create an emotional atmosphere. The research project in general is concerned with the way emotions are managed at a professional, expert level within the setting of residential care.[6] Within the following example the emotional atmosphere is one that indicates an interactive production of a shaming situation. An observational episode is analysed in order to show whether and how shaming is used as an educative tool. In analysing a scene from everyday life in residential care, particular attention is paid to the question of how institutional order and sanctioning practices are created and produced in the context of structures of power and control in the interactive relations between practitioners and children. One aspect of this is a structural examination of the way practitioners go about enforcing house rules within the institutional setting of the residential group home. Another aspect is an analysis of the practices of social workers in sanctioning norm infringements and in enforcing children's compliance with these sanctions. Such sanctioning practices in turn are an indication of the emotional labour of practitioners. In analysing the observational episodes, an empirical structure of meaning is reconstructed in which: (a) the trajectory of shaming of children is construed as an educative tool used to produce conformity; and (b) the emotional labour of practitioners is construed as an action aimed at monitoring and steering children's perceived feelings.

> I arrive at the unit a little before 12. The doorbell does not work, so I have to knock. Anna opens the door for me. Today, she has not brought a dog, so I can safely walk into the office. I put down my things and observe Anna as she completes a form. I ask her what she is doing. She explains to me that there is a daily room check by the residential child care worker on duty in the morning. That worker then records on the form who has given cause for complaint. Complaints are entered when a bed has not been made, for example, or when a child's room looks messy. She explains that today all the rooms are tidy, except Sina's: she has not made her bed. I ask what the point of this is. Anna explains that a room inspection is carried out every day in order to check who has tidied their room. This is followed by my question of what this means for Sina on this occasion. For Sina, it means that tonight, she is not allowed to watch TV, for example, or use the laptop or computer, in other words any electronic media. Anna records a 'happy face' smiley for today against all names except Sina's. Sina gets a so-called 'sad face'. In addition, Anna highlights this with a yellow marker. In this connection, she explains to me that these entries are important in informing the colleagues who are on duty this afternoon of the fact that Sina has not made her bed. She says she won't be here this afternoon herself and the colleagues on duty in the afternoon have to be able to rely on the entry itself. Then she puts the folder away and we go into the kitchen, where she offers me a coffee.

The episode can be framed conceptually by stating that emotional labour is structurally embedded in the rules of the institutional setting. The children and young people as well as the practitioners working in the residential group home are operating within an institutional arrangement in which they reproduce everyday practices of living together through daily routines. The *check sheet* used is part of a daily room inspection. Documentation is an everyday routine activity and its functions are control and regulation. Non-compliance is recorded by way of a 'sad face', compliance by way of a 'smiley'. A 'sad face', as a symbol of non-compliance, means that the child or young person concerned is not allowed to use 'electronic media' for that day. The sanction has a regulatory function in dealing with norm deviations. The 'sad face' creates a difference between the defined norm and children's deviant actions as regards tidiness and order. The check sheet structures the way practitioners act towards this end and represents evident legitimation for demanding the child's compliance with and acceptance of the sanction. It is linked to a timed punishment for the child in question. The way the sanction is communicated verbally and interactively involves a potential for producing emotions. In the following extract, 10-year-old Jasmin has been given a 'sad face'. The episode shows that the tensions this produces can demand an emotional labour from practitioners. What will be analysed is how the practitioner Katrin goes about obtaining compliance with and acceptance of the sanction in her interaction with Jasmin and where she applies emotional labour:

> More by chance than deliberately, I observe what is happening between Katrin and Jasmin in the adjacent room while I am standing in the kitchen. They are sitting on the sofa in the playroom facing each other. I move closer in order to be able to follow their conversation. Jasmin: 'Woah man, it's super unfair I can't see my nan on the weekend. All the others can visit their families except me.' Katrin explains to her that there are different visiting arrangements for each child. At the moment, the arrangements in her case mean that she cannot see her mother, for example. In this context, she also tells her that she has not tidied her room today. Because of this, she won't be allowed to watch tonight's film with the other children of the residential group. Wide-eyed, Jasmin looks at Katrin; then she pulls a face, the corners of her mouth turn downwards, her eyebrows pull into a v-shape and she frowns. Suddenly, Jasmin starts screaming loudly and I am startled by this. It looks like she is about to cry. Katrin puts her arm around her shoulders and bends her head over Jasmin's shoulders so they can look at each other. They are locked in an embrace and in close physical proximity. Jasmin grabs Katrin's arm which is lying on her shoulder and squeezes it firmly. In a

tearful voice that suggests protest, she says: 'Those rules are crap, they're not fair.' After that, she starts screaming and kicks her feet. Katrin holds her legs. She complains: 'All the others are watching TV tonight, except me. And what am I gonna do? Am I just meant to sit around the dining room looking stupid, or what!?' Katrin responds in a calm voice while putting her arm around her: 'Yes, those are the rules.' Jasmin: 'Crap rules.' She gets up and leaves the room.

Katrin, the specialist practitioner, is working on Jasmin's emotions, which she herself has elicited. In interpreting the episode, the focus will be on Katrin's emotional labour and on the practices used in sanctioning the 10-year-old. As Jasmin 'has not tidied her room', she is not allowed 'to see the film tonight with the other children of the residential group'. The sanction communicated by Katrin is directed at Jasmin's deviant behaviour. Since Jasmin's behaviour is defined as deviant by the 'sad face', she is handed a media ban in accordance with the institutionally defined system of sanctions. In addition, the punishment of Jasmin has an exclusionary character because she is denied the opportunity to join her peers in a social event. Jasmin's reacts to the sanction by means of bodily and linguistic representations. Katrin's move to put her arm around Jasmin's shoulders and seek eye contact with her creates physical closeness. This is not just a random reaction by the practitioner, but a goal-oriented mode of action. By acting in this way, the professional practitioner produces an emotional atmosphere aimed at shaping the girl's affective relation to the world. The 10-year-old grabs the arm Katrin has laid on her shoulder, squeezes it and says: 'Those rules are crap, they are not fair.' She speaks in a tearful and protesting tone which indicates her position as regards the situation and Katrin. She feels unfairly treated and considers the rules to be unjust. She shows this by starting to kick her feet and screaming loudly, so that Katrin holds down her feet. Jasmin's statement 'All the others are watching TV tonight, except me. And what am I gonna to do? Am I just meant to sit around the dining room looking stupid, or what!?' expresses a perception of inferiority and exclusion: she is excluded from the film evening and realises the exclusionary effect of the sanction. With the statement 'Yes, those are the rules', Katrin confirms both the sanctioning rule and the sanctioning practice. She thus establishes an exclusionary practice of banning Jasmin from the film evening, and, rather than opening a potential space for negotiation, the practitioner closes it off by referring once more to the validity of the rule. As might be expected, Jasmin declares: 'Crap rules', gets up and leaves the room.

The episode involves two relevant semantic contexts: (a) the production of emotions; and (b) emotional labour. The sanctioning practice is a means for restoring an institutional order embedded into the production of emotions within asymmetrical power relations. In this episode, Jasmin complains about her exclusion from that evening's group activity and the associated injustice. However, she cannot do anything about it because the practitioner acts as a representative of the institution and enforces the sanction against her. Jasmin's power resources are not sufficient to be able to change the situation in her favour. She is powerless and inferior while facing the superiority of the institutional order. Her verbal and bodily representations show that Jasmin is conscious of her inferior position, since it leads her to break off her interaction with Katrin and leave the situation, thus using the remaining power potential at her disposal. The fact that Jasmin acts in this way can also be read as her rejecting the shaming character of the sanction. The episode implies an educative relation aimed at ensuring that the 10-year-old complies with the applicable norms of the house rules. Here, education involves using sanctions to generate pressure to conform with and accept an established normative order. At the same time, this conformity-oriented educative relation creates a position of inferiority which implies a shaming atmosphere. This is, firstly, because Jasmin cannot do anything about the sanction and, secondly, because the sanction means that she is excluded from the film evening. There is no room for negotiation and equally no possibility of making amends. She has done something wrong for which she is punished and she cannot escape this punishment: she has to bear it. As a result, by perceiving her powerlessness vis-à-vis the sanctioning actions of Katrin, Jasmin recognises herself as being deficient in this situation. The potential space for influencing the situation is closed off by the practitioner and it is this closure that produces a shaming atmosphere. According to this analysis, shaming is a tool used in educative practice that is already built into the structure of the house rules at the institutional level and that is produced through emotional labour at the interactive level.

In Katrin's emotional labour, a physical closeness is expressed that is aimed at steering and influencing emotions during the process of sanctioning. Katrin positions herself for this by putting her arm around Jasmin, seeking eye contact with her and thus establishing a physical closeness. While the practitioner's emotional labour is concerned with steering and influencing feelings, at the same time her work on

Jasmin's emotions aims to get her to recognise her deviant behaviour and to bear the associated consequences. Shaming is used here, firstly, as an educative tool for achieving compliance with the normative expectations of the institution, and, secondly, as leading into an emotional labour aimed at influencing the emotions it has produced in Jasmin so as to obtain her acknowledgement of the blame and the sanction assigned to her.

Discussion

Emotional labour takes place on the basis of practitioners' subjective judgements and perceptions in order to (re)produce, preserve or restore normal states (see Wagner, 2013, p 170). Emotional labour – in the sense of work on the emotions of others – has a normative background against which practitioners evaluate and categorise the feelings they perceive in children and young people. This normative orientation is centred on the boundary between that which is appropriate and that which is inappropriate. This raises questions relating to the normative regulation (and normalisation) of feelings. The empirical analysis of the observed episodes shows emotions being normatively regulated in a directive manner. This is particularly evident in educative relations, where the production of an emotional atmosphere – which include a shameful semantic – is linked to attempts by practitioners to generate pressure to conform to and accept established norms. This usually comes after the children or young people have infringed rules or norms laid down in the institutional setting and where this infringement has been sanctioned by the practitioners in a way that has an exclusionary effect. Especially in the sanctioning mechanisms, what becomes visible here are asymmetrical power structures within which it is above all the absence of any room for negotiation that characterises interactions between the two parties. The associated impulses involve the practitioners taking a position that sets a boundary, which means that the eliciting of feelings becomes an educative tool. In the context of the episodes discussed here, the emotional labour of the practitioner aims for the child to acknowledge the blame that is assigned to her for the deviant behaviour. With regard to the analysis of the interaction between Jasmin and Katrin, an emotional atmosphere with a semantic of shaming is created. In this atmosphere, an educative relation is developed with the goal of steering the child into negative emotional trajectories so that she will accept her guilt and punishment. This constitutes a forceful and directive intervention in the emotional experience of the child.

In the production of emotional atmospheres, implicit expectations of children's and adolescents' feelings are made explicit by professionals through physical representations and linguistic signatures. The emotional labour is the means for it. The professionals create an emotional atmosphere around themselves in order to influence the service users' perception of the situation. As part of the emotional atmospheres, emotional trajectories are created, in which the experience of emotions and possibilities of action are influenced (see Slaby, 2011, p 38). Constitutive for the emotional atmospheres and the trajectories of emotions is the interactively produced pulling power in which a subject becomes involved by the actions of another subject. Although the path for the experience of emotions is marked out at this point, a subject who is influenced by the pulling power of emotional trajectories can also escape them in principle. Whether service users feel emotionally affected by emotional atmospheres is related to their emotional response. The atmosphere created by Katrin pushes 10-year-old Jasmin into an inferior position and aims to make the girl feel guilty for her misbehaviour. Besides feelings of shame, feelings of anger or even fear can also be considered. In the analysed situation Jasmin is pulled into a trajectory of emotional atmospheres, but uses her available power resources to evade them. In this context, it could be discussed whether the emotional response of Jasmin to the emotional atmosphere produced by the professional indicates anger. It could also be considered that an angry reaction serves to escape the feeling of shame. The 10-year-old would have every reason to feel ashamed because she is in a powerless and deficient position, but this does not necessarily lead to feelings of shame. As a consequence, Jasmin does not allow herself to be influenced by the trajectory of shame created by the professional through emotional labour. This consideration points to the fact that acts of shaming do not have to lead to a subject feeling shame. This can be followed by considerations that subjects are able to defend themselves against the degrading, deficient and pejorative pulling power of shame. Anger can be discussed in this context as an emotional response in which the available power resources are used to escape the trajectory of shame.

Conclusions

To recognise and minimise shaming structures in the interaction between practitioners and service users is an essential criterion for the quality of professional practice (see Bolay, 1998, p 29). Awareness by practitioners of the power of shame must be seen as one category in the professional knowledge system used in practice. Arrogations of authority in the definition of problems, unjustified and unrealistic behavioural expectations, and the reproduction of spirals of submission and of relations of dependency all have shaming dimensions. They demand a high degree of reflexivity from practitioners in professional relationships in order to be able to uncover their own position of power, both behind the scenes and 'on stage'. Knowing about the issue of shame and shaming and engaging with it in a critical and reflexive way are criteria for evaluating the quality of someone's professional practice. The aim is to recognise and deconstruct negative emotional trajectories that lead to a degrading, devaluing and humiliating spiral of shame and shaming. In this regard, the emotional labour of practitioners is intertwined with relations of power and domination in which acts of shaming appear as the tool of a conformity-oriented education. Yet it is also true that in normative terms the professional actions of social workers are aimed at creating a potential space for autonomy and emancipation (see Sünker, 1989). That also applies to the way they deal with their own emotions and the emotions of others in their professional practice (see Schröder, 2017). This is not to say, however, that practitioners engaged in educative processes should only elicit positive emotions. Children also need experience of dealing with negative feelings such as guilt or fear. The challenge for professional practice consists in being able to offer a prospect for autonomy within the experience of negative emotions.

Notes

[1] In Germany, residential childcare is one of the services for which provision is made in the Child and Youth Services Act. It is a legal requirement that staff providing these services are appropriately qualified. This means that residential group homes will have social workers on their staff who are qualified to degree level.

[2] The quotations from German articles and books have been translated by the author of this chapter.

[3] Societal relations of production encompass the reciprocal relationship of the subject in its relation to the socially produced structures. This involves spatial, temporal, normative, social and cultural horizons in which the form-determination of society is produced via (socio)political, economic and civil society control processes that place the subject in a relationship with society.

[4] The shared perspective consists in using coordinated and cooperative working processes in order to develop prospects for regaining autonomy of action or for living a daily life based on self-determination and independence (Sünker, 1989; Dewe et al, 2001).

[5] These discussions of emotional labour have their origins in the studies by Hochschild (1990), as well as the studies by Strauss et al (1982) and by Dunkel (1988).

6 The data material underlying the research project is embedded into an ethnographic research strategy and consists of observation protocols, field notes and the transcription of informal conversations and structured interviews. Data evaluation during the research project did not follow any stringent methodology. In this analysis, grounded theory has been used to this end as an aid in the ordering, categorising and sorting of the material (Dellwing and Prus, 2012).

References

Abels, H. (2007) *Interaktion, Identität, Präsentation. Kleine Einführung in interpretative Theorien der Soziologie* (4th edn), Wiesbaden: VS Verlag für Sozialwissenschaften.

Böhnisch, L. and Lösch, H. (1979) 'Das Handlungsverständnis des Sozialarbeiters und seine institutionelle Determination', in H.-U. Otto and S. Schneider (eds) *Gesellschaftliche Perspektiven der Sozialarbeit*, vol 2, Neuwied and Berlin: Luchterhand Verlag, pp 21–40.

Bolay, E. (1998) 'Scham und Beschämung in helfenden Beziehungen', in H. Metzler and E. Wacker (eds) *Soziale Dienstleistungen. Zur Qualität helfender Beziehungen*, Tübingen: Attempto Verlag, pp 29–52.

Dellwing, M. and Prus, R. (2012) *Einführung in die interaktionistische Ethnografie. Soziologie im Außendienst*, Wiesbaden: Verlag für Sozialwissenschaften.

Demmerling, C. and Landweer, H. (2007) *Philosophie der Gefühle*, Stuttgart and Weimar: Verlag J. B. Metzler.

Dewe, B. (2009) 'Reflexive Sozialarbeit im Spannungsfeld von evidenzbasierter Praxis und demokratischer Rationalität: Plädoyer für die handlungslogische Entfaltung reflexiver Professionalität', in R. Becker-Lenz, S. Busse, G. Ehlert and S. Müller (eds) *Professionalität in der Sozialen Arbeit. Standpunkte, Kontroversen, Perspektiven* (2nd edn), Wiesbaden: Verlag für Sozialwissenschaften, pp 89–109.

Dewe, B., Ferchhoff, W., Scheer, A. and Stüwe, G. (2001) *Professionelles soziales Handeln. Soziale Arbeit im Spannungsfeld zwischen Theorie und Praxis*, Weinheim and Munich: Juventa Verlag.

Dörr, M. and Müller, B. (2005) '"Emotionale Wahrnehmung" und "begriffene Angst". Anmerkungen zu vergessenen Aspekten sozialpädagogischer Professionalität und Forschung', in C. Schweppe and W. Thole (eds) *Sozialpädagogik als forschende Disziplin*, Weinheim and Munich, pp 233–52.

Dunkel, W. (1988) 'Wenn Gefühle zum Arbeitsgegenstand werden. Gefühlsarbeit im Rahmen personenbezogener Dienstleistungstätigkeit', *Soziale Welt*, 39(1): 66–85.

Gerhards, J. (1988) *Soziologie der Emotionen. Fragestellung, Systematik und Perspektiven*, Weinheim and Basel: Juventa Verlag.

Gildemeister, R. (1984) '"Berufliche Identität" als integratives Konzept sozialpädagogischer Kompetenz', in S. Müller, H.-W. Otto, H. Peter and H. Sünker (eds) *Handlungskompetenz in der Sozialarbeit/ Sozialpädagogik II. Theoretische Konzepte und gesellschaftliche Strukturen*, vol 2, Bielefeld: AJZ Verlag, pp 251–72.

Graßhoff, G. and Schweppe, C. (2009) 'Biographie und Professionalität in der Sozialpädagogik', in R. Becker-Lenz, S. Busse, G. Ehlert and S. Müller (eds) *Professionalität in der Sozialen Arbeit. Standpunkte, Kontroversen, Perspektiven* (2nd edn), Wiesbaden: Verlag für Sozialwissenschaften, pp 307–18.

Hochschild, A. (1990) *Das gekaufte Herz. Zur Kommerzialisierung der Gefühle*, Frankfurt am Main: Campus Verlag.

Hornstein, W. (1995) 'Zur disziplinären Identität der Sozialpädagogik', in H. Sünker (ed) *Theorie, Politik und Praxis Sozialer Arbeit*, Bielefeld, Kleine Verlag, pp 12–33.

Kunstreich, T. (2005) 'Kritische Theorie/historischer Materialismus', in H.-U. Otto and H. Thiersch (eds) *Handbuch Sozialarbeit/ Sozialpädagogik* (3rd edn), Munich and Basle: Reinhardt Verlag, pp 1084–97.

Landweer, H. (1999) *Scham und Macht. Phänomenologische Untersuchungen zur Sozialität eines Gefühls*, Tübingen: Mohr Siebeck.

Messmer, H. and Hitzler, S. (2011) 'Interaktion und Kommunikation in der Sozialen Arbeit. Fallstudien zum Hilfeplangespräch', in G. Oelerich and H.-U. Otto (eds) *Empirische Forschung und Soziale Arbeit. Ein Studienbuch* (1st edn), Wiesbaden: Verlag für Sozialwissenschaften, pp 51–76.

Moesby-Jensen, C. and Nielsen, H. (2015) 'Emotional labor in social workers' practice', *European Journal of Social Work*, 18(5): 690–702.

Müller, B. (2011) 'Gefühle, Emotionen, Affekte', in H.-U. Otto and H. Thiersch (eds) *Handbuch Soziale Arbeit* (4th edn), Munich: Reinhardt Verlag, pp 455–62.

Müller, C. W. (1997) 'Gefühlserziehung und Soziale Arbeit', *Neue Praxis*, 3: 211–18.

Müller, S. (2001) *Erziehen-Helfen-Strafen. Das Spannungsverhältnis von Hilfe und Kontrolle in der Sozialen Arbeit*, Weinheim and Munich: Juventa Verlag.

Neckel, S. (1991) *Status und Scham: Zur symbolischen Reproduktion sozialer Ungleichheit*, Frankfurt am Main: Campus Verlag.

Olk, T. (1986) *Abschied vom Experten. Sozialarbeit auf dem Weg zu einer alternativen Professionalität*, Munich: Juventa Verlag.

Rose, B. and Wulf-Schnabel, J. (2013) 'Von der Schwierigkeit, die Lohnarbeitsverhältnisse zum Thema zu machen', *Widersprüche*, 128: 87–109.

Sartre, J.-P. (2016 [1943]) *Das Sein und das Nichts. Versuch einer phänomenologischen Ontologie* (16th edn), Hamburg: Rowohlt Taschenbuchverlag.

Schaarschuch, A. (1995) 'Das demokratische Potenzial Sozialer Arbeit', in H. Sünker (ed) *Theorie, Politik und Praxis Sozialer Arbeit*, Bielefeld: Kleine Verlag, pp 48–71.

Schaarschuch, A. (2006) 'Dienstleistung. Das aktive Subjekt der Dienstleistung', in B. Dollinger and J. Raithel (eds) *Aktivierende Sozialpädagogik. Ein kritisches Glossar*, Wiesbaden: Verlag für Sozialwissenschaften, pp 91–107.

Schaarschuch, A. and Oelerich, G. (2005) 'Theoretische Grundlagen und Perspektiven sozialpädagogischer Nutzerforschung', in A. Schaarschuch and G. Oelerich G (eds) *Soziale Dienstleistung aus Nutzersicht. Vom Gebrauchswert Sozialer Arbeit*, Munich and Basle: Ernst Reinhardt Verlag, pp 9–27.

Schäfter, C. (2010) *Die Beratungsbeziehung in der Sozialen Arbeit. Eine theoretische und empirische Annährung*, Wiesbaden: VS Verlag für Sozialwissenschaften.

Schoneville, H. (2013) 'Armut und Ausgrenzung als Beschämung und Missachtung', *Soziale Passagen*, 5(1): 17–35.

Schröder, C. (2017) *Emotionen und professionelles Handeln in der Sozialen Arbeit. Eine Ethnographie der Emotionsarbeit im Handlungsfeld der Heimerziehung*, Wiesbaden: Springer VS.

Slaby, J. (2011) 'Affektive Intentionalität: Hintergrundgefühle, Möglichkeitsräume, Handlungsorientierung', in S. Slaby, A. Stephan, H. Walter and S. Walter (eds) *Affektive Intentionalität. Beiträge zur welterschließenden Funktion der menschlichen Gefühle*, Paderborn: Mentis Verlag, pp 23–48.

Strauss, A., Fagerhaugh, S., Suczek, B. and Wiener, C. (1982) 'Sentimental work in the technologized hospital', *Sociology of Health and Illness*, 4(3): 249–78.

Sünker, H. (1989) *Bildung, Alltag und Subjektivität. Elemente zu einer Theorie der Sozialpädagogik*, Weinheim: Deutscher Studienverlag.

Sünker, H. (1995) 'Theoretische Ansätze, gesellschaftspolitische Kontexte und professionelle Perspektiven Sozialer Arbeit', in H. Sünker (ed) *Theorie, Politik und Praxis Sozialer Arbeit*, Bielefeld: Kleine Verlag, pp 72–101.

Thiersch, H. (2009) *Schwierige Balance: Über Grenzen, Gefühle und berufsbiographische Erfahrungen*, Weinheim: Juventa Verlag.

Wagner, T. (2013) *Entbügerlichung durch Adressierung? Eine Analyse des Verhältnisses Sozialer Arbeit zu den Voraussetzungen politischen Handelns*, Wiesbaden: Verlag für Sozialwissenschaften.

Winkler, M. (1988) *Eine Theorie der Sozialpädagogik*, Stuttgart: Klett-Cotta.

Winkler, M. (1995) 'Bemerkungen zur Theorie der Sozialpädagogik', in H. Sünker (ed) *Theorie, Politik und Praxis Sozialer Arbeit*, Bielefeld: Kleine Verlag, pp 102–21.

Winkler, M. (2004) 'Aneignung und Sozialpädagogik: einige grundlagentheoretische Überlegungen', in U. Deinet and C. Reutlinger (eds) *'Aneignung' als Bildungskonzept der Sozialpädagogik* (1st edn), Wiesbaden: Verlag für Sozialwissenschaften, pp 71–92.

Winkler, M. (2006) 'Kleine Skizze einer revidierten Theorie der Sozialpädagogik', in T. Badawia, H. Luckas and H. Müller (eds) *Das Soziale gestalten. Über Mögliches und Unmögliches der Sozialpädagogik* (1st edn), Wiesbaden: Verlag für Sozialwissenschaften, pp 55–80.

Wulf-Schnabel, J. (2011) *Reorganisation und Subjektivierung von Sozialer Arbeit* (1st edn), Wiesbaden: Verlag für Sozialwissenschaften.

PART III

Shame and professionalism: social worker perspectives

7

Shame regulation as organisational control: evoking, containing and diverting shame to create compliance

Matthew Gibson

Introduction

This chapter considers how those invested in an organisation seek to regulate feelings of shame in employees to generate compliance and conformity to organisational rules, standards and expectations. It first outlines the terrain relating to organisational control in social work services to argue that the place of shame regulation has been overlooked. Secondly, it analyses what shame is from a constructivist perspective, which lays the foundations for an analysis of how leaders and managers engage in a process of regulating others' shame. Thirdly, it provides a framework for understanding how leaders and managers go about regulating shame in other people so that any feelings of shame as a result of undertaking tasks the organisation expects them to do are contained and diverted, while ensuring that shame is evoked as a result of any transgressions. Finally, these arguments are discussed in terms of their relevance and importance for practice.

Organisational control

Organisations are created with a purpose. In order to fulfil that purpose there needs to be forms of control within the organisation over the workforce. Conceptualising organisational control has a long history in organisational theory. Weber (1978), for example, argued that bureaucracies provided the benefit of a set of rules that ordered employee behaviour while facilitating efficiency and fairness. The consequence of such organisation, he argued, was that this also provided a highly ordered and rigid system that limited individual freedom, creating what he referred to as the 'iron cage'. Paying a workforce and organising them into clearly defined spheres of activity, within a hierarchy, while enforcing strict and systematic discipline within the office, was meant to ensure that the organisation would achieve its aims and objectives.

In terms of social work organisations, however, the bureaucratic iron cage was not so rigid that it did not allow for some flexibility. Lipsky's (1980) classic paper on front-line practice in public service organisations identified the need for practitioners to exercise discretion in implementing bureaucratic rules, procedures and policies. While this facilitated flexibility in the face of complex real-life situations on the one hand, it enabled variation in practice methods and outcomes on the other. Such a situation was desirable while those who financed and operated the welfare state believed public servants to be public-spirited altruists, as such discretion was considered beneficial to the equitable and efficient process of implementing policy. While many in the early days of the welfare state held such a view, this was not sustained, requiring new forms of organisational control.

Le Grand (1997) argues that cultural and economic changes in the 1970s and 1980s led to a perception by some, and ultimately in those who held power, that public servants should be seen more as self-interested actors and, as such, required greater levels of control over their day-to-day activities and decision-making processes. Indeed, Evans and Harris (2004) argued that professional discretion should be seen as neither 'good' nor 'bad', as it can be a means to positively or abusively use delegated power. As notions of practice standards and consistency gained currency in political and economic discourse throughout the 1990s and 2000s, professional discretion became a threat to political accountability and policy initiatives were created with the express intention of controlling the social care workforce. The Integrated Children's System, an IT system for children and family social workers to manage and record their work, is a case in point. A policy idea that began in the 1990s and came to a climax around 2009 (White et al, 2010) was observed by Wastell et al (2010), in their two-year ethnographic study, to have resulted in practice that revolved around the computer system, forcing social workers to do things in certain ways at certain times. Such highly formalised rules and procedures diminished professional discretion and created a more modern iron cage that has been heavily criticised across the sector (see Munro, 2011).

In contrast to the iron cage as a mechanism of organisational control has been the idea of the 'panoptic gaze'. It was originally an idea by the English philosopher Jeremy Bentham, who imagined a structure that sat inside an institution which inspected people, and which gave the impression that everyone was being watched at all times, even when they were not. He argued that this 'panopticon' created 'a new mode of obtaining power of mind over mind' (Bentham, 1791, p 1) as it embedded the control of behaviour into the individual by virtue of them believing they could be sanctioned for misbehaviour. This idea was popularised by Foucault (1977) as a way to represent power within society that no longer needed physical force or violence but rather used the threat of surveillance to force compliance to social norms and rules. It is the gaze of another, whether real or imagined, within organisations that bring self-consciousness to the foreground, as individuals constantly evaluate themselves against organisational rules, standards and expectations (for an intensive elaboration of the meaning of being looked at for shame by Jean-Paul Sartre see also Chapter 3). Indeed, as Deetz (1995, p 87) stated, 'the modern business of management is often managing the "insides" – the hopes, fears, and aspirations – of workers, rather than their behaviors directly'. While researchers have focused their attention on the role of management in the creation of employee identity (eg Alvesson and Willmott, 2002; Nair, 2010), the role of emotions as targets and resources for organisational control has been somewhat overshadowed (Creed et al, 2014).

A more recent move in the study of organisational control has been to consider how culture can be used as a medium to control employees. Thompson and McHugh (1995), for example, suggested that compliance could be generated by socialising employees into specific roles within the organisation. This active form of socialisation uses culture to promote specific values, norms and symbols that affect motivation and identity (Alvesson, 2002). The role of shame in this process, however, has been neglected. Shame can be seen not only as a product of culture, which generates the social boundaries for what is considered shameful, but also constitutive of culture, in that it provides foundations for directing what people do and how they do it. To understand this process, and how a person can then seek to influence this process to change how someone feels, we first have to look at what shame is.

What is shame?

Thoits' (1989) review of emotion theory states that 'there are almost as many definitions of emotions as there are authors' (p 318), and within this there are many competing and contrasting theories of shame. A review of different theories of shame can be read elsewhere (see Gibson, 2019), but for the purposes of this chapter I will outline a constructionist theory of shame, and use that as the basis for analysing social work practice in an organisational context.

At the heart of constructionist accounts of emotion is a relational perspective of human life, where a person is engaged in interactions with their social environment embedded within a particular culture. Over time, a person learns culturally specific ways of perceiving, understanding and communicating about their interactions; emotions are one element of this learning process. Specific dimensions of experience, such as situational cues, social stimuli, the experience of pleasure/displeasure, physiological arousal/relaxation, changes in somatosensory sensations, appraisals and expressive gestures, can be learnt as an 'emotion'. To say one feels an 'emotion', such a shame, means one is communicating that the situation fits a socially agreed-upon set of knowable features, such as specific social situations, personal thoughts and bodily sensations (Averill, 1980; Wierzbicka, 1992). From such a perspective, an emotion is not a thing, but rather a process. This process is both macro, operating within a social group over a long period of time, and micro, operating within a person over a short period of time. To define shame is, therefore, to define the components of the process. Figure 7.1 outlines the process and components that result in an experience of shame, which will be defined later.

Situated complex

At the core of emotional experience is a 'feeling' about 'something'. This 'feeling' relates to the sensations within the body, which can change as a result of changes within the body itself or as a result of interactions with the environment. Ceunen, Vlaeyen and Van Diest (2016) refer to the awareness of these bodily sensations as 'interoception'. Bodily sensations are complex but can be broadly defined by both their 'valence', that is how pleasurable or displeasurable it is, and 'arousal', that is, how activated or deactivated our physiological state is (Russell and Barrett, 1999). The 'something', meanwhile, relates to the focus of the feeling. Barrett (2006) argues that emotions involve evaluating, or appraising, situations for their personal value and relevance. An emotional experience consists of multiple components, with our interoception, appraisals and actions at their heart, which Burkitt (2014) refers to as a 'complex', and can be considered to be experienced within a specific situation. Indeed, what we do (actions) and what we think (appraisals) can change our bodily state, while our bodily state can change what we do and think (eg Ortony and Turner, 1990; Damasio, 1994; Frijda et al, 2000).

Figure 7.1: A constructivist framework for experiencing shame

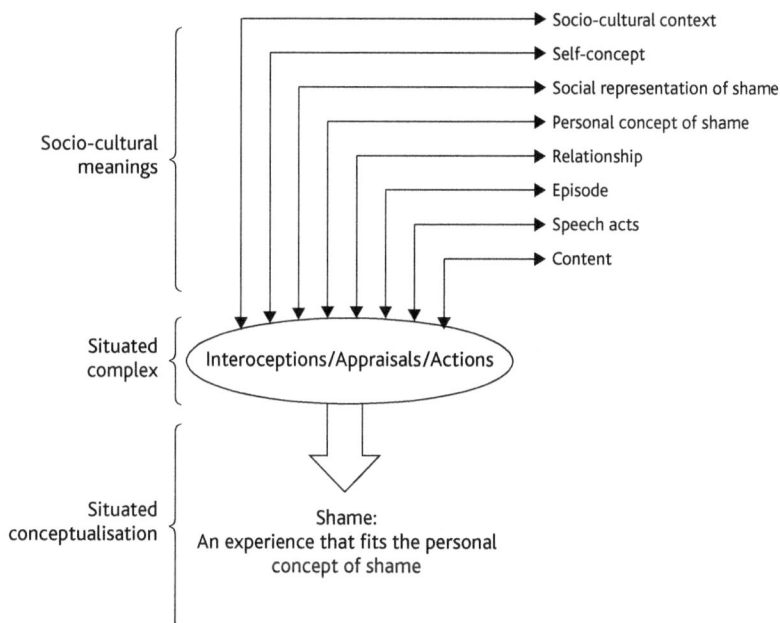

Socio-cultural meanings

How a person comes to construct meaning is of central importance in emotional experience. Cronen, Pearce and Harris (1982) provide a useful framework for outlining how humans construct and manage meaning in social situations that help us define the multiple layers of meanings and their influence on emotional experiences. They firstly argue that all interactions have 'content' that provides the information about the interaction. This may be verbal or non-verbal, but this information says little about what kind of message or interaction it is. They argue then that this content needs to be placed in context to have wider meaning. 'Speech acts' (Austin, 1975) provide the underlying intention of the content. These can be considered to be actions performed by speaking or gestures, such a compliment, an insult, a threat, an assertion or a question. Cronen, Pearce and Harris (1982) then argue that this content and the speech acts are contextualised within a specific 'episode' (Pearce and Cronen, 1980). Episodes can be considered a discrete situation, distinct from others. For example, a home visit or a court hearing can be considered to be episodes, as they have a beginning, middle and end within a specific time and place. The episode brings together knowledge of the other person and provides expectations about how the conversation should progress in terms of speech and non-verbal behaviour (Cronen, Pearce and Harris, 1982). Within these episodes, Cronen, Pearce and Harris (1982) argue that people have implicit agreements between each other regarding the nature of the relationship, which provides the relational meaning of the episodes. For example, a manager, in relation to their social workers, may consider themselves to be 'collaborative and reflective' or 'a dominant manager with obedient workers'. Such beliefs about the nature of the relationship contextualise the subsequent episodes, speech acts and content. While it may be easy to see such relationship dynamics as co-workers, supervisor/supervisee, manager/social worker, employer/ employee, appropriate interactions between such individuals will be informed by higher-level contexts.

For emotional experiences we have to outline a distinction between personal and social concepts of emotions. At a social level, we can consider an emotion as a 'social representation', which Moscovici (1973, p xiii) defines as a 'system of values, ideas and practices'. He argues that social representations have two functions. The first is to establish an order that enables individuals to orient themselves in, and master, their social and material world. The second is to enable communication to take place among the members of a community by providing them with a code for social exchange and a code for naming and classifying various aspects of their world. By collectively elaborating on personal experiences, over time societies are able to construct a shared, but not consensual, way of understanding and communicating about their emotional lives. Scherer (1992) argues that aggregated data on experiences of emotions simply reflect the social representations of the emotion. The culmination of the research on shame, therefore, provides the details of what we collectively understand it to be in English-speaking societies.

The 'social representation of shame' can be understood as an unpleasant, activated bodily state, as a result of a negative evaluation of the self due to failing to live up to a standard (eg Cooley, 1902; Goffman, 1956; Lynd, 1958; Lewis, 1971; Scheff, 2000; Tangney and Dearing, 2002; Gilbert, 2003; Brown, 2006; Turner and Husman, 2008; Chase and Walker, 2012; Leeming and Boyle, 2013; with regard to the aspect of devaluation see also Chapter 2). Also linked to our social understanding of shame, as highlighted by qualitative studies on shame experiences, are avoidance behaviours, such as withdrawing from social situations, hiding from others and attempting to escape from the experience (Gilbert and Andrews, 1998; Tangney and Dearing, 2002; Brown, 2006; Turner and Husman, 2008; Chase and Walker, 2012; Leeming and Boyle, 2013).

This social concept of shame is constructed by individuals within a cultural group, who, in turn, develop their own personal concept of shame through their group. Deviations in individual understanding of what shame is occur as a result of inconsistencies in communication within different groups of the same culture and/or because of personal experiences that provides personal meaning to the experience (Moscovici, 1961). While the social representation of shame and a person's personal construct of shame may be similar, they may not necessarily be the same.

An experience of shame relates to the self. How we understand who we are is therefore a central component of a shame experience. We develop ideas about who we are, who we are not and who we ought to be through social interaction (Rosenberg, 1979; Stryker, 1980; Higgins, 1987; Markus and Wurf, 1987). These multiple representations a person holds about themselves can be considered the self-concept (Markus and Wurf, 1987). Such self-concepts provide standards for a person, which makes it is possible to evaluate the self in the moment against such standards. Of course, people do not develop notions of themselves or social representations of shame, nor indeed come to understand the meaning of content, speech acts, episodes and relationships in isolation. We are social beings and it is through social interaction that we come to develop a set of shared meanings and definitions that include the rules and expectations for behaviour. While such shared definitions are sometimes held as conscious beliefs, they are more commonly held as implicit taken-for-granted understandings (Ridgeway, 2006). These shared meanings create boundaries for what is expected and what is not, what is normal and what is not, and how to act and how not to, which seem objectively correct and natural within that context. Such boundaries are created, and are reinforced, though social interaction, creating a form of power that is relational, distributed and often invisible within the social group (Foucault, 1977).

Situated conceptualisation

As a person engages with their world, perception and understanding about the current situation is achieved through the different levels of socio-cultural meanings. These meanings influence the sensations in the body, appraisals of the situation and actions of the person, which in turn may influence the meaning attached to the situation. Our feelings are as complex and novel as our social interactions. None are ever really the same. The social representations of shame, however, and our own personal construct of shame, provide a way of feeling and categorising it as shame. Some emotional experiences may be very close to these concepts, making the term shame highly appropriate, while others may only slightly resemble them, making the term relevant but not wholly applicable. We may all have said we have felt shame in a situation but that term may not have fitted very well, so we may have used other terms too, such as fear, humiliation, embarrassment, anger, mortification and so on. Barrett (2006) argues that we 'feel' an 'emotion', such as shame, when we put all the information in a situation together, which can be done automatically, habitually or purposefully, and the resulting experience fits our personal concept of shame. Feeling shame is conceptualising the situation as shame. This can be done through social interaction or in the imagination of the person (Barsalou, 1999; Barrett and Russell, 2015).

What is shame regulation?

As the previous section outlines, by shame we mean the processes involved in generating an experience that can be categorised as shame. By regulation we mean inducing, influencing or altering the emotional experience with the intention of either trying to make someone feel or avoid feeling shame. Furthermore, I make a distinction here between the actions of one person seeking to evoke, change or divert the feeling of shame in another, that is, emotion regulation (Gross, 2008), and the actions of a person seeking to feel, change or avoid feeling shame themselves, which is better classed as emotion work (Hochschild, 1979). There is an interaction between trying to make someone feel shame, for example, and how the other person then responds to these attempts. They may or may not end up feeling shame; a point to be discussed later.

So why would someone want to regulate the feeling of shame in another? In many ways, we all engage in this activity to a point. As discussed, we live within specific socio-cultural contexts and these contexts provide boundaries for what is acceptable and what is not. Acting or being outside of these boundaries is seen negatively, and when framed as individual responsibility shame is the likely outcome. Creed et al (2014) refer to these taken-for-granted boundaries as 'systemic shame' and define it as an ever-present and all-encompassing form of disciplinary power that produces conformity to established rules within the community. Such boundaries provide the means by which behaviour can be judged within a certain social group. While many fear breaking these cultural rules due to how they may feel as a result, there are people who have cognitive, emotional and/or moral commitments to such ways of being – Creed et al (2014) define them as institutional guardians – and they police the behaviour of others through criticising, blaming and shaming transgressions. We all have commitments to certain institutions and ways of being and so we are all, at some point, institutional guardians who may serve to regulate shame in others. By evoking shame, or the threat of shame, we provide a consequence to transgression and a possible motivation to conform to the rules and expectations. Regulating shame is a quick way to try to generate compliance.

Shame regulation as organisational control

Shame is a social emotion, in that the standards by which a person, their behaviour, thoughts and feelings are judged are generated within specific social groups and cultural contexts. Shame can be regulated, therefore, through influencing socio-cultural meanings. The structure of organisations, with formal processes, procedures and hierarchies, provides plenty of opportunity to influence, shape and dictate many aspects of the social situations within the organisation. Primarily, however, this occurs through the medium of discourse.

Discourses can be considered as groups of statements that provide a language for representing, or talking about, a topic. These statements structure knowledge, which makes it possible to construct the topic in a certain way, privileging certain ways of being and rules for doing things, while limiting others. They construct meaning about the world by constituting social subjects, social relations and systems of knowledge (Burr, 1995). Within any society there are many competing and conflicting discourses that provide different ways of understanding historical, present and future events, circumstances and outcomes. Some discourses will be supported and promoted by individuals and groups for particular purposes, while others will be disregarded and discredited. Within a particular social group, however, individuals will not be expected to be aware of the range of discourses and people are not necessarily free to choose among them. Rather, Foucault (1977) argued people are provided with dominant discourses through interaction within their social group, which in turn structures their social world.

Socio-cultural context

By attending to, and mobilising, discourses, people construct ways of understanding who they are, what they are doing, why they are doing it and the nature of their relationship to others. By promoting certain discourses, while silencing and disrupting others, the socio-cultural context and, therefore, the taken-for-granted knowledge and individual and group standards for thinking, feeling and acting within an organisation can be altered. Such action not only directly influences the boundaries for what is considered shameful and praiseworthy within the organisation but also what and how people seek to structure and manage what others do and how they do it.

Of course, there are those with power and influence who are able to mobilise, silence and disrupt certain discourses related to social work practice that sit outside of any social work organisation. Politicians, journalists and regulators, for example, play a vital role in this process and can apply great social pressure while also formalising and sanctioning certain ways of thinking and behaving. Indeed, the notion of social workers failing to protect service users and, therefore, being blamed for incompetence has not always been an acknowledged one (Gibson, 2019). This has been the result of the idea of professional altruism being disrupted and a discourse of individual responsibility instilled (eg Le Grand, 1997). Neither has the notion of assessing and referring people to other services. This has come about through the wider disruption of state-run services and the instilling of a discourse of choice and competition (eg Buchanan and Tollison, 1984). Such changes have altered the boundaries for shameful behaviour, with social work professional bodies changing their codes of ethics, organisations changing their policies and practices and social workers changing their way of working over time.

Organisations, and the leaders and managers of such organisations, are not passive in this process, however. Indeed, there is scope to mobilise, silence and disrupt in-house certain discourses so as to avoid shaming an organisation. Whether an organisation seeks to provide or commission wider support services, or focus more squarely on meeting statutory obligations, or seek to do both, for example, is determined by how the organisation, the service and the work is framed. This framing occurs through discursive practices and while shame may not seem to be explicit in this process, it provides the foundations for it. It is the boundaries for shame that provide the context for social work practice.

Self-concept

Within the dominant organisationally sanctioned discourses, leaders and managers can seek to exert control over employees by outlining the ways in which the latter should undertake their work so the organisation is able to achieve its aims. Managers can define people directly by explicitly outlining the characteristics considered necessary to perform certain functions and roles (Alvesson and Willmott, 2002). Equally, people can be defined indirectly, by making reference to the characteristics of others in different groups. A manager, for example, may comment that 'their' work is harder than 'other' social work roles, that is, requires a more resilient type of social worker in comparison to the softer and less intense work of a different type of social work. What such action achieves is defining the boundaries for shameful behaviour by outlining and promoting a clear set of standards for the role and a set of characteristics for performing the role.

Furthermore, managers can provide a particular interpretive framework for employees to understand the meaning of their work, retelling stories and providing reference points for important elements of the work. This is clearly seen in stories of tragedies in social work, which serves to remind workers of the possibilities for shame if they do not follow protocol correctly. Such action establishes and expands the set of standards and further defines the boundaries for shameful behaviour within the organisation. Moreover, morals and values can be explicated to extend and deepen the idea of the kind of person who undertakes this type of work and how they should undertake it. Finally, a clear set of knowledge and skills can be constructed to further outline what workers are expected to know and be able to do (Alvesson and Willmott, 2002).

Such discursive practices construct a notion of an ideal worker (Gibson, 2019). Indeed, employees are usually able to articulate a full or partial set of characteristics, behaviours and attributes that are considered desirable within the organisation, and conversely a set that are undesirable. With such standards defined, outlined and communicated, workers become aware of the systemic boundaries for shame and seek to prevent being shamed by avoiding undesirable, questionable and proscribed behaviours. It is possible that such standards become internalised by workers, resulting in changes to their own identity standards. The failure to live up to such standards, in such cases, evokes shame as a result of personal feelings of failure and inadequacy. It is not necessary, however, for a worker to assimilate such organisational standards as their own for them to conform to the standards. Indeed, knowledge of the standards can be sufficient to seek to avoid transgression of them and, therefore, being shamed by others.

Relationship

Managers are able to organise the formal relationships within the organisation, which has the effect of regulating feelings of shame, either by evoking shame, or the fear of shame, or by containing and diverting shame. Firstly, organisations have some kind of hierarchy. Some may be more progressive and have flatter management structures while others may organise through more traditional hierarchical bureaucracies. Either way, there exist lines of accountability, with some employees being provided with greater levels of power than others. Such power relationships are explicit and concomitant to this are the possibilities for praise, acknowledgement and pride on the one hand and criticism, judgement and shame on the other. Certainly, in situations where the organisation is asking social workers to do things that are difficult (eg Morriss, 2016), feelings of shame are always a possibility. Supervision by a 'superior' allows employees to receive formal acceptance of such actions. Such supervision can contain any feelings of shame, by enabling the worker to feel accepted while experiencing shame, and directing their feelings away from shame, by reframing the situation as positive and necessary, ensuring that worker can continue to perform their duties (Bion, 1962). On the flip side, however, the hierarchy can be cast as a symbol of shame, seen in stories of workers who have been shamed by managers, which are told and retold within organisations. The formal organisation of these relationships embed the symbolism for the boundaries for shame: shame or the threat of it is evoked when close to those boundaries. Indeed, the workers may know what these boundaries are but they also know that these boundaries are being policed, by whom, and with what consequence.

Secondly, organisations create a sense of group affiliation (Alvesson and Willmott, 2002) by creating categories of workers. Everyone may be a social worker, but they may be a different 'type' of social worker, placed in a different location, doing different types of work, within a specific team. Such creation of 'us' and, to an extent, 'them', generates a sense of belonging and feelings of group membership. In the context of a hierarchical power structure, one's team can become a safe haven, providing solace and comfort when faced with shame and distress. Similarly to the relationship with those higher up the chain, workers can either receive emotional containment of their shame from their work community or judgement and criticism. Organising social workers into small teams can, therefore, embed organisational standards, support group monitoring and regulate the thoughts, feelings and actions of those within the groups.

Episode

Many of the episodes that social workers engage in are defined by institutions and processes outside of their own organisation. Social work as a practice has legal and political foundations, and individual organisations may not have much influence over, for example, attending court hearings or engaging in computer work. What leaders and managers are able to do, however, is select the situations social workers engage in and modify these situations as most useful to the organisation (Gross, 2008). Who should be involved in certain situations, what work needs to be prepared prior to those situations, to what quantity and quality, how they should present themselves in such situations are all organisationally definable? Social workers are routinely engaged in such organisationally defined episodes with concomitant sets of standards and expectations and consequences for failing to meet them (see also Chapters 8 and 9).

These episodes can be seen as the enactment of the self-concept and relationship contexts as defined previously. Where leaders and managers want to contain any feelings of shame as a result of undertaking tasks on behalf of the organisation, such as removing a child from their parents, they can organise the episodes to ensure social workers have debriefs and supervision following such episodes. They may also, however, embed the possibility of being shamed in any episode by defining and promoting the formal disciplinary procedures. Such actions regulate the shame in social workers by alleviating or evoking shame in organisationally defined 'appropriate' ways. This heightens a sense of self-consciousness in social workers while highlighting the standards against which they are measured. This generates self-regulation and surveillance in workers towards conformity.

Speech acts and content

With the socio-cultural context set, ideas about the right kind of person needed to do the work, the relationships defined and the episodes outlined, the conditions are set to guide, shape and direct the conversations and social interactions within the organisation in particular ways. What people say, how they say it and how they act while interacting with others transfers meaning. Given the context, institutional guardians seek to police and reinforce the boundaries for shame in the organisation. They may attempt to inspire and persuade social workers or criticise and threaten them. They may embrace or ignore workers, smile or pull faces, offer friendly gestures or act cold and aloof. Such verbal and non-verbal communication is not only constituted by the wider context but it also influences it.

Such speech acts and content of communication may seek to regulate feeling shame by redirecting a person's attention away from the situation that is evoking shame towards something more palatable, such as focusing on some other aspect of their work that is considered good by those in the organisation (Gross, 2008). Alternatively, they may seek to redirect attention towards something they have done that is considered shameful within the organisation. Furthermore, they may seek to change how the worker responds to the situation (Gross, 2008), such as by reframing it as being praiseworthy (in the case of seeking to avoid shame) or shameful (in the case of seeking to evoke shame). Such strategies define and redefine the boundaries for feeling shame by evoking and containing such feelings.

Discussion

Shame is a powerful feeling. The anxiety of feeling inadequate, of getting things wrong and being seen to be a failure are strong drivers in social interaction. Avoiding shame can drive behaviour and self-presentation. While this can occur on a conscious level, it can also be habitual and, therefore, unconsciously dictate why we act in the way we do. This applies to social workers as much as it does managers, leaders, civil servants and politicians. There is an ongoing process of shame avoidance that occurs at all levels and interactions (Goffman, 1956). When people are, however, shamed, this only serves to reinforce the need to avoid being shamed in the future. The process of feeling shame is not to be found in nature, but rather in how we are nurtured.

Feeling shame relates to a set of standards. Yet we are not born knowing a set of standards that we must live up to. Rather, these are created by people in groups, and then applied back to the people within the group. In many cases, these standards provide a loose consensus about the way people should think, feel and act. In some contexts, however, those with power and influence within a group may come to the view that a greater level of control is necessary over members to generate greater levels of conformity. As the standards for thinking, feeling and acting are constructed, they can be reconstructed and applied with ever-greater heavy-handedness. While this process has been theorised as the use of power (eg Foucault, 1977) or identity construction (eg Alvesson and Willmott, 2002), and has been related to shame (eg Scheff, 2000; Creed et al, 2014), the process as shame regulation has been overlooked. Yet the very experience of this process is indeed feeling shame, or at least seeking to avoid feeling shame. Indeed, it is the experience of shame that is the powerful social force utilised to achieve compliance.

Organisational theory has outlined how bureaucracy within organisations can create a form of iron cage for workers (Weber, 1978). Embedded into such cages, however, are formal processes for discipline, hierarchies with power and possibilities for judgement, criticism and expulsion from the organisation. The experience of shame is embedded into the iron cage. Furthermore, the panoptic gaze of managerial discourse and practice has highlighted how the standards and expectations within organisations live in the minds of workers, resulting in self-surveillance and self-presentation (Foucault, 1977). Such processes necessarily result in feelings of shame, often hidden, in workers when paired with the possibilities for failure, criticism and judgement. Shame is, therefore, embedded into the organisational panoptic gaze. Equally, organisational theorists who seek to outline identity regulation processes ignore the lived experience of shame in imposing new identity standards onto employees (Alvesson and Willmott, 2002), while those who acknowledge shame in organisational processes have yet to consider the mechanisms through which shame is evoked in daily practice (Creed et al, 2014).

This chapter has outlined a framework for understanding how these wider organisational, institutional and social processes relate to the lived experience of shame. This framework allows us to see how the processes involved in experiencing, or anticipating the experience of, shame, can be influenced, manipulated and changed to regulate this feeling in workers. While organisational leaders and managers may proclaim that the shaming of workers is abhorrent, the practice should not be seen as a form of managerial misbehaviour. Rather, the shaming takes place within a wider context that frames such action as justified. Indeed, Creed et al (2014) argue that episodic shaming of employees is strategic and purposeful as such actions are guided by the boundaries for systemic shame within the organisation. From a shame regulation perspective, we can see that attempts to contain, alleviate or divert feelings away from shame are also strategic and purposeful. Managers do not want workers feeling shame for doing things that they are employed to do.

Attempts at regulating shame in others may create the desired effect of evoking or containing shame, but this is not necessarily the case. Everyone carries with them their own set of contexts, personal experiences, ideas of who they are and want to be and concepts of emotions. Seeking to regulate someone else's feelings, especially around ideas of ability, capability and character, can result in a range of emotions for the target of the regulation. Anger and humiliation are possible feelings that may generate feelings of resistance more than compliance. Even feeling shame may not result in the level of conformity intended. Indeed, people may seek to influence, manipulate and sabotage efforts to regulate someone else's feelings, or in some cases simply leave the environment, claiming it has toxic effects.

All of this may sound like setting boundaries for shameful behaviour has dark underlying intentions. However, rather than seeing this process as good or bad, it should be seen as simply a social and cultural process that exists and can be heightened within organisations. Being aware of such a process provides opportunities for ethical, humane and creative practice. Indeed, some behaviours and actions *should* be seen as shameful. Hurting or harming vulnerable people is widely seen as immoral. The question is where is the line between acceptable and unacceptable professional behaviour? That is where the boundaries for systemic shame should lie. Conflict is created when pressures from outside the profession of social work impose ideas about practice that are at odds with the ideas for good practice within the profession. It is at such crossroads that we see social workers being shamed for failing to meet administrative tasks, performance targets or other business processes that have little bearing on the actual quality and effectiveness of their work with people. Aligning the boundaries for shame with professional ideals, practice and research evidence is most likely to gain widespread professional agreement. That is, ensuring that workers are not shamed for taking time to work with people or trying new things they genuinely believe would help would facilitate innovation and creativity, and that those who do cross the boundaries of acceptable behaviour are not treated in such a way that it humiliates and demeans them. A humane system is not one without shame. It is one that is shame-aware, offers ways of repairing damage and treats people as human beings, worthy of acceptance, even in the face of failure.

References

Alvesson, M. (2002) 'Culture as a constraint: an emancipatory approach', in M. Alvesson, *Understanding Organizational Culture*, London: Sage, pp 118–44.

Alvesson, M. and Willmott, H. (2002) 'Identity regulation as organizational control: producing the appropriate individual', *Journal of Management Studies*, 39(5): 619–44.

Austin, J. L. (1975) *How to Do Things with Words*, Oxford: Oxford University Press.

Averill, J. R. (1980) 'A constructivist view of emotion', in R. Plutchik and H. Kellerman (eds) *Theory, Research and Experience*, New York: Academic Press, pp 305–39.

Barrett, L. F. (2006) 'Are emotions natural kinds?', *Perspectives on Psychological Science*, 1(1): 28–58.

Barrett, L. F. and Russell, J. A. (eds) (2015) *The Psychological Construction of Emotion*, London: Guilford Press.

Barsalou, L. W. (1999) 'Perceptual symbol systems', *Behavioral and Brain Sciences*, 22(4): 637–60.

Bentham, J. (1791) *Panopticon: or, the Inspection-House*, np.

Bion, W. R. (1962) *Learning from Experience*, London: Karnac.

Brown, B. (2006) 'Shame resilience theory: a grounded theory study on women and shame', *Families in Society*, 87: 43–52.

Buchanan, J. and Tollison, R. (eds) (1984) *The Theory of Public Choice*, Ann Abor: University of Michigan Press.

Burkitt, I. (2014) *Emotions and Social Relations*, London: Sage.

Burr, V. (1995) *An Introduction to Social Constructionism*, London: Routledge.

Ceunen, E., Vlaeyen, J. W., & Van Diest, I. (2016) 'On the origin of interception', *Frontiers in Psychology*, 7: 743.

Chase, E. and Walker, R. (2012) 'The co-construction of shame in the context of poverty: beyond a threat to the social bond', *Sociology*, 47: 739–54.

Cooley, C. H. (1902) *Human Nature and the Social Order*, New York: Scribner's Sons.

Creed, W. E. D., Hudson, B. A., Okhuysen, G. A. and Smith-Crowe, K. (2014) 'Swimming in a sea of shame: incorporating emotion into explanations of institutional reproduction and change', *Academy of Management Review*, 39(3): 275–301.

Cronen, V. E., Pearce, W. B. and Harris, L. M. (1982) 'The coordinated management of meaning: a theory of communication', in F. E. X. Dance (ed) *Human Communication Theory*, New York: Harper & Row, pp 61–89.

Damasio, A. (1994) *Descartes' Error: Emotion, Reason, and the Human Brain*, London: Vintage.

Deetz, S. (1995) *Transforming Communication, Transforming Business: Building Responsive and Responsible Workplace*, Cresskill, NJ: Hampton Press.

Evans, T. and Harris, J. (2004) Street-level bureaucracy, social work and the (exaggerated) death of discretion. *The British Journal of Social Work*, 34(6): 871–95.

Foucault, M. (1977) *Discipline and Punish*, Harmondsworth: Penguin.

Frijda, N. H., Manstead, A. S. and Bem, S. (eds) (2000) *Emotions and beliefs: How feelings influence thoughts*. New York: Cambridge University Press.

Gibson, M. (2019) *Pride and Shame in Child and Family Social Work*, Bristol: Policy Press.

Gilbert, P. (2003) 'Evolution, social roles, and the differences in shame and guilt', *Social Research*, 70(4): 1205–30.

Gilbert, P. and Andrews, B. (eds) (1998) *Shame: Interpersonal Behavior, Psychopathology, and Culture*, New York: Oxford University Press.

Goffman, E. (1956) 'Embarrassment and social organisation', *American Journal of Sociology*, 62(3): 264–71.

Gross, J. J. (2008) 'Emotion regulation', in M. Lewis, J. M. Haviland-Jones and L. F. Barrett (eds) *The Handbook of Emotions*, New York: Guilford, pp 497–512.

Higgins, E. T. (1987) 'Self-discrepancy: a theory relating self and affect', *Psychological Review*, 94: 319–40.

Hochschild, A. R. (1979) 'Emotion work, feeling rules, and social structure', *American Journal of Sociology*, 85(3): 551–75.

Le Grand, J. (1997) 'Knights, knaves or pawns? Human behaviour and social policy', *Journal of Social Policy*, 26(2): 149–69.

Leeming, D. and Boyle, M. (2013) 'Managing shame: an interpersonal perspective', *British Journal of Social Psychology*, 52: 140–60.

Lewis, H. B. (1971) *Shame and Guilt in Neurosis*, New York: International Universities.

Lipsky, M. (1980) *Street-Level Bureaucracy: Dilemmas of the Individual in Public Service*, New York: Russell Sage Foundation.

Lynd, H. (1958) *On Shame and the Search for Identity*, New York: Harcourt, Brace & World.

Markus, H. R. and Wurf, E. (1987) 'The dynamic self-concept: a social psychological perspective', *Annual Review of Psychology*, 38(1): 299–337.

Morriss, L. (2016). 'AMHP work: dirty or prestigious? Dirty work designations and the approved mental health professional', *British Journal of Social Work*, 46(3): 703–18.

Moscovici, S. (1961) *La Psychoanalyse: Son Image et son Public*, Paris: Presses Universitaires de France.

Moscovici, S. (1973) 'Foreword', in C. Herzlich (ed) *Health and Illness: A Social Psychological Analysis*, London and New York: Academic Press, pp ix–xiv.

Munro, E. (2011) *The Munro Review of Child Protection: Final Report: A Child-Centred System*, London: DfE.

Nair, N. (2010). 'Identity regulation: towards employee control?' *International Journal of Organizational Analysis*, 18(1): 6–22.

Ortony, A. and Turner, T. J. (1990) 'What's basic about basic emotions?' *Psychological Review*, 97: 315–31.

Pearce, W. B. and Cronen, V. E. (1980) *Communication, Action and Meaning: The Creation of Social Realities*, New York: Praeger.

Ridgeway, C. L. (2006) 'Linking social structure and interpersonal behaviour', *Social Psychology Quarterly*, 69(1): 5–16.

Rosenberg, M. (1979) *Conceiving the Self*, New York: Basic Books.

Russell, J. A. and Barrett, L. F. (1999) 'Core affect, prototypical emotional episodes, and other things called emotion: dissecting the elephant', *Journal of Personality and Social Psychology*, 76(5): 805–19.

Scheff, T. J. (2000) 'Shame and the social bond: a sociological theory', *Sociological Theory*, 18(1): 84–99.

Scherer, K. R. (1992) 'On social representation of emotional experience: stereotypes, prototypes, or archetypes?', in M. von Cranach, W. Doise and G. Mugny (eds) *Social Representations and the Social Bases of Knowledge*, Bern: Huber, pp 30–6.

Stryker, S. (1980) *Symbolic Interactionism: A Social Structural Version*, Menlo Park, CA: Benjamin Cummings.

Tangney, J. P. and Dearing, R. (2002) *Shame and Guilt*, New York: Guilford.

Thoits, P. A. (1989) 'The sociology of emotions', *Annual Review of Sociology*, 15(1): 317–42.

Thompson, P. and McHugh, D. (1995) *Work Organizations: A Critical Introduction*, London: Macmillan.

Turner, J. E. and Husman, J. (2008) 'Emotional and cognitive self-regulation following academic shame', *Journal of Advanced Academics*, 20: 138–73.

Wastell, D., White, S., Broadhurst, K., Peckover, S. and Pithouse, A. (2010) 'Children's services in the iron cage of performance management: street-level bureaucracy and the spectre of Švejkism', *International Journal of Social Welfare*, 19(3): 310–20.

Weber, M. (1978) *Economy and Society: An Outline of Interpretive Sociology*, London: University of California.

White, S., Wastell, D., Broadhurst, K. and Hall, C. (2010) 'When policy overleaps itself: the "tragic tale" of the Integrated Children's System', *Critical Social Policy*, 30(3): 405–29.

Wierzbicka, A. (1992) 'Defining emotion concepts', *Cognitive Science*, 16: 539–81.

8

Claim, blame, shame: how risk undermines authenticity in social work

Mark Hardy

Introduction

Concerns have been prevalent for some time now regarding the quality and outcomes of social work practice, particularly as this relates to decision-making regarding risk, which is often perceived to be poor, as exemplified most clearly by high-profile service failures. Consequently, the profession finds itself subject to constant scrutiny and continual reform, while social workers themselves practise in a risk-averse climate, very much aware that 'poor judgement' can and does lead to disciplinary action, with all that this entails in terms of professional repute, social standing and continued employment. How do practitioners cope with these expectations? In this chapter I will describe how this situation has emerged, and its impact on front-line social work practice, via an account of the impact of risk thinking in social work, which intersects with debates regarding the nature of such work and its relationship to the purposes and activities of the state. I will also highlight how the emotional and practical consequences of working in a context in which blame and shame are real concerns relate to incidences of precautionary practice. The central argument of this chapter is that because of unrealistic expectations of infallibility, social work decision-making has taken on an 'absurd' character, and so I explore the value of existential philosophy in enabling practitioners to preserve the authenticity of their practice. I conclude with a call to develop a collective *parrhesia* to challenge unrealistic expectations regarding the quality, accuracy and value of social work practice.

Histories of social work suggest that a radical shift has occurred in the nature and ethos of practice since around the early 1990s. Underpinning this shift is the confluence of three related political, institutional and intellectual developments: neoliberalism, managerialism and risk. The first of these refers to the rise to prominence of certain key precepts – reason, responsibility and rationality – in the institutions and practices of government. Relatedly, managerialism entails a much more explicit emphasis on efficiency, value for money and effectiveness, stressing accountability and transparency as vehicles for quality and excellence in practice. Risk, meanwhile, although not completely novel, has nevertheless assumed significant prominence as both rationale and organising principle for practice. Although each of these three strands have impacted on social work in significant ways, their cumulative effect is most apparent when we explore the impact of the rise of risk.

Risk in social work

Risk has been an overt concern in social work since around the early 1990s. Its focus on predicting and managing the likelihood of service users causing harm, either to themselves or others, arguably represents a significant departure from social work's traditional priority of addressing the welfare or therapeutic needs of individuals and families. From the 1980s onwards, however, a number of high-profile incidents led to political and public concerns about the ability of social workers to prevent harm being caused by or to service users. Originally, this was in relation to childcare, with cases – Maria Colwell, and later Victoria Climbié – having significant effects on trust and faith. Subsequently, the focus fell on mental health, with notable cases such as those of Jason Roberts and Christopher Clunis assuming iconic status (Warner, 2006). There have also been concerns directed at community care following abuse of power in work with vulnerable adults (Butler and Drakeford, 2003; Lymbery and Postle, 2015). More recently, the case of Peter Connolly – 'Baby P' – in England represents a potent example of what Epstein characterises as 'extreme failures' (1996, p 114), which continues to resonate via its impact on ongoing developments in social work education, organisations and practice (see Shoesmith, 2016, for an insightful 'insider' account). Consequently, since the early 1990s, social work has arguably been transformed from a profession with a commitment to enhancing individual well-being via inclusionary psychosocial means to one with a paramount concern to prevent harm via administrative and exclusionary approaches.

Although there are various accounts of how and why these shifts have arisen, in the UK at least it is arguably no coincidence that they followed the election of a reforming Conservative government in the late 1970s, determined to establish neoliberal principles and practices within the structures of government. Various scholars have outlined the changes to social work associated with the rise of neoliberal thinking across institutions and practices of 'the social state' (eg Kemshall, 2002; Garrett, 2009; Cummins, 2018). Stephen Webb (2006), for instance, emphasised how the logics of risk, regulation and security intersect with neoliberal perspectives regarding individual responsibility, choice and freedom. These differ markedly from the collectivist commitments that informed the history and development of social work, and so their rise to prominence has impacted on the work's nature, objectives and ethos in ways which potentially compromise its integrity and effectiveness. Because of its predominant focus on harmful events that may or may not happen in the future, risk contributes to a lack of due regard being paid to actual, existing need. The energies of practitioners and the resources of agencies are fixated on the future to the detriment of the here and now. This further accentuates social exclusion, prompts over-reliance on coercive approaches to practice and downgrades the significance of social context in assessment and intervention, thus undermining long-standing commitments to social justice (Parton and Kirk, 2010). Risk also triggers particular kinds of organisational responses, which are as concerned with the standing and legitimacy of the agency as the right, proper or moral response to individuals facing difficult circumstances. Agencies prioritise the identification, prevention and reduction of risk, emphasising the rights of the wider community to be protected from social work clients. Significantly, as a result, social work becomes increasingly risk-averse. Practitioners become participants in a repressive framework, 'unreflective co-conspirators' (Stanford, 2008, p 210) in the politics of risk, whereby the logic of risk functions as a 'predominantly morally conservative and repressive social, political and cultural force in contemporary social work' (Stanford, 2008, p 209).

Concerns about risk also feed into the emphasis within policy discourse on standardisation of practice via the reduction of practitioner discretion. The assumption here is that service failures result from poor decision-making by practitioners, and that the limiting of practitioner discretion therefore represents a means of eliminating risk. Consequently, we have witnessed a shift in the basis for decision-making away from informal, tacit, subjective knowledge generated via 'time spent' engaging with individuals and families, to seemingly more objective data. Professional decision-making increasingly occurs on the basis of evidence-based guidelines and decision support tools based on validated empirical research implemented in accordance with prescriptive managerial and policy directives on how to respond to different cases on the basis of risk categories. Decisions are made drawing on actuarial data rather than interpreted based on individual professional judgement.

As the nature of the services that are offered by agencies has become increasingly focused on the identification and management of risk, practitioners' responsibilities have shifted. They are 'not so much for the cure or reform of clients ... but for their administration according to the logic of risk minimisation' (Rose, 1996, p 349). Risk practices are therefore seen as part of the apparatus via which the de-prioritisation of need in favour of risk enables the displacement of governmental commitments to welfare provision (Culpitt, 1999). In line with the priority attached to individualism and responsibility within neoliberal thought, service users are deemed to have contributed to their own misfortune by 'individual failing and moral ineptitude' (Lavalette, 2011, p 1). Being 'a risk' or 'at risk' is a manifestation of either a failure to fulfil one's responsibility to function capably within society, or a moral lapse indicative of a flawed identity which itself comes to be a risk indicator.

To many, it does appear that there has been a notable and meaningful shift in the rationale for social work practice, from focus on the welfare of the individual to a disproportionate concern with the harm that service users may cause to themselves and, more alarmingly, others. These shifts reflect wider social changes, captured in the notion of a 'risk society' (Beck, 1992). Consequently, it is now commonplace to suggest that the traditional humanistic components of practice have been usurped, while the professionalism of workers has been eroded. Practitioners increasingly practise defensively, erring on the side of caution in line with the precautionary principle, summed up by Lewens as 'better to be safe than sorry' (2007, p 10). This manifests in risk-averse decision-making, the avoidance of positive risk-taking, overuse of exclusionary interventions and, sometimes, the deliberate but poorly substantiated 'risking' of service users whose needs and circumstances suggest this is unwarranted (Oberdiek, 2017). As a consequence, social work can no longer be conceived of as relational and empowering but instead as bureaucratic and disempowering (Rogowski, 2010; Bamford, 2015; Gibson, 2019b).

This critique represents the critical consensus regarding the rise of risk among observers of social work. In its generality it risks reifying both an 'ideal type' as well as a 'golden age' of social work (Hardy, 2015). But undoubtedly, within social work practice, risk is a 'real' 'thing', and so has an impact, not least through risk aversion, which 'abounds' in social work (Fenton, 2019, p 70, Whittaker and Havard 2016). Perhaps more than any other factor it is concern about the prevalence and consequences of risk aversion which underpins many of the concerns that critics have regarding the practical consequences of risk on social work (Cooper, Hetherington and Katz, 2003; Featherstone et al, 2018). The power of risk arguably reflects the medium through which it is communicated. Actuarialism quantifies risk, with numeric values 'purporting to act as technical mechanisms for making judgements' (Rose, 1999, p 198), thus lending credence to what is, in effect, predictive guesswork (Hardy, 2016). In this way, organisations can counter criticism that over-reliance on partisan relationship-based knowledge undermines objectivity in decision-making. There is little sense here, however, that within organisations risk may be recognised as a socially constructed 'artefact' rather than an objective phenomenon, or that risk assessments, rather than being accurate approximations of truth, instead represent subjective political and moral judgements which are eminently contestable. Rather, the expectation is that competent professionals should be able to predict and consistently and accurately differentiate between low- and high-risk eventualities and thus prevent harm occurring. This aim is regarded as both ontologically legitimate and epistemologically achievable.

Claim

So, where do these expectations – infallibility, and the related notion that 'blame' is an appropriate response to 'error' – come from? Efforts to fundamentally reform public services in the UK are commonly associated with the Conservative government that held power from 1979 to 1997 and instigated sweeping changes to the organisation, delivery and ethos of the public sector under the rubric of 'New Public Management' (Clarke and Newman, 1997). The subsequent Labour government, elected in 1997, shared this focus on quality and value, and arguably accelerated this process, including via its commitment to evidence-based policy and practice (Davies, Nutley and Smith, 2000). Alongside this focus on 'knowledge-based excellence', it sought to embed systems and processes of audit and accountability, targets and measures – effects which were captured, thus demonstrating value for money so as to ensure that reforms delivered (Barber, 2007). However, as critics have pointed out, these standards, targets and their associated 'rituals of verification' (Power, 1997) were introduced, precisely because of the well-established difficulties of accurately measuring the outcomes of social interventions, as proxies for, rather than measures of, actual change (Pawson, 1989). Their prevalence enabled the view that the *perception* of success matters as much if not more than the *reality* in retaining or enhancing individual, professional and institutional legitimacy in politics, public service and professional activities more generally. This perspective became deeply entrenched within the agencies of the public sector and then beyond, as subsequent governments extended competition and choice (Newman and Clarke, 2009). The tendency to accept 'the influence of electoral calculation in framing governmental social policies' (Bamford, 2015, p 73) was also evident in social work agencies.

Although a shift from authority- to evidence-based practice represents one of the most significant 'knowledge-based' developments in social work over the past quarter-century, emphasising strengths without acknowledging limitations risks overstating the case. In any case, orthodoxy provokes critique, and a parallel strand of social work thinking, based upon wholly different epistemological presumptions, has challenged the dominance of empirical practice. This perspective emphasises that social work is characterised by uncertainty, ambiguity and complexity (Parton, 1998). Indeed, Fook (2007) suggests that social work is *defined by* its relationship to uncertainty, while Webb (2001), in his influential critique of evidence-based practice, claims that empiricism disregards the reality and constraints on actual decision-making processes in social work: 'A more complex relationship exists between social work interventions and decisions made by social work agencies ... governed by imperatives which fall outside the workings of a rational actor' (Webb, 2001, p 63), including unquantifiable moral considerations (White and Stancombe, 2003). Social circumstances and relationships are inherently inter-subjective, reflecting the variable and (to some extent) individualised nature of the human beings involved. Uncertainty, ambiguity and complexity seriously complicate the ability of practitioners to make accurate predictions regarding the impact of social work intervention as well as judgements regarding future service user behaviour. Consequently, and of necessity, practitioners must make decisions in circumstances in which complexity represents a real 'confounding variable' in efforts to generate and apply accurate generalisable knowledge.

Expectations regarding accuracy and effectiveness were less stringent in what Oldfield (2002) refers to as the era of welfare. Social work remained 'below the radar' while there was general congruence between its underpinning principles and those of society more generally. However, faith in the ability of science to falsify and certify knowledge claims grew as consensus regarding the capacity of particular methodologies to challenge uncertainty developed, thus contributing to the increasing belief that professionals could and should be both accurate and effective in their judgements and interventions. As this view became politically institutionalised, and against the backdrop of a culture in which 'excellence' was increasingly normalised, it became difficult for organisations and practitioners to acknowledge (never mind justify) the actual everyday reality of 'run-of-the-mill' social work, which, like all professional activities, is characterised by variability rather than uniformity in quality. This reality jars with the now politicised and corporate culture within social work organisations. Hubris is the norm in this climate and a counterproductive vice, not least because the expectations it projects have meaningful effects (Button, 2016).

Social workers, like all professionals, are fallible – or, as Nietzsche (1994) would have it, 'human, all too human'. Following the death of Peter Connolly, Munro's (2012) review of child protection practice concluded that the ability of social workers to make accurate decisions is hampered by their burdensome bureaucratic workloads and the degree of scrutiny to which they are subject, both of which impact on the time available for face-to-face practice or spending time with people. Paradoxically, measures put in place by successive governments to ostensibly enhance service quality and improve decision-making undermined the conditions necessary to facilitate these. As O'Connor puts it: 'New public management systems contribute an additional layer of complexity, as evidenced in practitioners' fears about blame and error' (2019, p 12). Consequently, despite high-level acceptance of the 'false hope of eliminating risk' (Munro, 2012, p 134), practitioners still must make judgements in far from ideal situations, based on less than full knowledge. In conditions of uncertainty, however, errors are inevitable.

It is important to stress, however, that despite this there is no substantial empirical data to suggest that social work practitioners are in any meaningful way 'better' or 'worse' than professionals in other domains of practice – law, healthcare, policing, journalism – when it comes to making decisions. Belief that the judgements of social workers – or the substantive knowledge which underpins them – are inadequate stems from the interplay between media hyperbole and political expedience – 'buck-passing' being an established part of the architecture of organisations (Hood, 2011). Unrealistic expectations, it seems, are not just based on incomplete knowledge, they are also positively damaging, precisely because they promote the idea that infallibility is possible and achievable. As Dingwall and Hillier aptly put it, 'claims lead to blame' (2016, p 23).

Blame

Over twenty years ago, Nigel Parton (1996) identified the influence of 'blaming systems' on social work, and although much has changed subsequently it seems that this idea continues to hold sway. This should not be surprising. In her seminal work on understanding risk as a cultural phenomenon, Mary Douglas (1992) argues that the impulse to blame, and the systems which develop to facilitate and sustain this, reflect deep-seated social needs to hold to account those who transgress social norms, for the sake of collective cohesion. Despite shifts in rules and norms, this instinct is perennial. Although Douglas was concerned with risk and blame at community level, her work has resonated with organisational theorists in particular (eg Matheson, 2017), and has been utilised in analysing risk in social work, not least because often those who attract blame are the very people who populate social work caseloads. The attribution of blame within communities is often a manifestation of power and so 'digs more deeply the cleavages that have been there all the time' (Douglas, 1992, p 34), coalescing around groups who are already disadvantaged and stigmatised. Additionally, blame is central to how government and agencies have adapted to a cultural context in which infallibility is the expectation, however unrealistic and unfair that may be. Within blame cultures, blame accrues not just to those who actually cause harm – a domestic violence perpetrator who assaults a partner or child, for example – but also to those in authority who, it is expected, should have anticipated and prevented the unforeseen outcome. Indeed, within social work this is especially the case. Parton suggests this is because of the distinctiveness of the role that social work plays, which is an essentially mediating one, between the individual and society, public and private, care and control. In addition, it is 'the only profession whose core is based on a socio-legal expertise, and continually attempts to mediate across the various tensions that inhabit the sphere of "the social"' (Parton, 2014, p 164). This is a difficult balancing act and so social work is especially vulnerable to accusations of 'error', particularly where that error concerns the well-being of children.

The essential ambiguity of the social work role is also emphasised by Merlinda Weinberg (2016). Although it is challenging to social work's preferred self-identity, this means that doing unequivocal good in social work is difficult. The roles and responsibilities that social workers fulfil across domains typically require the exercise of both liberatory and constraining authority, often within the remit of the same case. Core social work aims and approaches – care and control, liberation and regulation, safety and justice – conflict with each other and with long-standing ethical commitments to autonomy, self-determination, unconditional positive regard and the like. Complex interpersonal situations and legal responsibilities require social workers to serve multiple stakeholders – the state, the client, 'the third' (Weinberg and Campbell, 2014). Consequently, 'the client in social work is commonly more than one individual, and each has differing and, at times, conflicting needs' (Weinberg, 2010, p 33). These 'paradoxes' make 'ethical trespass' inevitable. This notion is drawn from Hannah Arendt's (1958) work on the issue of 'dirty hands' in politics, whereby decision makers and actors 'are required to do wrong in order to do right and so on the path towards some greater good, inevitably cause suffering and incur a moral cost' (Mroulije, 2019, p 146). Aspirations to 'moral purity' within social work, as exemplified particularly within virtue ethics, are revealed as idealised, distinct from the practical reasoning required to decide between competing options in situations characterised by complexity and plurality (Evans and Hardy, 2017). Significantly, if ethical trespass is inevitable due to inherent ambiguity, this suggests that, consequently, social workers will routinely be regarded by one or more of the interested parties as having made the 'wrong' decision, and thus as blameworthy. This helps us to understand why social workers commonly regard themselves as 'damned if I do, damned if I don't'.

Shame

Although distinct, blame and shame can be practically difficult to disentangle. Recently, there has been significant theoretical work on the role of shame, which enables us to make some sense of this overlap, and so we are better equipped to understand how wider systems impact on individual practitioner subjectivity and agency via what the philosopher Peter Sloterdijk (1987) identifies as a form of 'psychopolitics', to which shame is central.

Shame is simultaneously a social concept, an experience and a feeling – lived, sensory and psychological. It occurs within social relationships, is interpersonal and represents a distinctive form of social suffering (Frost and Hoggett, 2006; see also Chapter 1). It also entails the experience of being judged, and has a moral basis, in that the operation of processes of shaming is dependent upon the perception by 'shamers' of an infraction of moral standards (Marar, 2018).

There is ongoing debate regarding the distinctions between anxiety, fear, shame and humiliation. It remains unclear whether these represent issues of definition or intensity and context, and questions regarding the extent to which people's vulnerability and resilience to shaming reflects individualised experiences, traits and resources, thus leading to variable and unpredictable impacts, can be raised. Nevertheless, as Liz Frost emphasises, potentially shame is 'a devastating emotion' (2016, p 437) with very real psychosocial consequences. It represents 'a powerful force in limiting human agency, capacity and potential' (Frost, 2016, p 434), thus emphasising the role that power and politics play when imposing a form of social suffering to which ostracisation is key. Walker (2011, cited in Frost, 2016) refers to 'the visceral experience of being shunned and expelled from human connectedness'. Like punishment, but not actually punishment, and therefore without explicit legal mandate or accountability, shaming deliberately causes hurt, resulting in 'serious identity damage' (Frost, 2016, p 435) via 'denigration and degradation' (Frost, 2016, p 440), with intentional effects on individual subjectivity. For some, this has devastating emotional consequences, as 'shame experiences the whole self as under attack' (Marar, 2018, p 32) and there is a well-established relationship between the experience of shame, humiliation and suicide (Mokros, 1995; Leask, 2013). As Guenther puts it 'There are many ways to destroy a person' (2013, p xi).

Of course, there are many who claim that there are both direct and indirect benefits associated with 'shaming' practices. Braithwaite's (1989) influential work on reintegrative shaming suggests that shaming is both just and effective as both an individual and general deterrent, and that is has been significant in the development of restorative and relational approaches in criminal justice and social work, particularly in communities with minority indigenous populations whose cultural cohesion has traditionally relied upon relational approaches to managing deviance. There have also been attempts to utilise shame more directly in social work practice, as either a mechanism promoting change or as a means of social control (eg Gal, 2011).

It is worth noting that Braithwaite drew a clear distinction between stigmatisation and shaming, arguing that the former is counterproductive whereas the latter represents 'the most important backstop ... when consciences fail to deliver conformity' (1989, p 82). However, his focus was the use of shaming within a framework of criminal law and a justice system which – whatever their limitations – are subject to multiple systems and processes of oversight and accountability. As such, there are questions about the applicability of 'shaming' within groups who are not 'deserving' of punishment (as they have not committed an offence) and about its use within organisations, such as social work agencies, as a covert means of regulating staff behaviour.

So, how extensive is fear of shame within social work organisations? This is a difficult question to answer. Given that concerns about service failure are long-standing, it should not be surprising that there has been a steady stream of research over decades testifying to the ways in which fear, blame and risk intersect (eg Smith, McMahon and Nursten, 2003; Dwyer, 2007; Braescu, 2011). In my own work exploring the impact of risk on social work practice, there were certainly instances of precautionary practice which practitioners attributed to fear of blame and what would follow (see Hardy, 2015, 2017). However, it would be an unsubstantiated generalisation to suggest that therefore shame impacts on most social workers across organisations all the time. Indeed, many organisations actively seek to militate against cultures of blame and shame via efforts to embed the principles of learning organisations. Here, practitioners are encouraged to acknowledge mistakes as a basis for individual and agency learning in line with lessons learned in high reliability organisations, such as aviation. Nevertheless, the fact that empirical studies do suggest that this is a real issue for some social workers in some agencies is significant in itself. For both practitioners and service users in these situations, this is problematic. For social workers, being shamed or working in a situation in which the fear of being shamed is pervasive is emotionally distressing, with potentially severe consequences for an individual's mental health, and has potential effects for career progression and retention. For service users, it means that they are subject to judgements and decisions that do not suit their needs and potentially subject to restrictions which unjustly inhibit their freedom to live their lives in the way they see fit. Gibson (2019a; see also Chapters 7 and 9) suggests that fear of shame can prevent social workers from working ethically. This is because it inhibits the practical expression of empathetic concern – concern for oneself affects willingness and ability to respond compassionately to others, which manifests most clearly in the coercive, exclusionary, punitive and risk-averse tendencies that are associated with the critique of risk in social work but also more ambiguously in a generalised lack of both procedural and relational authenticity as well as withdrawal and avoidance (Musil et al, 2004).

These issues have wider significance than social work, as they touch on enduring issues within political philosophy. The Italian philosopher Giorgio Agamben's analysis of the role that state power plays in the designation and denial of social status – the distinction between 'bios' and 'bare life' – particularly enables us to think critically regarding the ethics of power in shame (Agamben, 1998, 2005). Like Foucault (2004), he seeks to illuminate the operation of power within society, with a focus on the ambiguous rationales underpinning those judgements which enhance freedom by limiting the autonomy of others or promote security via the infliction of harm. Agamben draws attention to the 'double movement' of both subjectification and desubjectification via which the individual enters 'the grey zone', the 'zone of indistinction' in which the differences between a fully engaged politically and relational existence and 'marginal life' are stark. The structure of shame enables this distinction via a double-bind, affirming the relational nature of life, the dependence of the individual upon others at precisely the point that others seek to disaffirm these relations: 'In shame, the subject ... becomes witness to its own ... oblivion as a subject. This double movement, which is both subjectification and desubjectification, is shame' (Agamben, 2005, p 106).

Both humiliation and shame rely on individuation and entail processes of dehumanisation – isolating, scrutinising, labelling, castigating, devaluing and doing violence against – but in each case the motivation for this end is distinct. Humiliation is motivated by an almost sadistic determination to permanently distinguish and exclude via the identification and isolation of 'the one who does not belong ... to build a sense of unity among those who remain ... leaving no avenues of escape or return ... frozen in time, fixed in a position on the margins of social life' (Guenther, 2012, p 61). By contrast, there is an ambivalence to shaming which manifests in an arguably ethical recognition of the possibility of, if not redemption, return. This offer of hope, however, enhances the power of 'an other to whose gaze I am exposed, but whose view of myself I cannot control' (Guenther, 2012, p 61). Dependency on the other for possible 're-entry' emphasises the intersubjective status of self-identity and in doing so reiterates the powerlessness of the shamed. Shaming, then, bears resemblance to scapegoating, as described by Mary Douglas (1995) in her account of its social and cultural utility in the Old Testament. As the bearer of the sins of the community, the scapegoat, although marginalised on the periphery, must be allowed to return, not least because they may be required to fulfil this function in the future.

In social contract theory, citizens give up certain rights in return for security, policed by state authorities. The processes of individuation Agamben regards as central to shaming reflect the distinction between 'friend' and 'foe' which the political philosopher Carl Schmitt (2010 [1934]) regards as the definitive sovereign power, from antiquity to the modern state. The power to make this distinction and act upon it is backed up with the right to do violence against the transgressor. It is 'in the fear of what humans can do to each other, that the state finds the justification for its own existence' (Svenden, 2008, p 116).

This enables the 'state of exception' wherein citizens of the state are stripped to 'bare life'. Esposito suggests that biopolitics supplants the traditional paradigm of sovereignty as the ultimate legitimator of power, but via a paradoxical route whereby rather than 'adapting the protection to the actual level of risk, it tends to adapt the perception of risk to the growing need for protection – making protection itself one of the major risks' (2011, p 16). At the extremes, 'life can be protected from what negates it only by mean of further negation' (2011, p 15).

Theorists of biopower, then, question the motivation and value of the sorts of redemptive rituals that social workers sometimes facilitate – normalisation, reintegration, rehabilitation – on the basis that the individual's rights are subsumed within the needs of the collective as these manifest in state sovereignty. The use of shame to regulate professional behaviour highlights the pervasiveness of biopower across domains of neoliberal society. It is therefore unsurprising that social workers – human beings, lest we forget – might be shame-averse, particularly in those agencies which actively make use of shame to 'prod and incentivise' (Button, 2016, p 61) in the face of unachievable ends.

Challenging the absurdity of infallibility

Existentialism

Expectations of infallibility are clearly absurd. But how might social workers respond to this absurdity? As we have seen, one option is to internalise it. Risk-averse practice, whereby practitioners respond to service users in ways that disregard the needs of individuals and families because of fear of the consequences for themselves is the result of this acceptance and represents a form of 'inauthentic' practice. Both absurdity and authenticity are key concepts in existential philosophy (Aho, 2014), which raises the possibility that this perspective may offer insights into how practitioners could make sense of and potentially change their circumstances.

Many well-known philosophers have links to existentialism, including Kierkegaard, Nietzsche and Heidegger. Other theorists are defined by their existential contribution, for example, Sartre, de Beauvoir and Camus. They concern themselves with questions pertaining to the perennial challenges of existence, including 'what is the meaning of life?

Who and what am I? How should I live? What happens when I die?' Clearly, answers to these questions are not straightforward. Nevertheless, certain key themes sum up the existential perspective. Kierkegaard suggested that anxiety, which in existential terms refers to the general sense of uneasiness regarding the purpose of life many human beings experience, lends a degree of ambivalence to the notion of freedom. Nietzsche added a moral element to this unease with his famous aphorism 'God is dead.' Here, he was suggesting that as the influence of Christian ethics waned, a gap would emerge in which people would have to decide for themselves which moral principles would guide their lives, rather than relying on religious teaching to make these choices for them. For many people, these issues provoke a sense of angst about existence in general, which often manifests in concerns about individual mortality and – as Heidegger emphasised – the relationship between being and time, our 'short-livedness'. Mortality and temporality are the defining truths of human existence. Simone de Beauvoir emphasises that such issues are further complicated by our relationship to others, with whom we are enmeshed in interdependent relationships but ultimately cannot rely upon because imminent mortality means they and these are only ever temporary. The nature of human existence, and the prevalence of these perennial issues in our minds, means that human beings approach life ambiguously. Camus concluded that ultimately life has no meaning. Optimistically, however, he suggested that this meaninglessness gives us freedom to live whatever life we choose. More pessimistically, we are therefore responsible for the choices we make – or as Sartre put it 'Man is condemned to be free.'

Absurdity and authenticity are linked in existential thinking (Webber, 2018). Life is absurd because it has no fixed meaning. There are no transcendental values which will enable us to make the 'right' decisions. Rather, 'the value system we live by is defined by us and us alone. And it is not absolute' (van Deurzen and Adams, 2016, p 25). All the meanings we attribute to our existence, the value judgements that humanity makes regarding what is 'good', worthy, virtuous or legal, are recognised by existentialists as arbitrary, relative and inconsequential. None will make any difference to the fact that soon you and I will be dead, as will all the people we care about. So, what should we do with the short period of existence open to us, given that none of it has any substance or meaning, and 'everything is permitted … nothing is justified' (Webber, 2018, p 152)? How do any of us live meaningful lives when life – in essence – is meaningless and how we answer this very question doesn't matter? This is an absurd situation to be in, and yet it defines what it is to be a human being.

On the one hand, the nihilistic logic of this position is hard to refute. On the other, while existentialists are surely correct in their specification of the paradoxes that define human existence, it is also true that very few human beings live their lives as though life does not matter. Occasionally, we might come across a true hedonist. Illness such as mania can lead afflicted individuals into reckless, irresponsible behaviour. And some people do commit suicide (though more often due to lack of hope than lack of meaning). But usually the opposite is the case and generally we take life seriously. Indeed, many of the resolutions that existentially informed thinkers suggest enable humanity to cope with meaninglessness also entail the creation of an artificial meaning – a reason to live. Authenticity is key here. In existentialism authenticity refers to the ability to accept responsibility to choose one's way of existence and identity in awareness of mortality. The only way to create meaning and live authentically is – paradoxically – to rebel against absurdity, to act in ways that suggest life, our choices, our responsibilities, matter, in full knowledge that in the end absurdity will triumph, as mortality always does.

Existential theory is utilised as a theory for practice by social workers, with notable interpreters, including Neil Thompson (2000) and Donald Krill (2014), developing models of application. Here, however, the issue is less that the utility of existentialism is enabling service users to solve particular problems, but whether it might enable practitioners to make sense of workplace situations which at the very least have the potential to generate distress and disempowerment. According to Mark Griffiths (2017, p 196), a notable existential social worker, authenticity 'describes the quality of a person who accepts responsibility for being who they are ... without concern for how others might judge them'. Authenticity, then, is dependent on acknowledging our limitations (that we will die, and so are fearful, dependent and time-limited) and disregarding the opinion of others in favour of being true to ourselves. We can see how this might apply with regard to responding to cultures of blame and shame in social work. The tendency for agencies to exaggerate their potential and thus promote unrealistic expectations is a clear manifestation of inauthenticity which reflects a belief that 'the truth' is not what matters, but instead perception. This inauthenticity is founded on existential dread, of declining legitimacy undermining the raison d'être of the sovereign state. In seeking to reduce this dread by reaffirming legitimacy, political actors exaggerate their utility and effectiveness in countering contemporary concerns – risk and security. Security represents a false promise in the face of the truth of mortality and so we can see why its elevation as the aim of life has absurd consequences for service users and for practitioners. Eventually, however, absurdity forces individuals to 'respond to the call of conscience and own up to our responsibility' (van Deurzen and Adams, 2016, p 219). Authenticity represents the remedy for absurdity.

Parrhesia

Foucault continually highlighted the disjuncture between the operation of power within society and the claims to knowledge that legitimise this. In his later work on the ethics of identity, he interrogated the nature of subjectivity as a basis for challenging conventional understandings of – in particular – sexuality. In doing so, he drew on and developed the notion of *parrhesia*. This Greek term refers to 'the dangerous exercise of freedom' (Foucault, 2010, p 67), a form of 'truth-telling' distinguished by the risk that the teller must take to communicate the truth. The risk entailed in truth-telling is a necessary condition of *parrhesia*, which ensures a distinction from more general claims-making based on an ethical comportment that is freely entered into despite potential dangers. In the main, the threats the truth teller risks are to his or her social and institutional status because of the relationships of power of which both teller and receiver are part. Foucault suggested that *parrhesia* is fundamental to self-care, itself a core component of the ethics of the self.

What truths would a social work specific *parrhesia* tell? Firstly, that professional expertise represents a form of informed guesswork, and there are no realistic expectations that technological, 'scientific' or knowledge-based initiatives will impact on the accuracy of that guesswork, other than very marginally. Social work will remain fallible. However, although we don't know exactly how fallible social work is (how could we?) there is no substantive evidence to suggest it is any more fallible than any other professional activity. There is evidence, however, which suggests that strategies to enhance the quality of practice and improve decision-making can have counterproductive effects because they raise expectations and therefore encourage precautionary practice, limiting service user choice and autonomy in ways that are unfair. This is not to suggest that service user self-determination ought to be the 'trump card' in balancing care and control. Rather, in the case of risk-averse decision-making due to fear of blame and shame, it is not warranted. This is unjust and inauthentic, undermining service user trust and faith in social work, as well as social workers' commitment to their profession.

What are the potential dangers in telling these truths? Clearly, they challenge the legitimacy of governmental authority by undermining the claim that 'agents of the state' – in this case social workers, though the point has wider resonance – possess knowledge and a skills base that enable them to accurately and consistently assess risk. They also threaten the notion of evidence-based policy and practice by calling into question the claim that given time, complexity can be unravelled to the extent that practice will be 'effective' (as opposed to 'relatively effective', the only claim that does not violate scientific logic). Crucially, however, given that as things stand practitioners are shamed for failing to live up to these expectations (Gibson 2019b), there seems little to be gained by continuing to accept the inauthentic status quo.

What might such a *parrhesia* achieve? Firstly, it is important that this perspective has traction within debates about both the nature and function of social work but also, more practically, regarding effectiveness, quality, priorities and resourcing. Making decisions about any of these issues on the basis of perception rather than the reality risks perpetuating and accelerating problematic aspects of the contemporary settlement. Secondly, it is important that those practitioners who either have been shamed or whose practice is affected by the fear of shame are able to achieve recognition of their experiences. As Frost (2016) makes clear, well-being is dependent on recognition, which can be important in recovery, but is also required to disrupt established dominant narratives so as to effect change in the future. Ultimately, it is important to remember that as an ethical practice of self-constitution and self-care, Foucault regarded *parrhesia* as an approach which was beneficial for the individual truth teller. But in truth-telling there are also potential wider benefits: for other social workers struggling with similarly absurd scenarios; for service users, who pay a real price for inauthentic practice in terms of their liberty and freedom; and for society and citizens more generally, neither of whom are immune to the paradoxical effects of absurdity. The significance of what is at stake here should not be underestimated, as summed up by Sloterdijk: 'In a culture in which hardened idealisms make lies into a form of living, the process of truth depends on whether people can be found who are aggressive and free ("shameless") enough to speak the truth' (1987, p 102). The ultimate remedy for inauthentic falsehood is the power inherent within truth.

Conclusion

Social work was once referred to as 'the invisible trade' (Pithouse, 1987). In an era in which accountability and transparency are seemingly axiomatic virtues, and in which the predominant technologies social workers utilise render them readily susceptible to surveillance and scrutiny (Hardy, 2020), it is perhaps unsurprising that this memorable phrase no longer resonates. Now, social work is a transparent endeavour, in which practitioners are not only visible but also find their every decision and action potentially subject to oversight. As we have seen, in such a working environment, although blame and shame may not be endemic, fear of their potentiality represents a real issue for social work practitioners and affects service users because of the intersection between fear and precautionary practices. This is likely to remain an issue while expectations of infallibility remain prevalent and influential. Existential thinking fits the absurdity of this situation and may well help some practitioners to make meaning in ways that enable them – at an individual level – to resist precautionary tendencies and engage authentically with the people with whom they are working. *Parrhesia*, meanwhile, brings together concerns with truth, ethics and practice in ways that potentially lend the concept critical purchase in efforts to change institutions and their activities. Of course, this is to invite opposition, and there is the possibility – intrinsic to *parrhesia* – that truth tellers risk the wrath of those who perceive them as a challenge to their power, status or authority. This is most likely, however, where truth has the actual potential to effect change. Authenticity is always a choice, and decisions come with risks. But as Anderson so aptly puts it (2019, p 496), 'risks are not simply dangers we face, but things individuals must take.'

References

Agamben, G. (1998) *Homo Sacer: Sovereign Power and Bare Life*, Stanford, CA: Stanford University Press.

Agamben, G. (2005) *State of Exception*, Chicago: University of Chicago Press.

Aho, K. (2014) *Existentialism: An Introduction*, Cambridge: Polity Press.

Anderson, A. (2019) 'Parrhesia: accounting for different contemporary relations between risk and politics', *Journal of Sociology*, 55: 495–510.

Arendt, H. (1958) *The Human Condition*, Chicago: University of Chicago Press.

Bamford, T. (2015) *A Contemporary History of Social Work: Learning from the Past*, Bristol: Policy Press.

Barber, M. (2007) *Instruction to Deliver: Fighting to Transform Britain's Public Services*, London: Methuen.

Beck, U. (1992) *Risk Society: Towards a New Modernity*, London: Sage.

Braescu, P. (2011) 'The blind side of mild fear', *Journal of Social Work Practice*, 26(1): 5–13.

Braithwaite, J. (1989) *Crime, Shame and Reintegration*, Cambridge: Cambridge University Press.

Butler, I. and Drakeford, M. (2003) *Social Policy, Social Welfare and Scandal: How British Public Policy is Made*, Basingstoke: Palgrave Macmillan.

Button, M. (2016) *Political Vices*, Oxford: Oxford University Press.

Clarke, J. and Newman, J. (1997) *The Managerial State*, London: Sage.

Cooper, A., Hetherinton, R. and Katz, I. (2003) *The Risk Factor: Making the Child Protection System Work for Children*, London: Demos.

Culpitt, I. (1999) *Social Policy and Risk*, London: Sage.

Cummins, I. (2018) *Poverty, Inequality and Social Work: The Impact of Neo-Liberal Austerity Policies on Welfare Provision*, Bristol: Policy Press.

Davies, H., Nutley, S. and Smith, P. (eds) (2000) *What Works: Evidence-Based Policy and Practice in Public Services*, Bristol: Policy Press.

Dingwall, G. and Hillier, T. (2016). *Blamestorming, Blamemongers and Scapegoats: Allocating Blame in the Criminal Justice Process*, Bristol: Policy Press.

Douglas, M. (1992) *Risk and Blame: Essays in Cultural Theory*, London: Routledge.

Douglas, M. (1995) 'The cloud god and the shadow self', *Social Anthropology*, 3: 83–94.

Dwyer, S. (2007) 'The emotional impact of social work practice', *Journal of Social Work Practice*, 21(1): 49–60.

Epstein, L. (1996) 'The trouble with the researcher-practitioner idea', *Social Work Research*, 20(2): 113–37.

Esposito, R. (2011) *Immunitas: The Protection and Negation of Life*, Cambridge: Polity Press.

Evans, T. and Hardy, M. (2017) 'The ethics of practical reasoning: exploring the terrain', *European Journal of Social Work*, 20(6): 947–57.

Featherstone, B., Gupta, B., Morris, K. and Warner, J. (2018) 'Let's stop feeding the risk monster: towards a social model of "child protection"', *Families, Relationships and Society*, 7(1): 7–22.

Fenton, J. (2019) *Social Work for Lazy Radicals: Relationship Building, Critical Thinking and Courage in Practice*, London: Red Globe Press.

Fook, J. (2007) 'Uncertainty: the defining characteristic of social work?', in M. Lymbery and K. Postle (eds) *Social Work: A Companion to Learning*, London: Sage, pp 30–9.

Foucault, M. (2004) *Society Must Be Defended: Lectures at the Collège de France 1975–76*, London: Penguin.

Foucault, M. (2010) *The Government of Self and Others: Lectures at the Collège de France 1982–1983*, Basingstoke: Palgrave Macmillan.

Frost, E. (2016) 'Exploring the concepts of recognition and shame for social work', *Journal of Social Work Practice*, 30: 431–46.

Frost, E. and Hoggett, P. (2006) 'Human agency and social suffering', *Critical Social Policy*, 28: 438–60.

Gal, T. (2011) *Child Victims and Restorative Justice*, Oxford: Oxford University Press.

Garrett, P. M. (2009) *Transforming Children's Services: Social Work, Neoliberalism and the Modern World*, Maidenhead: Open University Press.

Gibson, M. (2019a) 'The role of pride, shame, guilt and humiliation in social service organisations: a conceptual framework from a qualitative case study', *Journal of Social Service Research*, 45: 112–28.

Gibson, M. (2019b) *Pride and Shame in Children and Family Social Work: Emotions and the Search for Humane Practice*, Bristol: Policy Press.

Griffiths, M. (2017) *The Challenge of Existential Social Work Practice*, London: Palgrave Macmillan.

Guenther, L. (2012) 'Resisting Agamben: the biopolitics of shame and humiliation', *Philosophy and Social Criticism*, 38: 59–79.

Guenther, L. (2013) *Solitary Confinement: Social Death and Its Afterlives*, Minneapolis: University of Minnesota Press.

Hardy, M. (2015) *Governing Risk: Care and Control in Contemporary Social Work*, Basingstoke: Palgrave Macmillan.

Hardy, M. (2016) 'I know what I like and I like what I know: epistemology in practice and theory and practice again', *Qualitative Social Work*, 15: 762–78.

Hardy, M. (2017) 'In defence of actuarialism: interrogating the logic of risk in social work practice', *Journal of Social Work Practice*, 31: 395–410.

Hardy, M. (2020) 'Discretion in the surveillance state', in T. Evans and P. Hupe (eds) *Discretion and the Quest for Controlled Freedom*, London: Palgrave Macmillan, pp 41–62.

Hood, C. (2011) *The Blame Game: Spin, bureaucracy and self-preservation in government*, Woodstock: Princeton University Press.

Kemshall, H. (2002) *Risk, Social Policy and Welfare*, Maidenhead: Open University Press.

Krill, D. (2014) 'Existential social work', in F. J. Turner (ed) *Social Work Treatment: Interlocking Theoretical Perspectives*, Oxford: Oxford University Press, pp 166–90.

Lavalette, M. (2011) 'Introduction', in M. Lavalette (ed.) *Radical Social Work Today*, Bristol: Bristol University Press, pp 1–10.

Leask, P. (2013) 'Losing trust in the world: humiliation and its consequences', *Psychodynamic Practice*, 19(2): 129–42.

Lewens, T. (2007) 'Introduction: risk and philosophy', in T. Lewens (ed) *Risk: Philosophical Perspectives*, Abingdon: Routledge, pp 1–20.

Lymbery, M. and Postle, K. (2015) *Social Work and the Transformation of Adult Social Care: Perpetuating a Distorted Vision?*, Bristol: Policy Press.

Marar, Z. (2018) *Judged: The Value of Being Misunderstood*, London: Bloomsbury.

Matheson, C. (2017) 'Four organisational cultures in the Australian public service: assessing the viability and plausibility of Mary Douglas' cultural theory', *Australian Journal of Public Administration*, 77(4): 644–57.

Mokros, H. B. (1995) 'Suicide and shame', *American Behavioural Scientist*, 38(8): 1091–103.

Mroulije, M. (2019) *Rethinking Political Judgement: Arendt and Existentialism*, Edinburgh: Edinburgh University Press.

Munro, E. (2012). *The Munro Report of Child Protection: Final Report: A Child Centred System*, London: Department of Education.

Musil, L., Kubalčíková, K., Hubíková, O. and Nečasová, M. (2004) 'Do social workers avoid the dilemmas of work with clients?', *European Journal of Social Work*, 7(7): 305–19.

Newman, J. and Clarke, J. (2009) *Publics, Politics and Power: Remaking the Public in Public Services*, London: Sage.

Nietzsche, F. (1994) *Human, All Too Human*, St Ives: Penguin.

Oberdiek, J. (2017) *Imposing Risk: A Normative Framework*, Oxford: Oxford University Press.

O'Connor, L. (2019) 'How social workers understand and use their emotions in practice: a thematic synthesis literature review', *Qualitative Social Work*: Online First, 1–18.

Oldfield, M. (2002) *From Welfare to Risk: Discourse, Power and Politics in the Probation Service*, ICCJ Monographs, 1, London: NAPO.

Parton, N. (1996) 'Social work, risk and the "blaming system"', in N. Parton (ed) *Social Theory, Social Change and Social Work*, London: Routledge, pp 98–114.

Parton, N. (1998) 'Risk, advanced liberalism and child welfare: the need to rediscover uncertainty and ambiguity', *British Journal of Social Work*, 28(1): 5–27.

Parton, N. (2014) *The Politics of Child Protection: Contemporary Developments and Future Directions*, Basingstoke: Palgrave Macmillan.

Parton, N. and Kirk, S. (2010) 'The nature and purposes of social work', in I. Shaw, K. Briar-Lawson, J. Orme and R. Ruckdeschel (eds) *The Sage Handbook of Social Work Research*, London: Sage, pp 23–36.

Pawson, R. (1989) *A Measure for Measures: A Manifesto for Empirical Sociology*, London: Routledge.

Pithouse, A. (1987) *Social Work: The Social Organisation of an Invisible Trade*, Aldershot: Gower.

Power, M. (1997) *The Audit Society: Rituals of Verification*, Oxford: Oxford University Press.

Rogowski, S. (2010) *Social Work: The Rise and Fall of a Profession*, Bristol: Policy Press.

Rose, N. (1996) 'The death of the social? Reconfiguring the territory of government', *Economy and Society*, 25(3): 327–56.

Rose, N. (1999) *Powers of freedom*, Cambridge: Cambridge University Press.

Schmitt, C. (2010 [1934]). *Political Theology: Four Chapters on the Concept of the Sovereignty*, Chicago: Chicago University Press.

Shoesmith, S. (2016) *Learning from Baby P: The Politics of Blame, Fear and Denial*, London: JKP.

Sloterdijk, P. (1987) *Critique of Cynical Reason*, Minnesota: University of Minnesota Press.

Smith, M., McMahon, L., and Nursten, J. (2003) 'Social workers' experiences of fear', *British Journal of Social Work*, 33(5): 659–71.

Stanford, S. (2008) 'Taking a stand or playing it safe: revisiting the moral conservatism of risk in social work practice', *European Journal of Social Work Practice*, 11(3): 209–20.

Svenden, L. (2008) *A Philosophy of Fear*, London: Reaction Books.

Thompson, N. (2000) 'Existentialist practice', in P. Stepney and D. Ford (eds) *Social Work Models, Methods and Theories*, Lyme Regis: Russell House Publishing, pp 201–13.

Van Deurzen, E. and Adams, M. (2016) *Skills in Existential Counselling and Psychotherapy*, London: Sage.

Walker, J. (2011) 'The relevance of shame in child protection work', *Journal of Social Work Practice*, 25(4): 451–63.

Warner, J. (2006) 'Inquiry records as active texts and their function in relation to professional practice in mental health', *Health, Risk and Society*, 8(3): 223–37.

Webb, S. (2001) 'Some considerations on the validity of evidence-based practice', *British Journal of Social Work*, 31(1): 51–79.

Webb, S. (2006) *Social Work in a Risk Society*, Basingstoke: Palgrave Macmillan.

Webber, J. (2018) *Rethinking Existentialism*, Oxford: Oxford University Press.

Weinberg, M. (2010) 'The social construction of social work ethics: politicizing and broadening the lens', *Journal of Progressive Human Sciences*, 21(1): 32–44.

Weinberg, M. (2016) *Paradoxes in Social Work Practice: Mitigating Ethical Practice*, Abingdon: Routledge.

Weinberg, M. and Campbell, C. (2014) 'From codes to contextual collaborations: shifting the thinking about ethics in social work', *Journal of Progressive Human Services*, 25(1): 37–49.

White, S. and Stancombe, J. (2003) *Clinical Judgement in the Health and Welfare Professions: Extending the Evidence Base*, Maidenhead: Open University Press.

Whittaker, A. and Havard, T. (2016) 'Defensive practice as "fear based" practice: social work's open secret?', *British Journal of Social Work*, 46(5): 1158–74.

9

Shame, mistakes and reflective practice in social work

Alessandro Sicora

This chapter focuses on the connection between shame and mistakes and presents some of the outcomes of recent exploratory research involving social workers and social work students.

Being wrong is an emotional experience. It is not only the recognition of a deviation from external reality and an internal change in what the subject believes and their consequent acts; it is also the condition of being stuck in wrongness with no immediate way out (Schulz, 2010). This is unpleasant, especially when accompanied by the sight of the damage done and when internal or external voices not only blame for the wrong action but also criticise the person as a whole. The shift from 'I/you made a mistake' to 'I am/you are a mistake', that is, 'I am/you are a failure as a practitioner or even as a person' is easy and common, and shame may be the resulting emotion. Even if criticism may be useful feedback, providing constructive opportunities to learn from mistakes, it is more often felt by people as an attack on, and a sabotage of, their self-confidence, and this commonly produces a defensive reaction, rather than leading to the person listening and reflecting. In these circumstances, learning from mistakes becomes almost impossible.

Shame as a state of being is, one hopes, rare among social workers, but many people may have experienced this feeling to some degree during their careers. Nevertheless, mechanisms of denial and self-defence strongly affect the quality of any intervention, and they may lead to a refusal to constantly engage in the 'maintenance' of personal work tools, such as continuing training. By contrast, understanding and sharing even the feeling of inadequacy produce more resilient social workers and better interventions.

To support the concepts outlined, this chapter presents some examples of reflective writing by social workers and social work students who performed in-depth structured reflection on some of their most significant experiences in relation to this issue during research workshops conducted by the author. Some of the outcomes included: a sense of lack of personal and organisational resources and skills, strong empathic reactions to difficult situations faced by service users, complex relationships with colleagues and managers.

Shame has only recently been seriously considered as relating to social workers in their everyday practice (Gibson, 2014; Frost, 2016). This emotion, resulting from the belief that one is lacking in some sense and unworthy of acceptance and belonging, is felt, under certain conditions, by both service users and social workers. In the case of the latter, it can hinder empathetic action, and is often related to lack of satisfaction with one's work, maintaining the job and the struggle to act professionally in an ethical manner (Gibson, 2016). In many cases, shame may be a consequence of a lack of reflection on, and understanding of, one's professional mistakes (Sicora, 2017). The sense of inadequacy induced by this emotion can be also caused or intensified by traumatic events (assaults perpetrated by service users, serious failures etc) or it may arise when users, colleagues, superiors, other professionals and so on continuously and pervasively give little respect, legitimacy and/or recognition (with regard to the question of recognition see Chapter 1 for more details).

The analysis of the forms of reflective writing by social workers and social work master's students, produced during periods of guided self-reflection, sheds more light on this topic. This analysis was conducted in order to identify some of the most common situations, thoughts and images of those involved in shameful situations experienced in field practice. Here, perceived professional incompetence can provoke shame, but incompetence alone does not explain the onset of this emotion, the dynamics of which are complex and involve deep-lying parts of the self. This emotion affects the 'knowing how to be' dimension of social workers more than their 'knowing how to do', even though it is often recognised in this latter area and not in the former. Being aware that shame is a widespread emotion with a significant negative impact on the quality of professional performance may provide a good opportunity to reflect deeply on the nature of social work and discover new ways to improve it.

Self-care, self-compassion and self-forgiveness may be exit strategies from toxic shame useful for both social work students and social workers. They are not easy escapes from the responsibility of working with people in social services; on the contrary, they may help in accepting the fact that mistakes and failures are part of any human reality and that hiding them is likely to produce more harm than when people recognise errors, stop and learn from them, repair the harm possibly caused and apply the new learning in similar future situations for the benefit of other service users.

Social workers and service users: an emotion in common

Shame, considered as a feeling of inadequacy (often summarised in sentences beginning 'I am not sufficiently' followed by adjectives such as 'good', 'capable', 'competent' and so forth; see also Chapter 3 analysing neoliberal expectations), is an intrinsic part of social work, which is a profession that touches the limits of human experience and social living in situations, for instance, of extreme poverty, suffering, dependence, deviance and end of life. Shame and recognition deeply influence the practice of social work and affect both social workers and service users (Frost, 2016). The former is avoided; the latter is sought. The acknowledgement that shame is a natural part of human nature limits the negative effects produced by such an emotion; for example, the reduction of empathy and the inability to recognise, reflect and learn from one's own failures.

Shame is often excluded from the emotions regularly acknowledged or discussed, perhaps being understood as an outmoded focus (Turnaturi, 2012) or regarded as a taboo subject. One could say that people often feel 'ashamed about their own shame' because if they name this emotion, they reveal what they are ashamed of and want to hide from themselves and others. The burnout of workers in social and health services can be understood as undergoing the shift from situations that can be labelled with 'I made a mistake' (or even 'you made a mistake' when the stigmatisation comes from the surrounding environment) to others summarised by the sentence 'I am a mistake' ('you are a mistake') (Sicora, 2017). Walker (2011) suggests that allowing social workers to talk about their feelings of shame (as well as of anger and fear) makes them more resilient and creative in their jobs, especially if they are culturally able to acknowledge their vulnerability. Being unable to express such feelings can cause burnout and professional distress. According to a recent Spanish study, self-acceptance is a dimension of personality positively correlated to resilience in social work students and social workers (Palma-García and Hombrados-Mendieta, 2017).

The public perception of social workers is closely linked to the topic of shame. Stereotypes and stigma have affected this profession since its beginning, and several research studies conducted in the US demonstrate that there is still a long way to go in terms of producing a better image for social work. Interestingly, during research for one of these studies respondents were asked how they would feel if their children chose a helping profession (psychologist, nurse, physician etc). Social work received the lowest percentage of respondents' expected 'happiness' (LeCroy and Stinson, 2004). A recent survey of the opinion of social workers in New Zealand concerning the public perception of their profession included two questions about pride and stigma as encountered in their professional and personal lives. It revealed the presence of these ambivalent emotions in many social workers due to hard work, difficult tasks, professional values and the complexity of an often misunderstood professional identity (Beddoe, Staniforth and Fouché, 2017).

On the other hand, many service users turn to the social services for help after failing their socially appreciable life projects. They feel all the weight and the discomfort of their 'fall', of whatever type it is: economic (eg the shame experienced by middle-class people when they lose their jobs and have to go to social services in order to claim for unemployment benefit, which is a completely new and shameful situation for them) or related to their social position, psychophysical balance or other forms of reduction of status. Also, going to mental health or addiction services is often difficult due to the labelling nature attributed by many people to such components of the welfare system. At the same time, some behaviours leading to situations of social exclusion appear to be dysfunctional attempts to alleviate the sense of discomfort produced by shame, and they trap people in a sort of vicious cycle from which it is hard to escape. For example, a significant correlation has been found between a tendency to feel shame and abuse and dependence on alcohol (Treeby and Bruno, 2012). This highlights the short circuit created in those who try to escape from the discomfort of 'feeling inadequate' by using a substance that generates an addiction capable itself of being a source of further shame.

Other forms of addiction follow the same pattern when, at the beginning, they 'promise' relief from some form of distress (of any kind, shame included) but then consume too much time, attention and freedom. They thus become difficult to control and, in the end, create more distress (shame, as well as impairment of social, occupational and relational functioning). Hypersexual behaviour, also known as sex addiction, is probably one of the most evident examples of this process since it involves forms of sexual behaviour that are often condemned by social norms but in which some people engage to cope with negative emotional states, even though they increase the sense of despair from which these people want to escape (Mosher, Hook and Grubbs, 2017).

Sometimes even experiencing emotions perceived as wrong is a source of shame, as in the case of many caregivers overwhelmed by the fatigue of care and torn by the unspeakable inner conflict between love and hate for their dear ones when they absorb all their time and energy, as in the case of those suffering from dementia or other serious debilitating diseases. Also, stories from survivors of trauma, especially in the case of long-term neglect or abuse, demonstrate that 'I felt bad' may easily shift into 'therefore I am bad' (Germer and Neff, 2013).

Operational definitions and research on shame in social work

This section focuses on some of the experiences of shame described by master's students undertaking internships and trained social workers during workshops aimed at raising awareness of the impact of shame. The trainer gave some operational definitions of shame and briefly described the state of research on shame and social work. He then asked the participants to reflect on and write about their own experiences of this feeling. Even though shame has been widely defined in the previous chapters of this book, here it is advisable to synthesise the main concepts provided in the workshops to stimulate more in-depth reflection on shame experiences.

Shame involves intense discomfort because, being closely connected to one's self-image and sense of dignity, it often implies a considerable reduction of self-confidence and a paralyzing sense of powerlessness. This emotion is typically social. It involves the desire to get away from others and can be accompanied by anger and resentment when it is connected with some form of humiliation (Anolli, 2010). Even though shame has a pervasive impact on the lives and relationships of individuals, it has long been ignored in research on emotions, as well as in the specific field of social work. Although those who feel shame rarely acknowledge it with ease, this emotion is an experience common to many social workers. It is correlated with satisfaction with their work and can threaten their ability to comprehend another's perspective and act professionally (Gibson, 2016).

In a recent scoping review, Gibson (2016) has highlighted several studies which directly, or more often indirectly, consider shame and social work in countries such as Australia, Brazil, Canada, China, Finland, Ireland, Israel, New Zealand, Norway, the UK, South Africa and the US. The author identifies three groups:

1. Research in which shame is clearly named and recognised. These studies consider situations including, to name the most common, professional mistakes and failures (as in the case of a user's suicide) and aggression perpetrated by service users against social workers.

In these circumstances workers often believe they have not reacted adequately or have felt and expressed emotions (fear, anger, etc) that they should not have shown and find difficult to admit to their colleagues. This group of studies suggests that these situations produce significant internal discomfort and are more common in social work than one might imagine.

2. Studies in which shame, although not explicitly named, is clearly recognisable, as they consider emotional states strongly associated with feeling devalued and inadequate (ie connected to an internal dialogue peppered with sentences like 'I am not competent enough' or 'I am not able to react adequately'; see also Chapter 2, which provides further theoretical information concerning devaluation). These feelings are often due to lack of legitimacy and recognition of the profession in the eyes of others, like service users, colleagues, managers, but also public opinion.

3. Other research studies that, while considering aspects of the personal and professional self negatively assessed by the workers, cannot be included in the two previous categories because they refer to a sense of guilt rather than shame. The former focus on behaviours judged negatively by the subject that engaged in them ('I did a bad thing'), while the latter are aroused by the fact that social workers perceive themselves as negative ('I am bad'). These studies provide some interesting insights into the emotional experiences of self-consciousness in social workers.

Experiences of shame in social work internship and practice

The previous section, 'Operational definitions and research on shame in social work', summarised work carried out during some training sessions for social work master's students and trained social workers in various regions of Italy. The participants were then invited to reflect on situations in which shame had been the dominant emotion during their internship, in the case of the students, or in their professional lives, in the case of the social workers. The purpose of reflection, carried out in pairs using a list of questions, was to conduct joint explorations of a little-known field and to share the learning that emerged from this. Over thirty questions, based upon Gibbs' (1988) reflective cycle – a tool aimed at considering an event in detail in order to grasp its full meaning and implications for future action – were asked. These were grouped into six stages: (1) description, (2) feelings, (3) evaluation, (4) analysis, (5) conclusion, (6) action plan. This was aimed at users recalling as many details as possible of the event under analysis during the first two stages, and then identifying what was positive and negative in the episode (stage 3) in order to analyse the dynamics involved in the event itself and go deeper into their understanding (stage 4). The core questions of the last two stages are 'what else could you have done?' (conclusion) and 'if it arose again what would you do?' (action plan).

Each pair had to work on a single episode. One person spoke; the other listened and asked the questions included in Gibbs' reflective cycle, plus any other clarifying questions to understand the episode better. At the end of the time available, the pair had to summarise the findings using a maximum of only 160 characters, including spaces, as if a text message sent by a mobile phone. The purpose of this limitation was to focus the participants on identifying the essence of the episode previously examined in detail and the related learning and understanding. Although the groups usually did not consist of more than thirty people, sharing all the answers would take too long, the essence of the narrative would be lost, and so too would be the possibility of opening a wide and frank debate on the most common aspects of shame emerging from the experiences of the participants. These can be called 'bonsai stories' because, although they are miniature tales, they often manage to contain all the essential elements of more complex narratives, similar to the bonsai, which has abundant and well-formed leaves and branches like other trees, but on a much smaller scale (Sicora, 2018). Even though they are very short, these reflective writings can be considered case studies, more precisely 'cases of local knowledge', as described by Thomas (2011), because they are examples of personal experiences from which to begin to broaden one's cognitive horizons. The further advantage of this technique is the anonymisation produced by this extreme synthesis. As will become clearer in what follows, where some of these 'bonsai stories' are presented, this extreme synthesis omits any personal data, perfectly protecting the privacy of the people involved in the narratives and making the tellers less shy in talking about their often quite personal and embarrassing stories. To further protect them, participants had the opportunity not to allow the trainer to make any use of their micro-narratives. During the debate they had the choice of whether to identify themselves as authors of the stories or not.

In order to provide an overall picture, albeit synthetic and not exhaustive, of the different meanings that shame assumes in social work, some of these 'bonsai stories' are quoted here. The first examples come from students, the others from workers. They have all been translated from the original Italian into English.

Most of the experiences of shame described by students arose from the unexpected discovery that the theoretical learning in the classroom did not make them sufficiently skilled to deal with real situations in field practice. In other words, books and lessons gave them only a part of the knowledge needed to be a social worker but somehow had provided the illusion of being sufficient to enable practitioners to cope with the everyday challenges of their jobs.

The following quotations exemplify such situations and, in a group discussion, were labelled as 'being a novice':

> At a mental health centre during an interview: shame from a sense of experiential inferiority.

> I was in a situation of shame during an interview with a mother and her daughter (they had to be protected from possible domestic violence): as a trainee I did not have the skills and tools needed in that situation.

> Feeling of shame and embarrassment during an interview with a woman in a multi-problem family. Fear of answering inadequately and invading her privacy.

> Sense of inadequacy caused by awareness of not having some of the skills required by my supervisor.

> Team meeting: they talked about the DAP [the acronym for the Italian Department of Penitentiary Administration] but with shame I did not understand the meaning.

> Sense of shame during my first interview because I felt inexperienced and was younger than the service user.

> Sense of shame because of the presence of someone I knew from my home town during the interview.

> Sense of shame during my first interview because I felt inexperienced and too young compared to the user.

The internal voices shaming students in these examples had different origins: the students themselves who thought that they were inferior because of a lack of experience, or other people (probably in some cases internalised, in others not), such as the supervisor (also known as 'practice teacher' in some educational contexts) and service users, who may be even more severe judges if they personally know the student or if they are older than them.

Age was again a factor, as well as the fear of making the wrong assessment because strong emotions, in causing the paralysing shame expressed in these two examples:

> Embarrassment during a meeting between a service user and a trainee because of the young age of both.

> Shame because I was unable to assess a situation with neutrality and felt emotionally paralysed when I knew that this user made the same mistakes again.

In their everyday practice, social workers often encounter behaviours and living conditions considered shameful by society: for example, deviant behaviours or extreme poverty. The first of these encounters can produce shame in students during their internship, as in the following example:

> Shame when I was going to the post office with a homeless person without my supervisor who was temporarily unavailable.

The discussion aroused by this 'bonsai story' in a workshop was particularly useful for developing greater awareness among students about the causes of shame and pride in situations encountered by social workers and in the profession itself. Stigmatisation, stereotypes and negative labelling affect not only service users but also the helping professions. A student asked rhetorically how the author of the episode summarised here would have felt if she or he had to accompany her or his favourite Hollywood movie star instead of a homeless person. Thinking critically also means investigating what lies behind social conventions in order to find the origins of inequality and the obstacles to social justice, which are two key concepts in social work. Reflections aroused by strong and even negative emotions, such as shame, give valuable opportunities and stronger motivation for learning from experience if these emotions are not pushed away, but are recognised, named and 'heard' as messengers of information able to furnish useful discoveries and improve professional skills. At the same time, students may discover that many unpleasant feelings are very common and that there is no need to be ashamed of them.

Workshops with social workers led to similar outcomes, first of all the weakening of the 'shame of shame', which is a taboo for practitioners who, according to the expectations of many people, should be objective, scientific and detached. It is acceptable that students may not have all the skills required for their future profession since any internship is part of the learning process in social work. On the contrary, it is less acceptable for those who, after successfully completing their studies, are now paid to do a job. However, despite the expertise acquired, no one seems immune from feeling shame in certain circumstances, as shown by the following examples of 'bonsai stories' written by social workers:

> Interview with a caregiver: I felt uncomfortable because I thought I was not competent and she was judging me negatively.

> First interview with a son for his mother with Alzheimer's: feeling of inadequacy; he expected me to be an expert on the subject, but I didn't feel trained enough.

These two sentences seem similar to some of those written by students. The feeling of being 'inadequately' competent and trained does not disappear with at the start of one's professional career but appears to fade away over time without perhaps ever disappearing completely. This is also true because contradictory and discordant expectations placed upon social workers by the public, the profession and government institutions exert strong pressure to avoid being shamed and, on the contrary, to attract praise (Gibson, 2019). Sometimes it is almost impossible to avoid blame from someone, as expressed in the following extract:

> [P]hone call in which accusations and negations were made: 'you are doing nothing for the children', second phone call after removing children from the family: 'you are doing nothing for their desperate mother'. I stopped the conversation.

Experiences of shame may generate new learning, as described in the first of the next group of 'bonsai stories', which are examples of how the organisational dimension is recurrent in developing more or less intense feelings of inadequacy. This can happen at the beginning of the career, as in the first two examples, one of which highlights the achieved learning ('I learned to say no'), or as in the last text, when a negative evaluation expressed by a manager is likely to be uncritically internalised by the operator:

> Shame because, at the beginning of my career, my incompetence was highlighted by a user in the presence of my superior. Sensation of fragility resulting from defence expressed by my boss. I learned how to contain anger more than I thought I was able to.

> First job. The administration asked me to accompany a group of elderly people to a holiday centre. Shame for not recognizing my role and anger at not being able to impose myself. At the next departure I refused, asking for a written service order that they could not make. I learned to say no.

> Shame at being blamed by a colleague for the incomplete assessment of a case. The evaluation procedure had not been completed because of the complexity of the case.

As stated by Gibson (2018, 2019; see also Chapter 7), professional practice is often shaped by the dynamic relationship between the intention of the management and the administration to strategically control pride and shame in others, and the individual experiences of social workers in dealing with these emotions. This is a typical social control mechanism operating through the definition of what is considered 'acceptable' and 'appropriate'. Engaging in professional action outside these defined boundaries should produce shame and, consequently, the attempt of the workers concerned to avoid this unpleasant feeling by adapting to the organisation's requests. In this process, being a scapegoat is not a rare experience in social work, as in the following case:

> Special commission: I expressed my favourable opinion on the placement in a day care centre of a 17-year-old girl with mental and physical disabilities. I prepared and sent the required documents. It turned out that the girl was already included in another social welfare programme, and this created problems in health management and funding between different agencies. I became a scapegoat in a context without rules and roles. I felt unprofessional and inadequate.

The expression of organisational control can even be aggressive, as in the first of the next set of 'bonsai stories'. The following two are examples of the power of group pressure and of team meetings as frequent scenarios for shaming:

> Excessive and unmotivated verbal aggression by my boss for my presumed professional mistake. Shame: desperate crying in front of colleagues even if in solidarity.

> After a month of work, during a meeting I felt inadequate because my colleagues pointed out to me that I had underestimated a serious episode without having reported it to the team immediately.

> Organizational meeting between multiple services with facility manager. Blame in front of everyone about the time taken to write my in-depth reports. Feelings of inadequacy, shame and anger.

Shame may be 'toxic', destructive and excessive (Potter-Efron and Potter-Efron, 1999), but, like any other emotion, it may also have a very benign and useful function: for example, when it alerts social workers to the conflict between the core values of social work and the driving forces exerted by organisations:

> Shame at belonging to a 'system' that does not reflect our way of considering the helping relationship.

> Shame when I was feeling not sufficiently warm and empathetic towards foreign users. Services are unable to help them because of a lack of resources (cultural as well).

This last extract seems to highlight the deep sense of identification that workers may have with their agencies, even when these show organisational inadequacy in dealing with new categories of problems and service users. Also in this case, as in the others, the storytelling makes broader reflection on the dynamics behind the emotion experienced by the practitioner possible. Shame may direct attention, for example, to the lack of resources, to the difficult relationship between organisation and workers and to many other issues of work in social and health services.

Concluding this brief selection from the numerous micro-narratives collected during the workshops described earlier in the chapter, the last 'bonsai story' seems to highlight an intense empathic link between the social worker and the service user during an interview about a very dramatic experience. The worker empathically feels the sense of shame expressed by the woman:

> I was young and it was my first experience at the municipality of Xxxxxx. A woman with economic problems and a drug-addicted son arrived in my office and confessed to me that her son had sexually abused her. I felt displaced, helpless and ashamed that a person older than me told me this.

Feeling shame and learning from it

The public, management and politicians are increasingly intolerant of professional mistakes, and they expect social workers to always know what to do, even in the most difficult situations. The clash of standards, rules and objectives of organisations, users and society as a whole produces a series of conflicting expectations and implies that, despite a social worker's best efforts, any decision taken by them can produce blame, disappointment and a sense of devaluation. Obviously, this feeling is experienced more intensely when those who shame the practitioner have more power (Gibson, 2016). At the same time, satisfaction in social work may be achieved through a process of balancing, establishing and recreating professional pride towards conditions for authenticity in practice. Shame and any other self-conscious emotions are an inherent part of social workers' experience. They therefore guide and constrain actions and interactions with users, colleagues and managers (Gibson, 2019).

The micro-narratives quoted in this chapter confirm these reflections, and the discussions aroused in the workshops in which they were formulated have shown that unexpressed shame can lead to an intense sense of isolation and personal crisis. Identifying and defining shame experiences can be the first step in developing personal and professional resilience, and in reducing the negative effects of toxic shame. It would be interesting to deepen the exploration of the dysfunctional compensatory strategies that social workers also develop as alternatives to the perhaps more difficult, but certainly more regenerative, attempts to reach full awareness of their discomfort about feeling 'inadequate' in their professional lives.

Recognising one's fragility and vulnerability is a key factor in the acquisition of personal and professional balance (Brown, 2015), especially in social work, where it is always very difficult to define the boundaries between what is personal and what is professional. Being aware of one's shame and even declaring it to others is certainly a part of this process, but shame, like any other unpleasant or pleasant emotion, may give social workers information on their internal and external worlds that would be difficult to obtain otherwise (David, 2016).

Starting from recognition of the structurally inherent complexity of social work and the existence of different forms of positive and negative impact that organisations can have on their workers, some recent research highlights the importance of social workers promoting their personal well-being and self-protection in the face of situations of concrete risk of stress and burnout. The development of adequate level of resilience in social workers is a difficult and complex process; nevertheless, it is vitally important for the reduction of compassion fatigue in the helping professions and improvement of the quality of any welfare system (Kapoulitsas and Corcoran, 2015). The skills and strategies necessary for this purpose should already be developed by the training received at university. Gio (2017) notes that most social work students reach the end of their studies unprepared to use self-care approaches to prevent burnout. The author states that the attitude and practice of self-compassion – that is, compassion directed towards oneself through attitudes of self-kindness and respect for one's deepest needs – is an effective approach for coping with recurrent stress in social work. A key step in this process is the recognition and acceptance of situations and emotions that generate discomfort, as in the case of shame. Similarly, O'Neill, Yoder Slater and Batt (2019) highlight the strong relationship between self-care and academic stress in undergraduate and post-graduate social work students and demonstrate that students who practise daily self-care experience much less stress and more successful results during their academic life. The authors suggest that social work programmes should be encouraged to teach self-care, particularly in light of workers' professional future and of the need to develop more resilient practitioners able to deal with the many difficulties of social work practice.

Neff (2011) identifies three components of self-compassion: self-kindness (this includes being understanding of ourselves rather than self-judgemental and fault-finding), recognition of our common humanity and connection with others (the appreciation for ourselves comes from the recognition that there is good in us as there is in all people), mindfulness (rather than ignoring or exaggerating our discomfort). Self-appreciation and self-compassion are closely related to each other and cannot be separated, even though they seem to be different: the former brings pride and approval, the latter healing from suffering for our own selves and lives.

Even now, little is known about self-compassion in social work, but a recent survey on social workers in the US shed new light on how self-compassionate social workers are and on what factors contribute to self-compassion among them. The findings suggest that self-compassion is fairly widespread among social workers and is positively correlated to, in order of importance, health status, educational level and relationship status. Self-compassionate workers are more resilient when dealing with their mistakes, inadequacies and any other factors leading to stress. At the same time, they are more effective at work, especially in relating with service users, and always find new energy even in the most difficult situations (Miller et al, 2019).

Not far from self-compassion is the concept of self-forgiveness. The latter can usually refer to specific mistakes and transgressions involving violations of rules, but it may also be appropriate when people suffer from a sense of failure at work even though responsibility for the negative outcomes cannot be attributed exclusively to them but is found in a complexity of actions and interactions of different factors and subjects (Woodyatt, Cornish and Cibich, 2017). In every field of human behaviour self-forgiveness may be reduced by self-destructive motives (very common in some forms of addiction, where these often provoke self-punishing tendencies) and increased by self-accepting and self-compassionate motives. These include the acceptance of wrongdoing, the reaffirmation of violated values and the maintenance of a positive self-regard (Mosher, Hook and Grubbs, 2017).

Of course, self-compassion and self-forgiveness cannot be easy escapes from one's ethical responsibilities when mistakes are made. Social workers have the obligation to repair their errors and learn from their mistakes, in order to benefit future users. In fact, errors are unpleasant but inevitable in all systems and fields of work and life. Through recognition of the inescapable trade-off between security (and its costs) and damage caused by mistakes, 'smart failures', that is, 'small-scale, reversible, informative, linked to broader goals and designed to illuminate key issues' (Penn and Sastry, 2014, p 2), may be considered, in certain and special circumstances, as an alternative to failures produced by the implementation of ordinary and normal strategies. For this reason, the development of adequate expertise through systematic and structured reflection is of primary importance

(Sicora, 2017) and being aware even of unpleasant feelings, like shame, can start and fuel the whole process.

By extending this reasoning, it can be said that giving a name to one's emotions, even those of discomfort, is one of the most effective strategies to recognise their informative value and reduce their negative impact, if any (David, 2016). It is not always an easy task when the identified emotions generate annoyance, even if not discomfort, and when, paradoxically, this reaction brings more discomfort than the original emotion that produced it. This is the case with meta-emotions, that is, emotions which people feel about their own emotions (Jäger and Bartsch, 2006). Capturing the full range of emotions present in oneself and in others is a central skill in the helping professions, of which the empathic relationship is an essential building block. The phrase attributed to the poet Rainer Maria Rilke 'If my devils are to leave me, I am afraid my angels will take flight as well' (Barritt, 2005, p 108) offers useful suggestions on how to reconcile with one's own emotional sphere as a whole, with both its luminous part and the darkest one.

The acquisition of knowledge suggested earlier in this section is an essential part of each path of resilience and self-reinforcement. Social workers can pursue this on their own, but it is much more effective and incisive when it is carried forward collectively as reflective practice. The latter practice is the result of a logical and strong connection among experience, reflection and action, forming together a never-ending cycle yielding deeper understanding and better effectiveness. The interior dialogue underlying this process is strongly influenced and, in turn, influences the environment of the reflecting person. Searching, learning and creating theory are parts of the overall operation (Sicora, 2017).

Meetings with colleagues, team activities, supervision and continuous education, as well as a specific attention to these topics at university, would certainly be useful to create adequate opportunities to talk, discuss and learn together about topics usually associated with shame, that is, issues which people want to hide or bury. It certainly takes courage to talk about one's shame and what has produced it, but to put aside natural reluctance to examine this emotion can lead to unexpected discoveries, greater work satisfaction and probably also better results when helping people through social work services.

References

Anolli, L. (2010) *La vergogna*, Bologna: Il Mulino.

Barritt, P. (2005) *Humanity in Healthcare: The Heart and the Soul of Medicine*, Oxford: Radcliffe.

Beddoe, L., Staniforth, B. L. and Fouché, C. B. (2017) '"Proud of what I do but often … I would be happier to say I drive trucks": ambiguity in social workers' self-perception', *Qualitative Social Work*, 18(3): 530–46, https://doi.org/10.1177/1473325017725801.

Brown, B. (2015) *Rising Strong: The Reckoning. The Rumble. The Revolution*, New York: Spiegel & Grau.

David, S. (2016) *Emotional Agility: Get Unstuck, Embrace Change, and Thrive in Work and Life*, London: Penguin.

Frost, L. (2016) 'Exploring the concepts of recognition and shame for social work', *Journal of Social Work Practice*, 30(4): 431–46.

Germer, C. K. and Neff, K. D. (2013) 'Self-compassion in clinical practice', *Journal of Clinical Psychology*, 69(8): 856–67.

Gibbs, G. (1988) *Learning by Doing: A Guide to Teaching and Learning Methods*, London: Further Education Unit.

Gibson, M. (2014) 'Social worker shame in child and family social work: inadequacy, failure, and the struggle to practise humanely', *Journal of Social Work Practice*, 28(4): 417–31.

Gibson, M. (2016) 'Social worker shame: a scoping review', *British Journal of Social Work*, 46: 549–65.

Gibson, M. (2018) 'The role of pride, shame, guilt, and humiliation in social service organizations: a conceptual framework from a qualitative case study', *Journal of Social Service Research*, 45(1), 112–28, https://doi.org/10.1080/01488376.2018.1479676.

Gibson, M. (2019) *Pride and Shame in Child and Family Social Work*, Bristol: Policy Press.

Gio, I. (2017) 'A call for self-compassion in social work education', *Journal of Teaching in Social Work* , 37(5): 454–76.

Jäger, C. and Bartsch, A. (2006) 'Meta-emotions', *Grazer Philosophische Studien*, 73(1): 179–204.

Kapoulitsas, M. and Corcoran, T. (2015) 'Compassion fatigue and resilience: a qualitative analysis of social work practice', *Qualitative Social Work*, 14(1): 86–101.

LeCroy, C. W. and Stinson, E. L. (2004) 'The public's perception of social work: is it what we think it is?', *Social Work*, 49(2): 164–74.

Miller, J. J., Lee, J., Shalash, N. and Poklembova, Z. (2019) 'Self-compassion among social workers', *Journal of Social Work*, 14 February, https://doi.org/10.1177/1468017319829404.

Mosher, D. K., Hook, J. N. and Grubbs, J. B. (2017) 'Self-forgiveness and hypersexual behavior', in L. Woodyatt, E. L. Worthington Jr, M. Wenzel, and B. J. Griffin (eds) *Handbook of the Psychology of Self-Forgiveness*, New York: Springer, pp 279–91.

Neff, K. (2011) *Self-Compassion: The Proven Power of Being Kind to Yourself*, London: Hodder & Stoughton.

O'Neill, M., Yoder Slater, G. and Batt, D. (2019) 'Social work student self-care and academic stress,' *Journal of Social Work Education*, 55(1): 141–52, https://doi.org/10.1080/10437797.2018.1491359.

Palma-García, M. de las O. and Hombrados-Mendieta, I. (2017) 'Resilience and personality in social work students and social workers', *International Social Work*, 60(1): 19–31.

Penn, K. and Sastry, A. (2014) *Fail Better: Design Smart Mistakes and Succeed Sooner*, Boston, MA: Harvard Business Review Press.

Potter-Efron, P. S. and Potter-Efron, R. T. (1999) *The Secret Message of Shame: Pathways to Hope and Healing*, Oakland, CA: New Harbinger Publications.

Schulz, K. (2010) *Being Wrong: Adventures in the Margin of Error*, New York: HarperCollins.

Sicora, A. (2017) *Reflective Practice and Learning from Mistakes in Social Work*, Bristol: Policy Press.

Sicora, A. (2018) 'Learning from mistakes in social work', *European Journal of Social Work*, 21(5): 684–96.

Thomas, G. (2011) *How to Do Your Case Study: A Guide for Students and Researchers*, London: Sage.

Treeby, M. and Bruno, R. (2012) 'Shame and guilt-proneness: divergent implications for problematic alcohol use and drinking to cope with anxiety and depression symptomatology', *Personality and Individual Differences*, 53(5): 613–17.

Turnaturi, G. (2012) *Vergogna: metamorfosi di un'emozione*, Milan: Feltrinelli.

Walker, J. (2011) 'The relevance of shame in child protection work,' *Journal of Social Work Practice: Psychotherapeutic Approaches in Health, Welfare and the Community*, 25(4): 451–63.

Woodyatt, L., Cornish, M. A. and Cibich, M. (2017) 'Self-forgiveness at work: finding pathways to renewal when coping with failure or perceived transgressions', in L. Woodyatt, E. L. Worthington Jr, M. Wenzel and B. J. Griffin (eds) *Handbook of the Psychology of Self-Forgiveness*, New York: Springer, pp 293–307.

Index

205